# Homing

*On Pigeons, Dwellings and Why We Return*

JON DAY

JOHN MURRAY

First published in Great Britain in 2019 by John Murray (Publishers)
An Hachette UK company

This paperback edition published in 2020

I

A CIP catalogue record for this title is available from the British Library

Paperback ISBN 978-1-47363-540-1
eBook ISBN 978-1-47363-539-5

Typeset in Bembo MT by Hewer Text UK Ltd, Edinburgh
Printed and bound in Great Britain by Clays Ltd, Elcograf S.p.A.

John Murray policy is to use papers that are natural, renewable and
recyclable products and made from wood grown in sustainable forests.
The logging and manufacturing processes are expected to conform
to the environmental regulations of the country of origin.

John Murray (Publishers)
Carmelite House
50 Victoria Embankment
London EC4Y 0DZ

www.johnmurraypress.co.uk

your way back to one, is a miracle-narrative of birds and men. Humane and beautifully navigated, it is hands down a book of the year' Andrew O'Hagan

'One of the delightful things Day's book does – and there are so many delights in this book – is raise the question of what it might mean to identify with both an individual and a flock . . . The book's quiet optimism about our ability to change, and to learn to love small things passionately, will stay with me for a long time' *Times Literary Supplement*

'*Homing* is a paeon to these underrated characters of the street scene' *Country Life*

'In this lucid and beguiling book, Jon Day has written a marvellously interwoven tale of our two species' Jonathan Raban

'Endlessly interesting and dazzlingly erudite, this wonderful book will make a home for itself in your heart' *Prospect*

'[Day has] succeeded in making that most familiar of birds seem mysterious, almost magical, and illuminated, brilliantly, the urge towards home' Malachy Tallack

'An intriguing and colourful patchwork of information: not just about the lifestyles, habits and abilities of these clever homing birds, and their – frankly obsessed – owners; but also the wider philosophical and scientific ramifications of this mysterious man-to-bird relationship . . . Day has done a fine job in exposing the homing pigeons' particular artistry and skill, and is touchingly honest about how his birds have taught him to stop being so restless, to settle down, as a father, and in his own new family' *On Yorkshire*

*Also by Jon Day*

Cyclogeography: Journeys of a London Bicycle Courier

Jon Day is a lecturer in English at King's College London. He has written for the *London Review of Books*, the *New York Review of Books*, the *Guardian*, the *Financial Times* and others. His first book, *Cyclogeography*, was published in 2015. He lives with his family in London.

## *Praise for* Homing

'A vivid evocation of a remarkable species and a rich working-class tradition. It's also a charming defence of a much-maligned bird, which will make any reader look at our cooing, waddling, junk-food-loving feathered friends very differently in future' *Daily Mail*

'Day beautifully interweaves the twin threads of his life . . . as he settles down with his partner and starts a family, while at the same time training his birds to fly ever further away. The book is awash with historical and literary detail, and moving moments . . . the author, his birds and brood reside happily alongside one another in the intangible bliss he calls home. This wonderful book captures so much of what that word means' *Daily Telegraph*

'Day draws us into the esoterica of an unfamiliar world . . . and makes it inviting to non-initiates . . . His big-hearted and quietly gripping book has one very satisfying finishing line' *Guardian*

'[Day is] an elegiac writer, scrupulous in his reasoning . . . His descriptions . . . are wholly gripping . . . By the end of this joyful, richly rewarding book, his house has become a home, and his avian charges infinitely more than flying rats' *Mail on Sunday*

'Day seamlessly weaves several stories together . . . *Homing* eschews the descriptions of beautiful landscapes and wildlife that we're so used to in the works of Robert Macfarlane, Helen Macdonald and John Lewis-Stempel, and yet this is nature writing at its best . . . I never expected to learn so much about the homing pigeon, and to have developed a newfound respect for the common feral one' *Financial Times*

'A beautiful book . . . *Homing* is a highly literary book, dense with quotes from the likes of Sebald and Solnit, Perec and Henry Green. That Day's own prose does not feel out of place amid such exalted company gives you an idea of what a very good book this is' *Observer*

'*Homing* did something I thought would be impossible – made me fall in love with the humble, familiar feral pigeon. It is both a repository of fascinating stories and memorable characters, and a deeply felt personal enquiry into the nature of "home". Every page of this beautifully written book brought me pleasure' Charlotte Higgins

'Day swoops and soars over many fields of art and science to unravel our instinct for home . . . His understated lyrical style expresses beauty without sentimentality . . . His description of the pigeons settling in at home is a cosy delight' *The Spectator*

'I love Jon Day's writing and his birds. A marvellous, soaring account' Olivia Laing

'Day's stories from the history of human–pigeon relations are well chosen and well told . . . this is a simple book telling a simple tale, and there's a great deal to like in the simple imagery of a young family and their pigeons growing up together in an east London home – whatever "home" means' *Literary Review*

'I totally love Jon Day's new book *Homing*. For people who recognise that feeling familiar to Freud, of being homesick for nowhere, Jon's sense of making a particular home, or of knowing

For Ivo

# Contents

## *Author's Note*

Some of the people I spoke to while writing this book did not wish to be identified. I have changed their names.

*Then felt I like some watcher of the skies*

John Keats, 'On First Looking into Chapman's Homer'

*Where thou art—that—is Home—*

Emily Dickinson

## 7.15 a.m., Thurso, 504 miles from home

The call came through at 8.26 a.m. on the Saturday morning, but I'd been waiting for hours by then, and was beginning to wonder if it would come at all. The message moved southward, rippling down the lines from the north, a single, urgent sentence: 'The birds are up.'

Brian, the race controller, sounded officious at the end of the line. This was no time for small talk.

'They were released into a light variable wind at a quarter past seven,' he said. 'Visibility was good. The first returns should arrive this evening. The clocks'll be struck at ten p.m. Have a good race.'

In London the sky was clear, with wisps of cloud scudding high overhead and a light breeze fingering the leaves on the trees. The morning was already hot, and it would only get hotter as the day progressed. Two weeks before, a band of high pressure had moved in to squat over the country and, despite the occasional thunderstorm, it had held. The grass had yellowed. The reservoirs were running dangerously low. There was talk of a hosepipe ban. Saddleworth Moor caught fire and burned for days, lighting up the evening sky with an orange glow. The heat had dried out the land and, in the process, had revealed the presence of ancient archaeological sites. Ghostly outlines of Roman villas and bathhouses appeared in the fields. The plane trees outside my house began to shed their bark in the drought, like snakes sloughing off their skin.

I had been awake since before dawn, worrying. I hoped I'd done enough to prepare the birds for the race. I hoped that they had been given enough food and water in the lorry on the way up. I wondered if they had any sense of the journey they were about to undertake. I tried to imagine what it might feel like to be them.

In the hours before Brian called I checked the weather forecast compulsively, as well as a website monitoring what it called 'space weather': the electromagnetic anomalies – sun flares and solar storms – which, some pigeon flyers believe, confuse their birds' navigational instincts. There was a chance of rain over the Midlands at noon – summer storms rolling in off the North Sea – but the flock wouldn't arrive there until later in the day, so should avoid the worst of it. The wind was calm. Solar activity was negligible. Conditions seemed promising for good returns.

Preparations for a homing pigeon race – which can feel as much a ritual as it does a competition – begin long before the birds are released. On Wednesday the previous week I had cycled to the clubhouse with the six pigeons I had chosen to enter cooing in the basket strapped to the front of my bicycle. For weeks previously I had worried about which birds to send. It had been a hard season, and I had lost many.

Two had gone missing on a training flight before the racing had even begun, when I released them into a dead sky from a car park at a junction of the M11. One would turn up again three months later no worse for his adventure, but the other I never saw again. I lost another to a hawk on a flight from Cambridge three weeks after the season had started. I lost one from Laceby, one from Berwick-on-Tweed, two from Whitley Bay. One cock had, for a reason known only to himself, taken off on a still day from the roof of my loft and flown away to start a new life on his own, out in the wide and dangerous world.

The birds I had selected for today's race were healthy and rested, and had been flying well around home for weeks. They were in full feather, having not yet begun their autumn moult. Some were sitting on eggs, which would make them particularly motivated to fly home quickly. At certain periods during the breeding cycle a pigeon's homing instinct is stronger than at others. Cocks that are driving hens to their nests to lay their eggs, or hens that are sitting on eggs that are just about to hatch, as mine were, are particularly favoured for longer races like this one.

When I arrived at the club I took my pigeons out of the basket one by one and passed them down the line to be marked. To ensure that no one cheats, no fancier, as pigeon racers are known, is allowed to mark his own birds. When they got to the marking station a rubber ring bearing a unique race number was attached to each bird's leg. This number was recorded on the race sheet alongside a description of the pigeon: sex, age and colouring. After they had been marked the birds were placed in communal baskets, the cocks and hens separated to prevent them harassing each other.

The marking is the moment the birds are registered for the race, but it also provides an opportunity for racers to get a sense of the form of their rivals' pigeons. As they are passed from hand to hand their weight and condition are quietly assessed. Do they feel sluggish and overfed? Are they in good feather, or too deep in the moult to perform? Are they well balanced in the hand?

The work was done largely in silence, with only the occasional grumble when a number was read out incorrectly, or a pigeon was put into the wrong basket. Those who had finished marking their birds stood to one side, smoking, discussing training strategies and breeding regimes, or moaning about the hawk attacks which, they said, seemed to be becoming more frequent. As they waited they checked the weather on their phones.

Once all the pigeons had been marked the baskets were fastened, the ties crimped with a small tin seal bearing a number and the image of a pigeon. Then the baskets were loaded onto a trailer while the flyers went inside the club to strike the clocks.

Next the birds were driven from the club to a service station on a motorway north of London, where they were loaded onto a larger lorry, along with pigeons from several other clubs. Thurso was an amalgamation race, which meant that birds from clubs across the South of England were racing against each other. The North London Federation, in which I was competing, was open to flyers who lived within a 33-mile radius of Wormwood Scrubs, but fanciers from Kent and Bristol had sent birds to Thurso, too.

After being loaded onto the lorry the pigeons were driven north through the night. They were supposed to arrive by Thursday evening, but the lorry broke down on the way up, and so it wasn't until Friday that the convoyer finally reached the liberation point: a nondescript car park on the east bank of the River Thurso, at the end of the A9, in the northernmost town in Britain.

One thousand or so pigeons were competing in the 2018 Thurso Classic, one of the longest and most prestigious pigeon races in the club calendar. My six birds would be flying with them. The liberation point was 504 miles to their home loft, in my garden in East London. But pigeons rarely fly as the crow does, choosing instead to follow low-lying land and avoiding large bodies of open water, and so the distance they would travel would likely be far greater. With a following wind they might fly at 50 miles per hour, and would be able to cover the distance in twelve hours or so. But Thurso was famously unpredictable, and it was the hottest race day anyone could remember. It would probably take them far longer to home, if they made it back on the day at all.

# I

# Homing In

There was a period in my childhood when my friend Nick and I used to rescue feral pigeons from the streets of London. Most seemed to die fairly quickly, succumbing to one of the many medieval-sounding diseases – 'canker' or 'one-eye cold' or 'pox' – which we read about in the pigeon-keeping books we discovered on an overlooked shelf in the local library. But one, a bird that for some reason we christened 'Psycho', thrived under our ham-fisted care.

We had found him in the gutter at the end of our road, huddled over himself and nursing a broken wing, looking like a collapsed umbrella. He put up no fight when we went to pick him up. We took him back to my house in a cardboard box, rigged up a crude splint for his wing, and installed him in an old rabbit hutch in the garden.

I remember Psycho as a handsome bird – his plumage oil-slick blue, deep and dark as a raincloud. But, looking back at photos of him, he was in fact distinctly scruffy: hobble-kneed and broken-toed, his ragged feathers framing a beady eye of flaming orange. A typical London pigeon.

Gradually, Psycho came to trust us. After a few days he would stand quite calmly on my wrist. Soon he would eat from my hand and perch on my shoulder. I liked to hold him and feel the softness of his feathers; his heartbeat fluttering against my fingers like a moth trapped in the hollow of my hands. The secret intimacy was thrilling. Soon, I imagined, the bond between us would be too strong to be broken: Psycho would accompany me to school,

*Psycho's healed wing.*

fly around the playground at lunchtime or wait, perched in some nearby tree, while I was in lessons. Having only a vague under-standing of how pigeon postal systems worked, I dreamt of send-ing him on secret missions to my friends' houses with messages tied to his legs, confident that he would always return.

Eventually Psycho's wing began to heal and his strength increased, so Nick and I forced him to make a series of rehabilita-tion flights around the garden. We took him out of the hutch and carried him away before throwing him into the air, watching as he flapped awkwardly back. Each time we'd take him slightly further before releasing him, and each time he seemed to have a better sense of what we wanted from him. For the first few flights he would flop onto the ground and look angrily back up at us, his feathers puffed up in indignation, or, if he made it to the hutch, stand on the roof with his head cocked, as if asking what he should do now. But after a few weeks he seemed to have got the hang of it. When we released him he would fly directly to the hutch without dawdling and go inside to feed.

These flights went on for a month or two, until one day I let Psycho out to fly around the garden as usual. He stepped out, looked around for a moment, and then took off, quickly climbing higher than he had ever flown before. I watched as he circled the trees, and then the rooftops of the surrounding houses. Once, twice he came around, disappearing behind a chimney stack before emerging on the other side. He seemed to be orienting himself, taking stock of the strange new territory he found himself flying over, only now being properly able to look down upon it. And then, as though noticing something far in the distance, on the edge of the horizon, he set his course and shot off over the block of flats that stood behind my house. I waited all afternoon for him to return, but he never did.

For weeks, by night, I dreamt of him. I imagined him living somewhere in the cracks of the city: a guano-eyrie tucked away under the rotting carcass of a railway bridge, or a wind-buffeted ledge on the brutalist clifftop of a high-rise. I wondered why he had left, what kind of a life he could have had out there over the rooftops. I wondered what kind of a place had called him back home.

Birds fascinate because they appear to be fundamentally alien forms of life – removed from our environment and from our concerns, free to float above us and forever out of reach. They leave no tracks, and their journeys are for the most part invisible. But what I loved about the pigeons Nick and I tried to rescue from the streets of London was that they lived in an almost-human world, and they lived in that world in almost-human ways.

Urban pigeons are feral rather than wild. They lack the romanticism of their charismatic cousins: the *Corvidae*, the hawks and the raptors, the migratory passerines. Ted Hughes could never have written a poem called 'The Pigeon in the Rain'. Instead they are what biologists call 'synanthropes': creatures that live alongside rather than apart from us, thriving in the environments human beings have created for themselves. Pigeons are particularly successful in cities, where they can skim a living off the bloat of our excess, and where tall buildings mimic the cliff faces on which their genetic ancestors – *Columba livia*, the rock dove – once lived.

Why have pigeons been so successful in cities when so many other birds have not? 'One answer' argues the biologist Bernd Heinrich in *The Homing Instinct*, 'concerns home-making. Almost all members of the *Columbidae* make flimsy nests and have two pure-white eggs per clutch. Nests of most species are on the ground or in trees. But the rock dove, a native of the Mediterranean region and North Africa, traditionally made its home on cliffs. It "sees" most of our human dwellings as almost perfectly designed safe home sites.' This environmental flexibility has allowed pigeons to thrive in a world increasingly dominated by people, particularly in cities, where they have come to be thought of not as wild creatures but as pests.

I had first become fascinated by pigeons after reading Arthur Ransome's *Pigeon Post*, the sixth volume of his Swallows and Amazons series to which, as a boy, I was addicted. In previous adventures the Swallows and Amazons had spent their summers sailing on the lake – a composite of Coniston Water and Lake Windermere in the Lake District – discovering Wild Cat Island and getting into trouble with the 'natives' in the process. In *Pigeon Post* (which now strikes me as a thinly veiled colonial fantasy) the Swallows and Amazons set out to map the moors and mountains surrounding the lake, prospecting for gold with all the self-certainty of children of Empire. While out exploring they use three pigeons – named 'Homer', 'Sophocles' and 'Sappho' – to stay in touch with home.

Ransome's prose was clunky and laboriously descriptive, but I found it no less captivating for that. I loved the way he allowed childhood to be a time of heroism. I loved the way he created, out on those lakes and moors, a world in miniature. Most of all I loved the quotidian, practical detail of his novels, the attention he paid to processes and to activities: sailing, fishing, making fire. They were things that I, a city-bound child, didn't have much experience of, but this didn't matter. I read his books not as stories but as instruction manuals for adventure.

It was in *Pigeon Post* that I first learned of the difference between the common rock dove and the modern racing homer. In the wild, rock doves nest in large colonies on cliff faces, but during the day they move inland to feed, and so the home territory over which they range is larger than that of many birds. This means they are very good navigators. *Columba livia*'s innate homing ability has been recognised since man and pigeon began living in close proximity several thousand years ago, and over the millennia the rock dove has been bred into an animal with an almost incomparable ability to find its way home.

Unlike that of other migratory animals a pigeon's navigational instinct is unrelated to seasonal change or environmental conditions. Salmon return once in their lives to the rivers in which they were born to breed in their turn; eels follow the Gulf Stream from their spawning grounds in the Sargasso Sea to grow to maturity in Europe's waterways. Geese and swallows traverse the globe in search of food and warm weather through the changing seasons, marking off the turning year as they do so. For pigeons, however, home isn't just some generically suitable territory but a specific location. A pigeon's sense of home is local and distinct, therefore: it is a place rather than an environment. In this, they are much like us.

And yet, despite the fact that they are non-migratory, the pull of home is for pigeons perhaps more powerful than that felt by any animal. Once their home loft has been imprinted on them – something that happens when they are around six weeks old – homing pigeons will return to it for the rest of their lives. Even if kept away for many years they will, once freed, often try to make their way back. Pigeons can fly thousands of miles and will cross oceans to get home. The love – if that is the right word – that pigeons feel for their homes is so acute that they will sometimes die for it. In his diary Samuel Pepys recorded that during the Great Fire of London, while people scrambled to save their lives and goods, 'the poor pigeons, I perceive, were loth to leave their houses, but hovered about the windows and balconys till they were, some of them burned, their wings, and fell down.' The longest pigeon flight ever recorded was made by a bird owned by the Duke of Wellington, which was liberated from Ichaboe Island, off the coast of Namibia, on 1 June 1845. It took 55 days to fly the 5,400 miles back to its loft in Nine Elms in London, where it was found dead in a gutter one mile from its home.

Pigeons are unshowy birds, instantly forgettable because so familiar. Their greys and blues, banded with lines of black, allow them to blend in with their environments: the dull slate of a cliff edge or the glass and steel of a skyscraper. Despite this, look closely and you will notice that they are beautiful. We think of pigeons as grey but they are composed of an oceanic palette: deep blues and greens; tawny whites, like the crest of a wave. Their necks, with their rainbow sheen, are expressive, part of a sophisticated communicative repertoire. The colour isn't created by pigment but by the physical structure of the feathers themselves, which are covered in a delicate latticework of threads. These disrupt the light that hits them so as to mix in the eye of the observer: a pointillist iridescence. At breeding time they dance for one another, performing elaborate mating paso dobles. 'Modesty', wrote the poet Marianne Moore, 'cannot dull the lustre of the pigeon.'

Their coos. Their liquid, gurgling coos. You can hear voices in them. Listening to a loft full of pigeons is like eavesdropping on a conversation in a distant room. Sometimes they sound like a bunch of gossips. 'Did you hear what he said?' they seem to say; 'Ooh, I never saw the like.' When disturbed on their perches they harrumph like spluttering sergeant majors. When courting they coo sweet nothings at each other.

More than many other birds, they are made of air: their bones are hollow and light, and their bodies contain nine balloon-like sacs which protect their inner organs from impact damage, and store exhaled air after it is passed from the lungs. Their breasts, the muscles of which power their wings, take up half their body mass: eight of their sixteen feathered ounces. Their blood is rich in haemoglobin, and their enormous hearts pump it around their bodies at a rate far higher than our own. This means they can carry oxygen to their muscles with great efficiency, but it also allows them remarkable powers of recovery and an astonishing capacity to heal. Birds ripped open by hawks can be sewn up and will be flying again in a matter of days. Their average body temperature is slightly higher than that of other warm-blooded animals – around 41.7°C – which makes them resistant to many diseases, being too warm for most pathogens to survive.

They are loyal and mate for life, the cock and hen taking turns to sit their eggs (hen from evening to midday; cock from midday to dusk) and both feeding their offspring with 'pigeon milk', a pre-digested slop enriched with fatty cells produced in their crops. They have always been symbols of the domestic and the homely. In *The Goshawk*, his diary of an attempt to train a bird of prey during the run-up to the First World War, T. H. White celebrated the pigeon's innate docility, even while he hunted them to feed to his hawk. 'What a peace-loving but prudent race they were', White wrote, 'not predatory and yet not craven. Of all the birds, I thought, they must be the best citizens, the most susceptible to the principles of the League of Nations.'

When not mangled or amputated by wire and string, their feet – which the poet Mina Loy described as their 'coral landing-gear'– are strong, cleanly reptilian. They have dusky, dusty eyelids, the colour of a summer's midnight. Their eyes are burnt orange, and with them they can see far further and with greater clarity than humans can. In the 1970s and '80s, the US Coastguard trained pigeons to recognise people lost in the ocean as part of a project called 'Sea Hunt'. Individual birds were placed in observation bubbles mounted on the bottom of helicopters and trained to peck at buttons when they spotted a scrap of coloured fabric floating in the grey sea. They were able to correctly identify the fabric 93 per cent of the time; human subjects managed the same task with 38 per cent accuracy.

They are more intelligent than we give them credit for, one of only a few animals – along with great apes, dolphins and elephants – that can pass what psychologists call the 'mirror self-recognition test'. If you mark a pigeon's wing and let it look in a mirror it will try to remove the mark, realising that what it is seeing is a reflected image of its own body. They can understand they are watching video footage of themselves even when it is replayed to them with a five-second delay. Three-year-old children find it difficult to do this with a two-second delay. Pigeons are able to recognise individuals from photographs, and a neuroscientist at Keio University has trained them to differentiate between paintings by Monet and those by Picasso.

When they fly they can look ungainly, but they are quick and manoeuvrable in the air, able to avoid all but the fastest of the hawks. As cliff-dwellers they have evolved a unique wing structure which allows them to take off vertically, flying straight up before levelling out, like miniature jump jets. They can accelerate from 0–60 miles per hour in under two seconds. There are faster birds – peregrine falcons, the pigeon's main predator, can reach 200 miles per hour on the stoop – but few can fly horizontally, under their own power, as quickly as a pigeon can. The fastest sustained average velocity ever recorded by a pigeon was 110 miles per hour. They can comfortably fly at 50 miles per hour all day long, but with a following wind can travel far faster, covering up to 700 miles in a single uninterrupted flight.

And they fly through a human world. Rather than soaring disinterestedly above, pigeons stay close to the land – following the dips and runnels of valleys, carving between the canyons of buildings and often flying at street level, below the height of rooftops. They live in our landscapes and within our infrastructure, making their homes under railway bridges, on windowsills and ledges, wherever they might remain unmolested. Some studies have suggested that pigeons navigate using human landmarks, too: on familiar routes they are known to follow roads and canals, and some have been observed going around roundabouts before picking the appropriate exit for home.

Four years ago, twenty years after Psycho had flown the coop, my girlfriend Natalya and I moved house, from the centre of the city, where I had lived most of my life, to the outskirts. We had found out we were going to become parents and, driven by excitement and a degree of fear, decided we needed to find somewhere to make a home of our own.

We had met a decade earlier, on the first day of university, as we moved into our rooms. We carried our cardboard boxes in front of us like shields, and smiled nervously as we passed each other on the tight winding staircase. Natalya was from the Wirral. She was tall and had long hair which curled wildly around her head. I liked her laugh, which was open and generous, and I liked her confidence: the way she seemed so sure of what she wanted from life. I think we fell in love at that moment, but it took us a few years to realise it. We spent evenings in each other's rooms, in pubs and punts. After our final exams were over we spent the summer drinking wine in sculpted gardens. We launched home-made hot air balloons into the sky from a meadow near our college, and watched them drift slowly over the river in the evening air. I knew then that wherever Natalya went, I wanted to make my home.

For the next few years we lived a typically itinerant life together, staying in a string of dusty rooms in houses filled with strangers. After leaving university we moved into a room above a pub in East London. We made the most of the freedoms of the place. By day we'd lounge on the flat roof and look down on the drinkers in the garden; by night we'd work behind the bar, or sit there long after last orders, making plans and wondering where our lives would take us.

For some the pub was the only home they had. There were the regulars, session drinkers in whose slow suicides, it sometimes felt, we were complicit: the huge, lonely man who drank eight pints each night but talked to no one; the sprightly Irishman who spoke with a thick accent despite the fact that, as his daughter told us after he'd died (a heart attack while changing a light bulb above the bar), he'd never lived in Ireland; the cockney coke dealer in his flat cap, his face bubbled with acne scars, who was perpetually on the cusp of violence.

After the precariousness of the pub became too much we found a cheap room in a tall, thin house in Hoxton which we shared with a band of speed-taking nighthawks. But the room we shared was tiny, with space for a mattress and little else, and our housemates would come home in the small hours and stay up until dawn, keeping us awake. So we soon moved on, to an ex-council flat rented from an unresponsive landlord, which never quite felt like a home either.

During this time, in between studying for various degrees, I'd scratched out a living working as a bicycle courier by day and writing – book reviews, essays, anything that would pay – by night. The jobs were not that dissimilar. Both were paid as piece-work, so you only earned what you delivered, and both were paid badly. Natalya had a more stable job working as an executive for a television company, and for a decade we lived a life that was footloose and free, but when we found out we were to become parents we decided we needed to find a home of our own.

Natalya had saved up enough money for a deposit and I, having completed my PhD, had got a job teaching English Literature at a university in London, finally making me a viable prospect for a mortgage. The city was on the cusp of the worst housing crisis in living memory, and we felt absurdly fortunate to be able to even contemplate buying somewhere in which to live. Still, we soon realised we couldn't afford much in the area where we had spent most of our lives together. Estate agents showed us a dismal parade of potential properties: one-bedroom flats on main roads, where the windows would wobble every time a bus passed by; studio spaces in converted schools; squalid maisonettes on the edges of rotting industrial estates.

When it became clear we would not be able to afford to stay in the inner city we started looking further afield, following the bus routes out to the suburbs. We calculated commuting times and investigated transport links, drawing an imaginary circle around those parts of the city we could reach by bicycle.

Eventually we found a place in Leyton, five miles east of where we were living at the time, which felt like it could become a home. It was a mint-green terraced house on a street facing a cricket ground lined with tall plane trees. At night the trees were lit with light bulbs, a legacy of the attention the area had received in the run-up to the 2012 Olympic Games. There was a kitchen, a sitting room, more than one bedroom. Up in the eaves of the roof, overlooking the cricket ground, was a room I could use as a study. The garden was mysterious and dark, thick with vegeta-tion and dank with the smell of fox. From it I could see a patch of sky, framed on three sides by the roofs of the surrounding houses. There was a gap between the terraces to the north, through which an elevated railway rattled. To the east, a block of flats thrust up from the High Road to block out the sky.

The house was not in a good state of repair. Rain got in around the windows on stormy days, and there was an infestation of wood-worm in the eaves. During the summer months, when the larvae hatched into beetles and left their boreholes to mate, their crunchy bodies would fall, spent, onto my desk as I wrote. In the hallway and the kitchen the walls were crumbling from damp. There were yellow patches around the bay windows and on the ceilings of one of the bedrooms. Silverfish frolicked on the countertops at night. An ominous crack ran down a wall at the top of the stairs.

We had no money to fix any of this, but we didn't particularly care. The house felt loved, and it was the kind of place in which we could imagine our lives unfurling together. We counted ourselves lucky to have found it.

Mick, the house's previous owner, had been a taxi driver, and in the hallway was a wall-sized map of London which he'd painstakingly cut out of a large format *A–Z* and reassembled so that Leyton was located right in the centre. It was disconcerting to see the familiar London map re-oriented like this – the City and West End tucked away to the far left; Chingford and Essex given far greater prominence than they usually are. South London was almost an irrelevance on Mick's map, relegated as it was to the bottom quarter of the wall.

The map was an old one, made before the A12 had cut through the area, and long before the development of the Docklands and Lower Lea Valley. The area around the Isle of Dogs, now dotted with skyscrapers, was marked an anonymous white – uncertain of its future, and the redevelopment which would turn it into London's second financial district just a few years later. The Olympic Park which now sprawls across the Lower Lea Valley was nowhere to be seen, not even, yet, a planner's dream. The map showed us at the centre of a new, unfamiliar landscape: a *mappa mundi*, with Leyton rather than Jerusalem at its heart.

The summer after we moved it felt as though the idea of home was undergoing a crisis. Not enough homes were being built in London, and those that were for sale were absurdly expensive – affordable only for middle-class people in professional jobs, with savings or parents to help us. Everywhere in the city people were being exploited by landlords, or priced out of the areas in which they had grown up. Local councils made deals with private developers, offering them land for a pittance on the condition that they built a few 'affordable' houses alongside their glittering towers and shopping centres. Artists were moved out, then teachers and nurses, then everyone else. The wealthy colonised once-downtrodden areas. Newspaper columnists wrote pieces about how they had given up on the city and were fleeing for the coast.

Home was becoming a geopolitical issue, too. All across Europe the walls were going up. In 2013, the then Home Secretary

Theresa May sent a fleet of billboard vans around London bearing the message 'In the UK illegally? Go home or face arrest.' She
wanted, she said, to create a 'hostile environment' for those who
had 'come here illegally'. Three years later, during the lead-up to
the referendum vote on Britain's membership of the European
Union, those advocating Brexit had drawn on the dog-whistle
rhetoric of home to push forward their miserable plans. UKIP
leader Nigel Farage posed outside Parliament in front of a mobile
billboard showing a line of men in hoodies and jackets with
'BREAKING POINT' written over the top.

In the papers and on Twitter there was talk of a divide between
the 'citizens of somewhere' – people who dwelt in the places in
which they had been born – and 'citizens of nowhere': the rootless metropolitan elite. Two weeks later, 52 per cent of the
population voted to leave the EU. Many said they did so to 'take
back control' of the borders of their homeland, and a wave of
anti-immigrant sentiment was unleashed. Theresa May, who had
since become Prime Minister, said she couldn't guarantee that
people who had settled here would be allowed to stay in the
country after Britain had left Europe. On radio phone-ins people
spoke of sovereignty, of borders, of laws, of fishing quotas. But
hovering behind these arguments was another, more abstract fear.
The politics of home – of what it means to belong to a place –
felt more vexed than ever in my lifetime. 'Where is your home?'
became a question asked with vicious intent, a question which
came to mean 'Are you one of us?'

Our daughter Dora was born a few months after we moved to
Leyton. It was a difficult birth and, although we didn't realise it
at the time, it took us all a long time to recover from it. In the
forty-second week of her pregnancy Natalya had been called
into hospital in order to be induced. This was presented as a
straightforward intervention: a sensible precaution against the
complications of an over-term pregnancy. In the hospital we felt
nervously excited about what was about to happen. Afterwards

we went for a Turkish in a café on the Holloway Road before getting the train back home.

Almost as soon as we arrived the contractions began. We called my sister Anna, who had trained as a midwife. She came round to find Natalya crawling on all fours, wearing the gardening kneepads she had bought especially for the purpose. Anna drove us back to hospital through the rush-hour traffic. I remember the sun glinting orange through the grubby windows of the car, the pulse of traffic mirroring Natalya's contractions. I remember, too, the excitement turning to fear. I had a sense of disconnected helplessness, my desire to take away Natalya's pain accompanied with the knowledge that there was nothing I could do about it.

Back in the hospital we were ushered into a cubicle. Around us people chattered and metal objects clinked together, as in a noisy restaurant. When Natalya's waters broke she was bustled into a side room. Impassive doctors arrived every few minutes to prod and measure her, as though she was a specimen in a laboratory. Our 'birth plan', a document we'd put together in hopeful innocence, unaware of the quickened realities of the maternity ward, was soon forgotten. As the contractions got stronger Natalya stopped talking and retreated into herself. I held her hand and muttered platitudes, telling her to breathe, ineffectually rubbing her back and her shoulders until she told me to stop.

Time, marked by the rhythms of her contractions, did strange things. I remember a doctor coming in and having a loud conversation on the phone about another patient who had miscarried. I remember the moment the midwives realised that the baby's heart rate was dropping, and the doctors decided they had to intervene. I remember Natalya's fear as they showed her the implements they would use. And I remember the bewildering, overpowering joy when our daughter was eventually born, tiny and miraculous – a scrap of flesh hanging from sharp bones, like clothes from a coat hanger, her minuscule shoulders covered in fine, downy hair, her mouth a raw, mewling hole – and the dazed responsibility I felt as the three of us gazed at each other in surgery afterwards.

We had been living in Leyton for two years, and Dora was eighteen months old, when we decided to try for another child. Enough time had passed from those all-consuming early months for us to have forgotten the sheer fatigue, the strange fugue state you inhabit as a new parent, and the occasional darkenings which can accompany it. Dora was beginning to speak and to possess herself. She asked us about siblings. Natalya and I were both from large families, and didn't want her to be an only child. But our bodies wouldn't do what we wanted them to. There were two bleak days, a few months apart, when what had been a pregnancy, a quickening, ceased to be.

A miscarriage isn't something it is easy to grieve for. To mourn an unborn child is not really to feel grief, or rather, it is not to feel grief for a person, but for the idea of one. Instead these miscarriages felt like interruptions to a narrative: curtailments of a projected future. Those speculative diaries you make in the first flush of discovering you might become a parent – born in autumn, cousin in the same school year, twenty-one when we are fifty – cease to exist in an instant. The sadness we felt was for a story that had never properly begun.

In *A Portrait of a Lady*, Henry James represents the loss of Isabel Archer's unborn child with a blank – an empty space – an un-narrated portion of the three years following her marriage to Gilbert Osmond, as though an unrealised life couldn't be written. For a man, especially a childless one like James, this experience of abstracted loss was doubly projected: doubly distanced.

We had told friends we were going to have another child, and we now had to tell them we were not. I felt sheepish, as though we were putting them under some obligation to respond empathetically. The skeletal plans we'd erected crumbled away in an instant. Natalya and I had always been honest with each other about what we hoped for in our lives together. But these miscarriages created a distance between us that I wasn't sure we knew how to close.

In his essay describing what is usually translated as the 'uncanny', but which should more properly be translated as the 'unhomely', Sigmund Freud placed the feeling of being unhomed at the heart of his psychoanalytical project. The '*unheimlich*', Freud wrote, refers to 'that class of the frightening which leads back to what is known of old and long familiar'. For Freud, to be unhomed was to be presented with strangeness in an environment you thought you knew intimately. Many of the examples of *unheimlichness* Freud provides in his essay describe moments of doubling: the feeling of alienation you experience when looking at a dummy, or a puppet; when you mistake a person for a thing or a thing for a person. But for Freud the *unheimlich* was at its most powerful, and its most unsettling, when it described a deeper sense of estrangement: an estrangement not from the world but from the self.

In one striking passage Freud associated this sense of estrangement with the experience of being lost in an unfamiliar city. Walking around the red-light district of some anonymous Italian town, he describes feeling discomfited by the 'painted ladies' he sees in the windows, even as he is continually drawn towards them. He tries to leave, but can't get away, and keeps returning to the same streets. Freud understood this moment to represent an unconscious desire to return. It is this desire – to home in on the things we can't admit to ourselves we want to know, be they thoughts or places – that, he said, underpins our unconscious attraction to the uncanny. Freud, exiled from his homeland by the calumny of war, made this sense of dislocation central to his understanding of the psyche. One of his most radical ideas was to acknowledge that people could become unhomed within themselves: that they could be unmoored from the familiarity of their own minds without ever going anywhere.

★

Over the next few months Natalya and I struggled to reconcile ourselves to our new situation. She would leave for work each morning, her long commute by bike or by tube into the city. I wrote upstairs in my attic room, as the washed-out summer turned to a freezing winter. We'd stopped talking to each other as much, and fought often. I turned in on myself, and Natalya was upset by my absences. Our daughter was shuttled between child minders and grandparents. As winter became summer we considered our lot. Natalya was bullish about our having another child.

'It'll happen or it won't,' she said. 'Don't worry so much.'

I feared that by talking about our failure, by showing my sadness, I might make her feel I was blaming her in some way.

We had thought that in having Dora and moving to Leyton we had found somewhere we could make into a home, but that winter we came to realise that in moving house we had lost something, too. Though we had not travelled far, the few miles which now separated us from our old lives began to feel uncrossable. The home we had left behind wasn't made of bricks and mortar, but of the geography of the area we had discovered together, and those other ties which bind us to the places we inhabit. However precarious, we had felt settled in our old flat and our old lives, and we had thought that having a family would root us ever more firmly. It was a shock to discover this would not necessarily happen.

To 'home in' on something means to target it: to get it in one's sights, to focus on it to the exclusion of everything else. But it also means to move *homeward*: to retreat from the world at large into the domestic sphere. Bernd Heinrich describes home not just as a physical structure – the nest or burrow in which an organism lives – but, in a wider sense, as a territory or location, and also as a feeling: a disposition to return. This feeling, he argues, is deep-rooted, something akin to hunger or fear, a universal and elemental sense that cuts across species boundaries. 'For other animals and for us,' he writes, 'home is a "nest" where we live, where our young are reared. It is also the surrounding

territory that supports us. Homing is migrating to and identifying a suitable area for living and reproducing and making it fit our
needs, and the orienting ability to return to our own good place
if we are displaced from it.' We had moved to Leyton to try to do
all of this. We wanted to make our good place together, and to
welcome new life into it. But as time passed we came to feel ever
more disconnected from a home which, I began to realise, had
been largely psychological. We began to feel not exiled, precisely,
but temporarily homeless, or, perhaps, unhomed.

It was during this period, possessed by a desire for home stronger
than I had ever felt before, that I began to notice the pigeons
again. A vast flock of them roosted on the roof of one of the
houses opposite, on the edge of the cricket ground. I'd watch
from the window of my study as they embarked on their daily
circuit: down to the pitch to pick at the grass, then to the bins
behind the flats to the north of the pavilion, then on to the railway arch around the corner and finally back up to the rooftop. I
watched for weeks as one pair made their nest in a little nook in
the awning above the shutter of a kebab house. Their routine was
regular and predictable: they seemed to know precisely when the
bins would be emptied, when the old woman who fed them
crusts of bread would begin her slow journey along the High
Road, when the gulls would move in to chase them off the roof.
I envied them the stable predictability of their lives. My boyhood
fascination with the birds had never left me, and it was then that
I decided, almost on a whim, to buy some pigeons of my own.

   I wondered if they could teach me something about home.
They would at least, I thought, be a distraction. Training and
caring for a flock would take time and attention, and the worlds
they provided access to would be novel and unfamiliar to me.
Perhaps I would meet new people and begin to form a sense of
community. I thought Dora might be interested in them, too,
and that keeping pigeons might be a good way of teaching her
about the stuff of life: about growing up, about sex and death.

But I wondered if they could also provide us with something that was harder to define. If I could successfully train a flock to home to our new house, I thought, then perhaps we would begin to feel more firmly rooted in the place we now inhabited. The pigeons would have to learn to navigate the territory just as we would. They would mature, eventually having offspring in their turn. They, like us, would learn to become parents. The idea was irresistible. The pigeon's domesticity and love of home − its *nostophilia* − might teach us to understand something about what it means to dwell. By making a home for the pigeons I hoped to make of the unfamiliar map on the wall of our hallway − with its white spaces and blanks, its alien street names and unfamiliar shapes − a place we could know as home.

## 7.20 a.m., Thurso, 504 miles from home

A pigeon race, like a bicycle road race before the age of television, is impossible to watch in real time, which makes it a fertile source of speculation and misinformation: of stories, in other words. No one quite knows what goes on in the skies once the birds are up. Might they hit a patch of bad weather? Will a hawk attack scatter them? Sometimes whole flocks go missing during a race, brought down by heavy rain, or confused by fog, or baffled by the subsonic rumbles of passing aircraft, never to be seen again. In the club the fanciers say these incidents are increasing in frequency: that more birds are lost from races year on year. Some blame the ubiquity of mobile telephones, believing that the radiation they emit confuses pigeons' internal navigation systems.

For their flyers, a pigeon race consists of two distinct moments: the liberation, when the birds are released, and the homecoming, when the time of their arrival back at the loft is registered using specially designed tamper-proof clocks. Pigeons being quicker than people, you can never witness both. It is a race, as the fanciers say, with one starting gate but a thousand finishing lines.

Every bird flies a different distance to their home loft, so the winner of a race is decided by average velocity flown – measured in yards per minute – rather than overall time taken. The first bird back may not be the eventual winner of the race. Aerodynamics can significantly influence the outcome. A pigeon can fly far

more efficiently as part of a flock than it can on its own. Training
your birds to break from the pack at the right time – when they're
near their loft, so they won't overfly it, but not too far away, so
that they waste energy battling the wind on their own – is the key
to winning consistently.

Wind direction is important, too. Most birds will approach
their loft not in a straight line from the liberation point but at an
angle following the prevailing winds. Having a loft to the wind-
ward side of this line allows you to 'have the drop' on your
competitors, whose birds must swing round and regroup before
coming in to land, and so confers a distinct advantage. But more
important than any of this is to ensure your birds want to come
home in the first place.

At 7.15 a.m., two hours before I receive the phone call from
Brian telling me the birds have been liberated, the baskets are
opened in Thurso. As soon as the flaps are down the pigeons
emerge and take flight, one after the other, like parachutists leaving an aeroplane in orderly sequence. A few linger on the lorry,
or stand by the side of the road, pecking at the ground. One or
two might not make it out of the baskets at all. But within a few
seconds most of them have formed up into a vast, wheeling flock.
For a minute or two they fly around the car park. As they climb
the air is filled with the clatter of wings snapping together: a
feathered applause. The sky is thick with them, and for a brief
moment the flock blots out the sun. They do not fly with the
elegant, murmurating fluidity of starlings: their flight is wilder.
More free. Feathers drift down to the ground like snow.

They circle the area as they work out which direction to fly in.
First they must strike a transit, noting the location of the sun and
its height above the horizon, comparing this with the height they
expect it to be at home using their highly accurate internal
chronometers, and using the differential to plot a directional
bearing. If the sun were obscured by cloud, they might use the
magnetite deposits in their upper beaks to attend to the weak pull

of the earth's geomagnetic field instead. Still, no one really knows the true nature of the maps they consult. Is it a feeling for them? A discomfort? A pull? I imagine it as a kind of incompleteness, as though they've left part of themselves behind. How home must tug at them.

Soon the pigeons have made their decision – a collective one, the product of the emergent intelligence of the group. The south, with all its claims on them, is calling. Within minutes they have gone. The skies in Thurso are clear.

It will take them hours to arrive back home. If dusk falls while they are still on the wing they will land in trees along the way, roosting up until dawn. But if they fly well they should make it back before nightfall.

# 2

## The Birds

It was a cold January morning in Blackpool, with mist clouding the tower and obscuring the sea, muffling the noise of the gulls, and the men of the fancy were gathering. As I approached the Winter Gardens I began to spot them. Most were elderly. Some wore flat caps and long coats, their pockets embroidered with the names and pictures of pigeons. Many carried small wicker baskets, inside which living things stirred.

At the entrance to the British Homing World Show of the Year, billed in its promotional material as 'the largest gathering of pigeon fanciers in the world', a one-man band played English folk songs to the indifferent crowd. Two people dressed as pigeons handed out flyers for a raffle. 'Win a Loft!' the flyers said. I bought two tickets. Outside, fanciers stood smoking, their hands cupping their roll-ups against the rain.

I had left the house in the dark while Natalya and Dora slept. At the bus stop on the High Road a group of Polish women wearing thick padded coats breathed steam into the cold air while waiting for the bus that would take them to their jobs in the City. From the bus we watched in silence as London rolled by, its greys bursting into colour as the sun rose. From the train England rumbled past: the blackened earth, the ice-topped ditches glinting in the sunshine. The trees were leafless and skeletal. Mist gathered in the dips of the fields and drifted over the surface of rivers.

In the Empress Rooms of the Winter Gardens, in their serried ranks of cages, the pigeons waited to be judged. Their feathers were immaculate, their toes buffed to a high shine, their wattles chalky white. They exuded health. Around the edge of what was usually the ballroom owners made last-minute adjustments to their birds. They boiled kettles to steam bent feathers back into shape, cleaned shit off feet with baby wipes, massaged dabs of Vaseline onto beaks. Primped and preened, the pigeons glowed. A frenzied background cooing filled the room. The smell – wood polish and sawdust – had a pungent undertone of animal, not unpleasant but strong, a sour, acidic muskiness I would grow familiar with over the coming year.

The birds were divided into categories according to breed and competitive experience. Pigeons that had competed in races were placed in 100-, 200-, or 300+-mile groups. Then there were the 'show racers': birds bred to look like perfect racing specimens but which might have never left their lofts in their lives. These were the bodybuilders of the pigeon world, their glistening frames packed with highly defined yet functionally underwhelming muscle. They had no sense of place, and would struggle to home from 10 miles away.

Down in the sales room feed merchants advertised their proprietary mixes ('Young Bird Feed: Packed with Protein!', 'Widowhood Mixture: Get Your Birds Bulked Up!'); loft makers announced their latest designs ('super fast trapping with built-in Sputnik!'); and quacks sold performance-enhancing elixirs and herbal cleansers ('All Legal, NOT Doping'). There were stalls piled high with nest bowls, mineral pickstones, and fake plastic eggs, which are slipped under hens at the end of the breeding season as a form of pigeon birth control. Some of the attendees wore face masks, and the British Pigeon Fanciers Medical Research Team were on hand to offer blood tests for those who feared they might be afflicted with Pigeon Fancier's Lung, a chronic disease similar to asbestosis caused by an allergy to the proteins found in pigeon droppings.

There were birds for sale, of course. All the famous Belgian breeders were there, having driven their lorries from the Lowlands overnight. It was still early in the season, and most were selling *Columba* futures, taking orders for pigeons which hadn't yet been born, but around the edges of the room were a few early bred young birds in cages, waiting to catch some buyer's eye.

In a room off the main hall was a display of fancy breeds. There were pouters, tall birds with preposterously puffed up chests, strutting aristocratically around in their cages; English carriers, originally used as messengers but now an ornamental breed, with their long necks and fleshy, faintly obscene wattles. Indian fantails waddled across the table tops like miniature white peacocks. There were black and white Jacobins, haughty birds with feathered hoods which made them resemble wealthy Manhattan widows, and Old German owls, their beaks so tiny they would struggle to feed their own young.

There were acrobatic varieties of fancy breed, too: tipplers, birds that will fly for hours around the loft; Birmingham rollers, which soar to a great height before tumbling backwards through the air, as though doing somersaults. There is some evidence that these birds possess a gene for epilepsy, and that it is this which causes their rolling behaviour: aerial seizures making them fall through the air until they wake up.

There was something unsettling about the fancy breeds, which are kept in existence by the dogged and brutal diligence of their owners. Only the most appropriate birds, those that carry the prized features of their tribe, are allowed to reproduce. But for a long time there was some debate over whether all these different varieties of pigeon were members of the same species at all. During the nineteenth century most fanciers thought that different breeds of domesticated pigeon – with their radically differing looks and behaviours – must derive from several distinct wild strains. Charles Darwin, himself a keen fancier, believed that all strains of domesticated pigeon were, despite their vast physiological and behavioural differences, derived from a single species – the rock dove – and that their variety had been created not by nature but by human intervention, through careful selective breeding. This observation would be crucial to the development of what would become his theory of natural selection.

Darwin first became interested in pigeons in the 1840s, after he had returned home from five years voyaging aboard the *Beagle*. He had been intensely homesick during the long voyage, and ten years after returning to London had finally decided to settle, moving to the village of Down (now Downe) in Kent, with his wife Emma, to start a family and try to recover from the strange illnesses which would afflict him for the rest of his life. At Downe, according to his biographer Janet Browne, 'Darwin was creating a private Garden of Eden, bringing back together the birds and beasts of the domestic world, either on paper or in the flesh, in order to discover their origins.'

Darwin soon established a pigeon loft of his own at his new home. He joined two London pigeon clubs and spent the next few years breeding and observing the birds, which he grew to love. 'I am getting on splendidly with my pigeons,' he wrote to his son William, away at boarding school, in 1856, 'and the other day had a present of Trumpeters, Nuns & Turbits; & when last in London, I visited a jolly old Brewer, who keeps 300 or 400 of the most beautiful pigeons and he gave me a pair of pale brown, quite small German pouters; I am building a new house for my tumblers so as to fly them in summer.' He wrote to the geologist Charles Lyell and his wife, whom he had invited to stay at Down: 'I will show you my pigeons, which is the greatest treat, in my opinion, which can be offered to human beings.'

Darwin loved his birds for their curious behaviour and endless variety, but he also loved them for the unfamiliar world they gave him access to. In his autobiography he described the respect he had for other pigeon fanciers, the 'little men' ('all pigeon fanciers are little men', he wrote to his son) that he encountered in the smoky pubs of London, amateurs who seemed to know far more about these birds than any scientist did. It was almost as if the fanciers were another species for him to investigate and classify. Often they argued about breeding. 'For instance', he wrote to

*Fancy breeds.*

Thomas Huxley, who would later become the most ferocious defender of Darwin's controversial theories:

> I sat one evening in a gin-palace in the Borough amongst a set of pigeon-fanciers, – when it was hinted that Mr Bult had crossed his Powters with Runts to gain size; & if you had seen the solemn, the mysterious and awful shakes of the head which all the fanciers gave at this scandalous proceeding, you would have recognised how little crossing has to do with improving breeds, & how dangerous for endless generations the process was.

Darwin was struck by the zeal with which the breeders he encountered protected the lineage of their birds: the way they seemed intent on keeping alive varieties of pigeon which would, he believed, otherwise quickly revert to their wild state. He came to think of the relationship between bird and breeder as mutually constitutive. 'Does man control the pigeon or does the pigeon control man?' he asked himself.

Darwin's interest in pigeons came during a turning point in his work on what he then called the 'transmutation' of species. At the time, the debate over variation was focused on the degree to which a species could change through selective breeding. Were species fixed, for all time, by God, or were they fluid, open to manipulation and modification by natural forces, which in the *Origin of Species* Darwin would liken to the 'invisible hand' of the pigeon breeder? Most of the fanciers Darwin spent time with in the London pubs believed their birds were the descendants of wild strains that had since become extinct, and that in selectively breeding them they were keeping ancient bloodlines pure and true. In his *Principles of Geology*, Darwin's friend Lyell agreed, arguing that although individuals within species can vary a great deal, species boundaries themselves were fixed and immutable. Darwin disagreed. 'If this were true,' he scribbled in the margin of his copy of the *Principles*, 'adios theory.'

Pigeons would provide Darwin with some of the evidence he needed to show that Lyell was wrong: they were the domesticated, unshowy versions of his Galapagos finches. As he bred them and attended closely to the development of their chicks, he soon realised that all pigeon breeds, whatever they came to look like as adults, developed in very similar ways. And when bred outside their own lines they quickly reverted to look much like the feral pigeons he'd watched on the streets of London on his return from the Galapagos. Each highly individualised breed, he surmised, carried dormant within it the residue of its ancient heritage, a residue he likened to invisible handwriting, written into the species but only revealed at a later stage of the animals' development. Tipplers, tumblers, pouters and homers, he concluded, were all haunted by the genetic memory of *Columba livia*. Still, he acknowledged how unlikely his theory seemed when you looked at the birds themselves. 'The amount of variation has been extraordinarily great,' he wrote, '[f]ormerly, when I went into my aviaries and watched such birds as pouters, carriers, barbs, fantails, and short-faced tumblers, etc., I could not persuade myself that all had been descended from the same wild stock, and that man had consequently in one sense created all these remarkable modifications.'

Despite the evidence he had gathered, Darwin's theory took a while to be accepted. One of the readers for Darwin's publisher of *On the Origin of Species*, a clergyman named Whitwell Elwin, called the book 'a wild & foolish piece of imagination, for an outline it is too much & for a thorough discussion of the question it is not near enough.' Rather than rejecting the book, however, he advised Darwin to cut everything in it that wasn't to do with pigeons. 'Everybody is interested in pigeons,' he said, and such a book would 'be reviewed in every journal in the kingdom and soon be on every table.'

Darwin loved pigeons not just because of what they taught him but perhaps because, after years of wandering, they provided him with a sense of home. After five years on the *Beagle*, and ten years of doubt over whether he wanted to settle down at all, his pigeons rooted him, with his family, in domestic life. He was a deeply affectionate father, and came to love the home he found in Kent, cut off from the world and its distractions. His house became his laboratory and retreat, giving him the space and time to formulate his world-changing thesis. 'Few persons can have lived a more retired life than we have at Down,' he wrote a few years before he died. 'My life goes on like clock-work and I am fixed on the spot where I shall end it.'

But his experiments with pigeons had given him cause to worry, too. Emma, his wife, was also his first cousin. They had ten children together. Three died in infancy, and three were infertile. Throughout the rest of his life, Darwin wondered if he had been partly responsible for these tragedies. From his life-long interest in the domestication of animals, and his observation of pigeons, he knew that ill health could be passed from parents to children, and that such heredity might have been the source of his own family's sadnesses: the illnesses and deaths that seemed to stalk them. 'My dread is hereditary ill-health,' he wrote in a letter to his second cousin, the clergyman William Darwin Fox, in 1852. 'Even death is better for them.'

★

Before I went to Blackpool I had contacted Ian Evans, general
manager of the Royal Pigeon Racing Association (founded in
1896, patron: the Queen) and asked if he'd show me around. We
met in the Renaissance Rooms, where a pigeon auction was in
full swing. Cages at the front held the birds which were to be
sold. Attendants wearing white coats would remove pigeons
from their cages as their lots came up and hold them in the air,
spreading their wings to display them to the crowd. The auctioneer, with the universal auctioneer's manner – he might as easily
have been selling sheep or Impressionist paintings as pigeons –
conducted proceedings. At the start of each lot he read out the
bloodline of the bird for sale in a rapid burble. He gave us a
potted biography, telling us how far it had flown, how well it had
performed against its peers, the names of famous dams or sires.
Pigeons that had done well in the national combine races – in
which they compete not just against the birds of the members of
the local club, but against those from the entire country – were
particularly valued. Any bird with a famous pigeon in its line
made the bidders take note.

'Now we have a lovely pair of Busschaerts,' announced the
auctioneer (he pronounced it 'Bush-arts'). 'They're nest mates.
Sire was son of Good Lady, dam is out of Shadow. These are
quality long-distance pigeons, gentlemen. Good up to seven
hundred miles, and priced fair for the working man.'

Every now and then something about a bird would catch a
buyer's eye and there would be a flurry of bidding. Then the
gavel would come down, the birds would be inspected, and
ownership transferred.

'Why'd you buy another one?' a woman asked her husband
after he paid £200 for a single mealy cock, a handsome pigeon
with bright eyes and clean bars across his wings. 'You've not got
enough room for the ones you've already got.'

Despite the insistence on lineage and breeding, selecting a
pigeon is something of a mysterious art. Bird watchers speak,
rather unfortunately, of a species' 'jizz', a word that describes the

ineffable, cumulative signature of those characteristics – shape, plumage, behaviour – which allows you to identify a bird from a distance, and the fanciers were searching for something equally difficult to define.

'Quality is important, but it's hard to describe,' said Ian, 'you know it when you see it, but most of the time you don't see it.' The flyers at the auction wanted to handle the birds they were thinking of buying, feeling for what they called 'balance', or spreading their wings as though fanning a deck of cards to check the condition of their flight feathers. A good racing pigeon should feel firm and compact, but should also fill the hand. The head should be larger than that of a feral bird or fancy breed (homing pigeons have been shown to have larger brains than non-homing varieties and, like London taxi drivers, they have a particularly pronounced hippocampus, the part of the brain associated with navigation). Their feathers should be fine and soft, with no visible pinholes or frets. The ten primary flight feathers which run along the edge of the wing to the wingtip should develop incrementally from the secondary flights closer to the pigeon's body. They should open smoothly, separating like fingers when the wing is spread.

In the auction, potential buyers held the birds close to their chests, cupping them in both hands, straightening their tail feathers absent-mindedly while they talked. Some gazed deep into the birds' eyes through jeweller's loupes: these were the 'eye sign' theorists, who believe that you can identify a winning pigeon by eye colour or patterning – some significant form, the perfect proportion of iris to pupil – characteristics which they found it almost impossible to describe. The use of eye sign is a matter of heated debate in the fancy press, where portraits of winning birds are often accompanied with close-up photographs of their eyes. Some fanciers subscribe to even more arcane methods. 'In France and Belgium,' the noted pigeon historian W. Anderson has written, 'many fanciers, apparently normal individuals in most things, pay no attention to anatomical points, but depend largely on making their selections on the "specialist" who uses the "divining rod."'

At the auction most of the pigeons were being sold for less than £50, but some went for far more: hundreds or even thousands of pounds. Many of the highest priced pigeons were old birds, proven racers or breeders, but no use for a novice. They couldn't easily be broken to a new loft: even if you kept them inside for a few years, once released they'd almost certainly return to their original homes. Instead they were sold as breeding stock, and would never again see the outside of a loft. What I wanted was some young birds, Ian said, born that year and not yet homed to a particular location.

I asked him how to spot a winning bird.

'You don't,' he said. 'You might as well buy anything and see how it does. But not from the auctions. You want to buy them from someone on the floor – and don't pay the first price they ask.'

Ian was forty or so, with short brown hair and boyish eyes, friendly yet slightly reticent until conversation turned to the subject of pigeons. He had been in the fancy his whole life, he said, and he spoke about his birds and their accomplishments with a quiet, subdued awe. In South Wales he kept and raced his flock of thirty birds, and had had some success in club and federation races. His pigeons had won from across the Channel, from Saintes, 400 miles to his loft, and from Tarbes. He remembered as a young boy getting a yearling hen back from Thurso on the day of the race and running up and down the valley telling the other fanciers.

'They didn't like me very much that night,' he said.

Ian's father had kept pigeons before him, and his grandfather, too. The fancy was in his blood. For years he'd worked for a European-funded project aiding start-ups in The Valleys, but a few months ago he'd got a job as the general manager of the RPRA, and now he spent his working life with the birds he had always loved.

He was elegiac when I asked him what he enjoyed about

pigeon racing. He celebrated the sport's roots in working men's clubs and mining institutes: institutions established for the betterment of the people. He liked the way the fancy connected flyers with the places in which they lived.

'There was a time everyone in my area would fly birds,' he said, 'and on Friday they'd all race them. You'd see them in the pubs, the baskets of birds there for marking, the clocks for striking. As kids we were brought up into it. You could make a name for yourself with a good bird. You could start a line and it could become famous.'

Pigeon racing has always been a working-class, counter-intuitively urban pursuit. The sport was first invented in the eighteenth century by miners working in the coalfields of Liège in Belgium, and it quickly spread throughout Europe. At the turn of the century English fanciers, who had previously focused on fancy breeds, took notice of the incredible journeys these European pigeons were undertaking, and began to establish their own racing clubs. William Tegetmeier, an amateur biologist and keen fancier who was Darwin's main correspondent on pigeon matters, described these new birds – the *pigeons voyageurs* – in 1868. 'In rapidity and power of flying,' he wrote, they 'far exceed any other variety of pigeon with which I am acquainted. [. . .] this power of flight is conjoined with an attachment to home that is not surpassed by that of any other pigeon.'

Pigeon racing was brought to Britain, almost single-handedly, by a solicitor's clerk named Alfred Henry Osman, who was born in Bromley-by-Bow in 1864, and would go on to found a dynasty of pigeon fanciers. He had always been more interested in pigeons than the law, and soon gave up his job to found a newspaper, *The Racing Pigeon*, and spend more time with his birds. He organised the first pigeon races in the country on Wanstead Flats, just up the road from our house in Leyton. These early 'flapping races' were competed for by pairs of pigeons and raced over short distances. One bird would be released and made to fly back to its mate, which was held aloft by its owner. The races were fast and lively, but they didn't test the pigeon's homing abilities at all.

Later Osman was involved in organising races in which pigeons were transported far from home before being released. These took place before the development of the special clocks which allow the times of pigeons' arrivals to be recorded – like factory workers clocking in for a shift – and so in the early years ringed birds had to be physically presented at the club in order to be timed in after a race. After the pigeons had landed their owners would run through the streets carrying them, and living near the clubhouse conveyed a distinct advantage. Once the use of pigeon clocks became widespread, during the early twentieth century, flyers from further afield could compete on an equal footing.

As pigeon racing increased in popularity it was taken up mainly by an urban proletariat displaced from the countryside by industrialisation. Over time the abilities of the birds improved. Only the most successful pigeons were bred from, honing their speed and navigational abilities. During the nineteenth century a bird that could home reliably from 200 miles was remarkable; nowadays pigeons routinely fly twice that, and the best can race comfortably from 700 miles away.

It's easy to imagine how men – for they were nearly all men, often miners and factory workers who spent their working lives underground or trapped inside windowless workshops – might be attracted by a hobby which allowed them to shake off their earth-bound feelings and take flight. In a sketch of Spitalfields in East London written in 1851, Charles Dickens described pigeon flying as a symbol of release and escape. 'If your occupation in town or country ever oblige you to travel by Eastern Counties Railway,' he wrote:

> you may connect with this impression, a general idea that many pigeons are kept in Spitalfields, and you may remember to have thought, as you rattled along the dirty streets, observing the

pigeon-hutches and pigeon-traps on the tops of the poor dwellings, that it was a natural aspiration in the inhabitants to connect
themselves with any living creatures that could get out of that and
fly into the air. The smoky little bowers that you may have sometimes seen on the house-tops, among the pigeons, may have
suggested to your fancy – I pay you the poor compliment of
supposing it to be a vagrant fancy, like my own – abortions of the
bean-stalk that led Jack to fortune: by the slender twigs of which,
the Jacks of Spitalfields will never, never, climb to where the giant
keeps his money.

The sport of pigeon racing was, from the beginning, closely
associated with city life. Until 1976 most British pigeon flyers
trained their birds on the railways. The Transit of Poultry Order
of 1919 allowed unaccompanied birds to be sent by rail across the
country, where sympathetic stationmasters would release them
into the air before sending their empty baskets back home by
return train. In this way pigeons allowed their home-bound
owners to travel by proxy. The liberation points from which the
races began – Peterborough, Wetherby, Berwick, and Thurso to
the north; Tarbes, Barcelona, and Rome to the south – became
talismanic: a litany of distant places many flyers would never even
see. If the Tour de France gave, as Roland Barthes argued in
*Mythologies*, French people their first look at a map of France, for
many British people, pigeon racing provided an imaginative
cartography which was just as powerful, and just as mysterious.

Ian loved the sport but was unsure about its future. Globally,
pigeon racing was booming – in East Asia and China in particular
it was becoming increasingly popular, with flyers paying huge
amounts of money for famous European birds. But in Britain
the fancy was dying. Active participation in pigeon racing has
declined precipitously since its heyday in the 1950s, when there
were a quarter of a million flyers in Britain alone. Nowadays,
the RPRA has only 20,000 members, and numbers are dropping

all the time. The problem was not just that young people weren't taking it up, but that old flyers were dying or giving it up. The clubmen were getting weary, and the world seemed increasingly hostile to their hobby. Neighbours objected to the presence of pigeon lofts, which they associated with smell and disease, and fewer people had the time to feed and train their birds twice daily, or to give them the careful attention they required during the moult and around breeding time. Young people didn't seem interested either.

'Too busy playing their computers,' Ian said. 'They don't like to be outside.'

The only new flyers coming into the sport were from abroad. 'The immigrants are keeping it alive,' Ian told me. 'It's quite a big sport in Poland, in Morocco. I think it reminds them of home.'

As small back-garden racers left the fancy, many clubs had become dominated by the 'mob flyers' who kept huge numbers of birds in enormous lofts and raced attritionally, entering dozens of birds into each race and not worrying if few of them made it home. Doping, too, was becoming more of a problem. It had always been there in the sport – the plot of Georges Simenon's first novel concerns a chemist who develops a pill that acts as a *Columbidae* purgative, lightening pigeons before races so they can fly more quickly – but now the substances being used were more effective than ever, and were increasingly difficult to trace. Unscrupulous flyers dosed their birds with tinctures of amphetamine and cocaine, pushing them until their hearts burst.

'Unfortunately, we have had to bring in rules on doping,' said Ian. 'There have been instances in Holland and Belgium where people have been caught. They do it for prestige, and money. But it's no good for the birds, or the sport.'

Others were packing up because of raptor attacks. Many fanciers were convinced that the RSPB and others had colluded in reintroducing birds of prey to urban centres, where they picked off pigeons on training runs, or when they flew through on race days. Of these, the most hated was the peregrine falcon, which the fanciers nicknamed 'Percy'. They hated Percy with a cheerful savagery which surprised me, and had developed many strategies to stop attacks. Some tried to protect their birds by attaching red flashing lights to their feet, or painting large dots onto their wings which, they hoped, would scare the hawks off. Others waited until they spotted a raptor flying around their loft and let off fireworks to drive it away.

'Sometimes a peregrine will attack, and it'll take one, or two,' Ian said. 'But the rest will panic and fly into things. A lot are killed, but the majority of losses are caused by the others panicking.'

Once a hawk learns the location of a loft they might come back and hit it every day, picking off birds one by one. In response the RPRA has set up a network called the 'Raptor Alliance' which monitors and reports hawk attacks on pigeons in the hopes of drawing attention to the issue. It didn't seem to be having much effect.

'The public are very much on the side of the hawks,' Ian said sadly.

I wondered what he thought of the ethics of pigeon racing. Recently PETA had started a campaign to have the sport banned. Was it cruel to remove birds from their lofts, send them miles across country, to an unfamiliar place, and force them to find their own way home?

'Well, you never really own a pigeon,' Ian said, 'they're not pets. There's a saying, "They're only your birds when the trap's shut." Pigeons aren't wild, but they aren't tame either. The way I look at it, every time you open the loft they're free to leave. If they didn't like it they could go. And some of them do. But those that stay, I think, must feel happy in their homes. There's something quite magic about it. Sitting outside, watching the birds come home, wondering where they've been and what they've seen on the way. Getting a bird in from a long race – anything over five hundred miles – well, there's no feeling like it.'

*

Ian had business to attend to with the judges, so in the afternoon I wandered around the show alone. It was at the back of the main hall, on a stall manned by a husband and wife, that I spotted them. There were twelve pigeons for sale, their beaks large, flat and leathery, as they are for the first few months after they emerge from the egg, like the backs of baby sea turtles. Tufts of yellow fledging down were still visible on their heads and around their necks, as though they were wearing ill-fitting blond wigs.

The pair that caught my eye were deep grey, or chalky blue – they seemed to change colour depending on the angle from which I looked at them – with two black bars running across the base of their wing covers. Their plumage was flat and dense, absorbing the light like velvet. The birds looked slightly awkward in their bodies, as though they'd not quite grown into them, but they did seem to have, I thought, remembering Ian's advice, good balance and poise.

Every now and then they gave out high-pitched squeaks – young pigeons do for the first few months of their life, which is where they get their common name: 'pigeon' is a French derivation of the Latin *pipio*, or 'little squeaking bird'. One was squatter and slightly bigger; the other taller and leaner, with a long, elegant neck. Their eyes, not yet the orange they would become as they matured, were unfathomably dark, the skin around them dry, the texture of old window putty. They were around a month old, weaned and ready to leave the nest, but not so mature that they would be unable to imprint on a new home. They were just beginning to flap experimentally around their cages.

The man on the stall passed one to me and I held it, spread its feathers, checked its eyes and feet as Ian had shown me. I felt its wings straining against my hand. I was given a studbook listing the performances of their immediate relatives, which didn't mean much to me. One of their grandparents, 'Dream Maker', was, I read, 'direct from Super Gaby, breeder of endless winners. Dream Maker is sire and grandsire to several champions including Lord of the Rings and Lady of the Rings.'

I asked how much they were.

'Sixty pounds each,' the breeder said. 'They're direct from Gaby.'

I said I had no idea who Gaby was.

'Gaby Vandenabeele. You've never heard of Gaby? How much would you pay?' he asked.

We agreed on £40 for both. It seemed like a lot of money for birds which looked no different from those I had seen pecking around Blackpool's waterfront before the show, but also incredibly cheap, for birds which might turn out to be champions.

The breeder gave me some forms which would transfer ownership of the birds.

'They're siblings, so you don't want to breed them together,' he said. 'I can sell you another direct Gaby so you can breed from those if you like?'

He gestured to a ragged and sorry-looking pigeon in a different cage, but my heart was set on the pair I had picked.

'You can always breed them with others,' his wife said, 'but then you lose the line.'

'You can't lose the line,' her husband insisted. 'You mustn't lose the line.'

'Oh, loads of people lose the line,' his wife said to me conspiratorially. 'It wants fresh blood.'

She took my money and placed the birds in two cardboard boxes lined with sawdust.

'Nice pair of blues,' Ian said later when I showed him what I'd bought. 'This one's especially good,' he said, holding up the slimmer of the two, which he said was a hen. I wondered what it was he had noticed in her.

I hung around at the show for a while longer, watching the prize-giving, listening to the speeches listing the various, unintelligible accomplishments of the flyers, and taking free samples of grain from the stalls so that I'd have something to feed the pigeons when I got home. But I was conscious of the long journey ahead of me, and that the birds would soon need feeding and watering. I didn't want to have to get them out on the train, as I thought the other passengers might object. So after a while, as the light began to fade in Blackpool, I said goodbye to Ian, picked up my two cardboard boxes, and left.

*8.20 a.m., The Moray Firth, 460 miles from home*

On the internet pigeon forums there is fierce debate over the
route the birds take as they head south from Thurso. No one
knows for sure. Many have made the journey before – racing
pigeons don't really come into form on long distances until their
third or fourth year, and for Thurso most flyers send only their
best – but this is the furthest my birds have ever been away from
home. They do not recognise the land they now find themselves
flying over.

I try to follow their likely journey on the map in front of me
as they fly. I try to think like them, anticipating what terrain
they will want to avoid, the line they might take between the
mountains.

Initially, I imagine, the pack breaks in two. The birds from the
clubs in the West of England will follow their own route, breaking down the middle of the country towards Inverness, before
continuing west of the Cairngorms. Those flying in my federation, all heading to London, will stay further over to the east,
hugging the coast.

Initially they follow the A9, twenty miles south across the
width of the peninsula, down to Latheron, on the north side of
the Moray Firth. When they get to the coast they have a choice.
The most direct route would take the flock out over the sea
towards Fraserburgh, sixty miles across wild open water. But,
although they can be trained to fly over the sea, most pigeons

don't like to do so, and will do anything to avoid it. Most stick to the land, following the curve of the coast as it bends south-west. Those that do break across the water will have the advantage over the ones that decide not to.

They follow the line of the road, passing over the towns and villages below: Dunbeath, Berriedale, Helmsdale, Brora. The names mean nothing to them. The land looks wild from up here, abstract slabs of green and brown, not the ordered patchwork of fields they will encounter further south. There is forest, and water. In the distance there is mountain. The air is sharp and they can smell the sea in it. They've been on the wing for an hour when they reach the middle of the Firth, where the wind is blowing gently from the north-west, and the air is still cool. They will need to fly for fourteen more if they want to make it home while the light remains.

# 3

## Homemaking

I had gone to Blackpool without a clear plan of what I would do with the pigeons once I brought them home, and when I got back to London that evening I had nowhere to keep them. So I put them in a large cardboard box which I left in the lean-to next to the kitchen, where it sat beside the washing machine and the dishwasher, under a drying rack, while I decided where they should live.

The next morning I went downstairs and opened the box. I was half expecting something terrible to have happened in the night. But they were still there, standing in the corner, huddled together and giving out faint squeaks of alarm as I loomed over them. I picked one up. I'd shown them to Natalya the night before, and after a few tentative attempts I'd learned to move with conviction so as not to frighten them, grasping them across their backs with my fingers under their bellies, pinning their wings to their sides. As I held them I could feel their hollow-boned lightness, the soft delicacy of their just-fledged wings aching to stretch.

For the next week the birds stayed in the lean-to. Dora, Natalya and I watched them as they made themselves at home. Every now and then they'd unfurl their wings and shake their feathers, making a sound like the riffle shuffle of a deck of cards. They stood skitteringly on the sink, struggling to get a grip on its metal surface. They fluttered up to perch on the shelves above, which I'd covered in newspaper to protect from their droppings, squeaking softly at each other as they settled. In the evening they flew up to the drying rack, puffed up their feathers so that they looked like old men snuggling into oversize raincoats, and fell asleep standing on one leg.

Dora was delighted by their presence. She liked to feed them, and stroke their heads as I held them for her. In the mornings I'd go in with my corn tin and rattle it before feeding them, hoping they would come to associate the sound with food, which would make it easier to train them to come into the loft when I eventually let them free. Next I'd clear out the newspaper strewn on the floor, which they had ripped to ribbons in the night. I'd clean the surfaces and lay fresh newspaper before going to work, as their shit was prodigious. Every other day I ran the tap into the sink so they could bathe in it.

But they were growing up quickly, and the longer they were kept inside the less likely it was that they'd stick around once they were given their liberty. If I waited much longer they'd be too strong on the wing and might fly far from home at the first opportunity, getting lost before they realised where they had gone. It was clear I needed to build them a home of their own.

There aren't many books about how to keep and train a team of racing pigeons. For the most part the fancy is an oral tradition. The pigeon racing newspapers to which I had subscribed were full of obituaries and nostalgic articles about the heyday of the sport, but they didn't contain much practical information for the novice flyer. Still, in the library I found a few books – Edgar Chamberlain's baroque and pompous *The Homing Pigeon*; Colin Osman's no-nonsense *Racing Pigeons: A Practical Guide to the Sport* – which described how to build a suitable home for the birds. One book, by an eighteenth-century mathematician and naturalist named Georges-Louis Leclerc, Comte de Buffon, was full of advice on how to construct a good loft. To successfully home a flock of pigeons you mustn't build them a prison or a cage, Leclerc advised, but instead construct a place in which they *want* to live, and freely choose to return to. He said that pigeons aren't really pets at all, but are instead creatures which might deign to live with you if you provide a home for them which they approve of, but which they will always be free to leave. 'They really are not domestics like dogs and horses,' he wrote, 'or prisoners like fowls: they are rather voluntary captives, transient guests who continue to reside in the dwellings assigned them only because they like it and are pleased with the situation which affords abundance of food, and all the conveniences and comforts of life.' The relationship between fancier and pigeons is like a marriage, Leclerc thought: an agreement between equals rather than keeper and kept.

In the wild pigeons live together in vast colonies, many hundreds of birds strong, but as mine matured they would need to be provided with a cell, or nest box, which would become their own home territory, and to which they would return for the rest of their lives. The stronger the connection the pigeons had with their territory within the loft the more motivated they would be to return to it. According to Leclerc, the only way to induce pigeons to home well was to appeal to their sense of the homely.

I had bought some wood and drafted in my brother Ben to help, and gradually the loft took shape. It was built of plywood, 12 foot long and divided into sections, so that, come autumn, I could separate the cocks and hens to stop them from breeding over the winter, when they could rest. It had wire and dowel windows, and a door fitted with shutters to protect against the foxes that roamed the garden at night. The roof overhung the loft on each side to stop the rain blowing in.

Though I only had two pigeons I planned on buying more, and so Ben built twelve nest boxes with hinged fronts and little doors, and we placed these in the section in which the cocks were to be housed. In the hens' section we built twelve V-shaped perches and fixed these to the walls. I left the third section empty in anticipation of the young birds I hoped I would breed the following spring. Finally, we built an aviary so that the pigeons could get outside into the weather when they weren't flying, and fitted an electric fence around the bottom to deter the foxes.

The loft was not the prettiest thing we'd ever built. The roofing felt was rumpled in the middle, and one of the doors was slightly warped so that it didn't close easily. But I was proud of it, and the pigeons seemed to like it, and they quickly settled into their new home. On the first day they flew its length and explored the nest boxes. They stood on the perches and pecked gently at each other as they sat in the aviary enjoying the thrumming rain. They stayed close together, seeming to take comfort from their proximity. That night I locked and shuttered the door and windows and hoped the foxes' screams wouldn't unsettle them too much. Soon it would be time to let them fly free.

A month or so before Dora was born, just after we had moved to Leyton, I found myself in B&Q on a Saturday night and experienced what I thought of then – looking back, with a sense of sheepish embarrassment – as my 'crisis'. When we had first moved, Natalya and I had been hit with a wave of DIY enthusiasm: we stripped walls and fitted bookshelves, we embarked on the ritual sanding of the floors. We picked out paint colours from little booklets and armed ourselves with the light bulbs and stepladders and mops with which, we hoped, we could assert some ownership over our new house. It felt as if there was something slightly performative about our newfound domesticity. Natalya was distracted and uncomfortable, dealing with impending motherhood with a wise pragmatism, and had no time for such silliness. But, standing there in the aisles, eyeing up hedge trimmers, I was suddenly struck by an overwhelming fear of just how small our world was about to become.

For the previous few years, while working as a bicycle courier, I'd enjoyed an exhilarating sense of freedom: pedalling sixty miles a day through London's streets, delivering parcels and contracts and anything else that couldn't be emailed or faxed. It was a low-paid and arduous job, but I had loved it. I loved the physical exhaustion it provided: the blissful, almost hallucinatory fatigue you experienced after a week on the bike. I loved the fact that it was, in the end, meaningless work: that nothing was at stake, but also that nothing would ever come of it. I felt unburdened, and thought my life would continue to spool out ahead of me uncomplicatedly, like the road passing beneath my wheels. Never have I slept so soundly. But in leaving couriering, moving to Leyton and getting what I still thought of as my first proper job, I had, almost overnight, lost that sense of freedom.

In his 'personal diary' *My Heart Laid Bare*, the poet Charles Baudelaire, noted urban wanderer and inventor of the *flâneur*, described what he called the *grande maladie* of '*l'horreur du domicile*': the horror of home. That winter, as we waited for Dora to arrive, I began to wonder whether I was suffering from Baudelaire's *grande maladie*: a fear that freedom lay behind me, that I'd be sapped by fatherhood and work and the demands of domesticity – by the pram in the hall – and that the home I was building with Natalya would become a kind of prison. I knew my anxiety was a deeply self-indulgent one, borne in large part by the privilege I had as a man. But, as a feeling, it was no less real for that.

As Natalya's due date approached I became gripped by a vague and manic wanderlust. I found myself dreaming about adventures I would never undertake: walking across Europe, cycling to Russia, sailing around Great Britain in a sleek wooden ketch. I became addicted to a series of YouTube videos in which men wearing plaid shirts and full beards restored wooden sailing boats – milling wood from trees they'd felled themselves, smelting lead keels and anointing the planks adoringly with varnish – before sailing them across the fathomless ocean. I told anyone who would listen that I was going to go on trips to the wild moors, smell the fresh dampness of the rained-on ground, catch glittering trout from lowland streams.

Natalya considered my proposals with bemused and patient indulgence. I couldn't even drive, she pointed out to me one day when I announced I wanted to buy a boat and sail it to the Frisian Islands, let alone sail. Besides, she said, I had other responsibilities now. I wondered if I was so interested in adventuring

because, according to most measures, my life was so settled. I
loved my family. I liked my job. I was not depressed. I was not ill.
I was not an alcoholic or addicted to drugs. I felt utterly sane.
Still, it sometimes felt as though something – the idea of escape,
rather than its reality – was missing from my life.

On Independence Day in 1845, Henry David Thoreau moved
from the village of Concord, Massachusetts, to a shack he had
built next to Walden Pond. He moved there, he wrote in *Walden*,
the book in which he described his year in the woods, to 'live
deep and suck out all the marrow of life, to live so sturdily and
Spartan-like as to put to rout all that was not life, to cut a broad
swath and shave close, to drive life into a corner, and reduce it to
its lowest terms.' In doing so he provided a blueprint for disaf-
fected urban dwellers that is still beguiling. *Walden* is a book
about an idealised adventure that took the form of a withdrawal
– into the woods; into the self – but what I found most striking
about it as I read it again that winter was that in it Thoreau also
described, meticulously and obsessively, the way he set about
making a home for himself in the woods.

He had built his hut – 'an airy and unplastered cabin'– on land
owned by his friend Ralph Waldo Emerson, claiming the timber
he used and the stones from which he built his chimney under
squatters' rights. (He bought the frame of the building from an
Irish navvy, whom he promptly evicted, along with his family –
in *Walden* he describes, without a trace of guilt, them walking
forlornly away in the early morning light.) In the book Thoreau
goes into great detail about the hut's construction, arguing that
making a house should be an essential human function: like
making music or writing poetry. 'There is some of the same
fitness in a man's building his own house,' he wrote, 'that there is
in a bird's building its own nest.'

At Walden Pond Thoreau withdrew into himself in order, he
said, to find liberation. He stopped reading the news and sending
letters, and began to contemplate nature to try to find a new way

of living. But in leaving home he had recreated, almost perfectly, the conditions of domesticity he hoped to flee. His life of isolation was partly a myth of his own creation. He lived only two miles from Concord, where his mother and sisters continued to live, and he often went into town to sell crops he had grown, or just for company. He lunched each week with his grandmother, and often visited his mother, sometimes taking his dirty laundry to her to have it washed.

Thoreau wasn't the first man whose adventures were supported – were only made possible – by the drudgework of wives and mothers. It is easy to see him as a hypocrite, dependent as he was on the invisible labour of the women in his life to indulge in his fantasy of withdrawal. But perhaps this is just another example of the way in which home is always an artificial construct, one that can constrain as much as it can liberate. Homes, as Thoreau knew, are always ideals as much as they are real places: as much imagined and felt as they are built.

As a noun, home refers both to 'the place where a person or animal dwells' and 'a place where something originates, flourishes'. As a verb it means both to make a home, and to make *for* home. Etymologically, this doubled meaning of home pre-dates European languages in the form of the Indo-European word *kei*, meaning both to 'lie down' and to 'hold something dear'. The Old Norse *heima*, meaning home, house or village, cognate with the Old English *ham*, is the source of many words in modern European languages which differentiate between the physical structure in which you live and the feeling of dwelling in it: *talo* and *koti* in Finnish; *Haus* and *Heim* in German; *huis* and *heem* in Dutch; *hus* and *hjem* in Danish. And in English, *house* and *home*.

Until relatively recently the structure we would understand as the home simply didn't exist. Four hundred years ago most people in the West lived together in communal spaces, often sharing rooms, even beds, with servants and sometimes with animals, too. Furniture was scarce, and privacy unknown. 'In the Middle Ages,' writes the architectural theorist Witold Rybczynski in *Home*, 'people didn't so much live in their houses as camp in them.'

All this began to change during the seventeenth century, particularly in the Netherlands, when the rise of a professionalised urban bourgeoisie meant that the place in which you lived became separate from the place in which you worked. Houses no longer had to accommodate the trades or animals of their owners, but were designed to be structures purely for living in. Families became more intimate. Children, rather than being seen as little adults to be sent off to work as soon as they were physically able, were thought of as worth nurturing in their own right.

The emergence of the home, and the privacy it brought with it, soon made its influence felt across the arts. Dutch domestic painting from the period celebrated interior design and furnishing, and paintings often functioned as visual catalogues of a wealthy homeowner's belongings. The novel, a literary form that emerged just after the period in which the home was invented, is also concerned above all to describe interiors of various different kinds: the interiors of buildings, but also those of people. With rising literacy and cheap printing, a form of writing emerged that was designed to be read *at* home, in private and in silence, and to be enjoyed during that other great invention of modernity: leisure time.

Arguably the first novel written in English, Daniel Defoe's *Robinson Crusoe*, describes in painstaking detail two different kinds of homing. The first is Robinson's nostalgic longing for his own home, for the civilisation he has been removed from. He thinks often of his life back in London, and, in one memorable scene, fashions a parasol from palm fronds, imagining himself back home in London as he struts upon the strand. The second is his attempt to make a home in the place where he finds himself: to claim the unknown island as known territory. The novel reads, in part, as a domestic homemaking manual: a survivalist *Mrs Beeton*. Cut off from civilisation, Crusoe tries to apply the staunch

Protestant values of hard work and order to the *terra incognita* of the island on which he finds himself marooned.

The novel pays a great deal of attention to the processes involved in homemaking: Crusoe keeps meticulous records of his materials, and of the passing days. He builds shelter, makes fire, collects tools from the wreck of his ship, and domesticates goats, processes that are all described in a level of detail which to modern readers can feel laborious. So begins, too, the long and violent association between the idea of home and Empire. For Crusoe, as for the colonial enterprise more generally, the wide world exists primarily as raw material, to be claimed and shaped by the labour of industrious settlers. But in establishing their settlements and claiming their territory, colonialists inevitably excluded – and often annihilated – those who had lived in these places before them.

The exclusionary comfort of such homemaking – the way the familiar creates a refuge in uncertain terrain – is there in the very fabric of the novel as a form, too. The critic Edward Said has written about the way in which novels like Defoe's seem particularly concerned not just to describe the process of homemaking, but to make a home for their readers, a home on the page. In 'Reflections on Exile', his magisterial essay on the experience of displacement, Said argued that literature itself – especially in the form of the novel – could be thought of as a kind of home, and reading as a kind of homecoming. 'Classical epics,' Said writes:

> emanate from settled cultures in which values are clear, identities stable, life unchanging. The European novel is grounded on precisely the opposite experience, that of a changing society in which an itinerant and disinherited middle-class hero or heroine seeks to construct a new world that somehow resembles an old one left behind forever.

The sensibility provided by this new kind of narrative, and the ideas it expressed, influenced our psychology. The historian

John Lukacs has argued that the prefix 'self' rose to prominence only about three hundred years ago, alongside the invention of the modern home, in words such as 'self-centred' and 'self-esteem', 'self-love' and 'selfhood', and that a host of other words pertaining to subjectivity – 'disposition', 'ego', 'embarrassment', 'sentiment' – took on their modern meanings around the same time. 'Their use,' Rybczinski notes, 'marked the emergence of something new in the human consciousness: the appearance of the internal world of the individual, of the self, and of the family.' If modernity made the home, celebrating its creation in art and music and novels, then the idea of the home made the modern person in its turn.

By the end of January my two pigeons – named by Dora over breakfast, with great simplicity, 'Eggy' and 'Orange' – had begun to settle in to their new home. At first they were wary when I came near, taking anxious flight whenever I entered the loft. Over the next few days, however, they grew used to my presence. In the mornings, in the thin light of the winter dawn, I would open the fox-proof shutters that covered the door and window at night. I would whistle and rattle a can of grain, sounds which they had come to associate with food. Next I'd go inside to change their water and feed them, scraping their shit from the floor with a palette knife. When I reached a hand out towards them they would begin to growl, flitting their wings out to hit my hand away.

In the evenings I would go to the loft and feed them again, talking to them, picking them up and spreading their feathers, getting them used to being handled. I wouldn't call them tame, but within a week they'd grown to tolerate me, and would no longer fly off in panic when I got inside the loft with them. They were getting stronger on the wing by the day. It was time to let them out.

Osman, in his *Racing Pigeons*, warned that I might have already missed my chance. 'The first adventure out of the loft', he counselled, should not be delayed too late. If it is left for longer than about a fortnight after weaning the fancier will find that as the birds become older, they are more eager to fly and have the necessary strength to fly short distances; they are too strong on the wing. When he opens his loft for the first time, these older birds will fly out with a joyous flap of the wings and by the time they have begun to tire they will be outside the area they know and will not be able to return home.

Really, Eggy and Orange should have been let out a week ago, or, at least, I should have put them in a basket and carried them around the garden so that they could have got a sense of the lie of the land around them. But there was nothing that could be done about that now, and when the weather improved after a week of rain and snow, I decided the day had come to release them.

It was a grey morning in early February, but not as cold as it had been for the past few weeks, and, though the sky was overcast, visibility was good. Ian had told me to cut down on food the day before I let the pigeons out of the loft for the first time, so that they'd be hungry and less inclined to travel far away on their first flight. At 7.00 a.m., the time I usually fed them, I went to the loft and opened the door. I sat on a chair in the kitchen to watch what would happen next. For a while, neither bird noticed that they had been given their freedom. But after a few minutes Orange saw the open door and hopped towards it. Soon Eggy followed. They jumped up onto the door frame and poked their heads tentatively out, testing the air. They stood there for a few minutes, looking around the garden, cocking their heads to one side to gaze up the wall of the house, scanning the sky for threats.

Then, quite suddenly, without any obvious reason for the decision, they took flight. First one and then the other bird hopped into the air and flapped awkwardly towards the cherry tree at the back of the garden. The branch they landed on bent alarmingly under their weight. After a moment they flew up onto the roof of the house. Here they settled for a while, walking along the eaves and surveying the horizon. I took my eyes off them while I cleaned out the loft and put some grain in their feeder. By the time I'd finished, they'd vanished.

I didn't see them again all day. As the hours passed I began to feel deflated. My project had failed. The home I'd built for my pigeons had not been homely enough. I would have to begin again, buy new birds, work out what had frightened them and how to avoid it in future. Perhaps the nightly wailings of the foxes had unnerved them. Perhaps they were simply too old to be tamed. I was sad to think that they would still be out there as night fell. I sent a text to Ian to tell him they'd vanished. 'You might have left it too late,' he replied. 'But don't worry. If they've gone I'll breed you up another pair.'

At four in the afternoon, just as it was getting dark, I went back into the garden for one last look. It was then, in the failing light, that I noticed a bird, silhouetted against the sky on the roof of the next-door neighbour's house. It looked familiar: sleeker, thinner, more finessed than the feral pigeons on the roof opposite. I watched it as it moved closer, cautiously at first, then more confidently.

After a few minutes it flew down onto the windowsill of our house, and when it landed I could make out the red tag on its leg that marked it out as one of mine. Orange had returned. The air was still, and my heart was beating quickly, but I didn't want to spook him, so I feigned indifference. I watched with a hard, quiet intensity, as though I could will him to fly into the loft by thought alone.

Orange looked around, cocking his head, and I went up to the loft and opened the door. As I was doing so I heard the flutter of another pair of wings: Eggy flapped in through the dusk and landed on the roof of the neighbour's house.

I began whistling softly and rattling my tin of grain, not wanting to be too loud in case I spooked them. After a minute or two Orange swooped down from the windowsill onto the fence, and then down to the garden path. He walked slowly, not hurrying, towards me, approached the door of the loft, and jumped in.

Eggy was more skittish. She was still waiting on the roof. Next there was the problem of what to do with Orange while I waited for Eggy to come in. If I left the door of the loft open, Orange might eat his fill and then leave again before Eggy had worked up the courage to come in. He needed to be secured, so I went into the house to fetch a cardboard box, put Orange in it, then left the box in the loft with the door open.

Eggy, who had watched this operation with interest, hadn't moved any closer, but she hadn't flown off either. I moved away from the door, stood in the shadows under the tree, and waited. Just before the last light finally faded, Eggy folded her wings, fell off the roof into a long, effortless dive, and landed on the path in front of the loft. She hopped up to the door frame and turned several tight circles, as though making sure nothing was about to creep up on her, until finally, with a soft flutter and a coo, she turned one last time and hopped into the loft.

I followed her inside, closing the door behind me, and released Orange from his box. I watched them both feed for a while, stupidly amazed by what had just happened. It felt magical, just as Ian had promised: a quiet miracle no one else knew about, or would particularly care about if I told them. The birds I had bought in Blackpool – then a pair of strange, unknowable creatures – had left the loft I had built for them and taken flight. They had seen my world from above. They had felt its winds. And afterwards, of their own accord, they had decided to come back to the place which was now, I hoped, their home.

## 10.45 a.m., Dundee, 362 miles from home

Whatever route they've taken – whether they've crossed the Firth or followed the coast as it arcs down to the south – by now the birds have found their rhythm. The day is heating up, and the further south they travel the hotter it will get. At ground level the temperature is already 20°C; one hundred feet above the ground, where they are flying, it is 12°C. With a negligible following wind they fly at 50 miles per hour: a sustainable velocity, one they can keep up for hours. They beat their wings three times every second, 10,800 times an hour, and burn around 5 calories – the equivalent of one peanut – per hour of flight. This amounts to only 0.000462962963 calories per wingbeat, but it adds up. During a long flight like this they might lose a third of their body weight.

When flying, they tuck their legs in behind their bodies, so as to achieve a more aerodynamic shape. As they breathe, air is drawn into their lungs before being exhaled into their air sacs, allowing their lungs to fully empty between breaths and making them far more efficient at extracting oxygen from the air than humans are. Their hearts pump thick, oxygenated blood around their bodies 700 times per minute.

They avoid the mountains. From Fraserburgh they follow the curve of the coast, east past Peterhead, where the ships are preparing to put to sea, over Longhaven and Cruden Bay and Whinnyfold, and then on, around to Aberdeen. Though the air is warming up the sea is wild, and for now they fly over the land, staying in sight of the waves.

They fly in scattered lines, not quite taking turns at the front, in the manner of geese, but still benefiting from the aerodynamic advantage of the turbulence thrown up by the beating wings of the group. Pigeons flying in flocks navigate together, and experienced birds – those most confident in their wayfinding – will teach the other birds the most efficient lines home, but still no one is quite sure how these collective decisions are made.

Near Dundee the birds feel the first flutters of fatigue. It was from near here that a homing pigeon named Winkie made one of the most famous flights in wartime history, on 24 February 1943. Winkie was assigned to the crew of a British Bristol Beaufort bomber which crashed into the North Sea after suffering engine trouble on its way to Norway. The crew survived the crash but were stranded in their life raft, bobbing about in the freezing waters. They had sent out a brief radio message before they ditched, but reception was bad and they were unable to communicate their precise location.

As their plane broke up a container housing two pigeons fell into the sea. Both birds got wet and covered in oil, and one escaped into the air before the crew had time to attach a message to it.

This bird was Winkie, a two-year-old blue chequered hen with the ring number NEHU40NS. Winkie took to the skies at 4.30 p.m. She flew 120 miles, over the ocean at night, arriving back to her loft in Broughty Ferry, nestling in the crook of the River Tay, at 8.20 a.m. the next morning. Though she carried no message, as soon as she landed her owner, a man named George Ross, alerted the RAF, and a quick-witted NCO calculated the crew's likely position based on the time of the radio broadcast, Winkie's fatigued state, and her time of arrival back home. He was able to narrow the search area significantly, and the crew were picked up fifteen minutes later.

Four lives were saved that morning. The rescued men held a dinner in Winkie's honour, and a year later she was awarded the

Dickin Medal for animal gallantry. When she died, after the war, her body was stuffed and donated to Dundee's McManus museum, where it is still on display.

In his poem about Winkie's flight Douglas Dunn describes how, during a war that was all about borders and homelands, pigeons were able to transcend the messy contingencies of human geography. Rather than calculating her route with map and compass, Winkie – like the birds flying over the Firth today – consulted her 'table of instinct', finding the Tay's dent and following it home without ever knowing its name. For the names of places matter less than we think they do, and the comfort we take from living with animals stems in part from their indifference to human concerns and human borders. 'Your mission doesn't matter' Dunn's poem continues,

> Nor what unvisa'd coasts
> You cross on your postal expeditions,
> Nor the direction you take, or whatever
> Nationality is claimed for the forests below
> Or who pretends to own the air and seasons
> And the pronunciation of rivers and mountains.

# 4

## Ranging

As Dora grew and we tried to settle into family life, Natalya and I had pushed the possibility of having another child to the backs of our minds. The question was one we would confront in the future, when we had more time and felt more rooted in place. For the past year I had been a judge for a literary prize, a job which involved a great deal of reading. I had withdrawn to my room at the top of the house, and Natalya had been left to pick up the slack. But a few months before I had gone to Blackpool things had eased. With the reading over we finally had time for each other once again. In October Natalya had found out she was pregnant. Our happiness had been immediate and over-powering, but it was tempered by knowledge of the possibility of another loss, and the dull pain that had accompanied those we had experienced the year before. As autumn gave way to winter, however, we had come to accept – first tentatively, then joyfully – the idea that we were to have another child. It was due in the summer, and we started planning our lives around its arrival.

January and February had been cold – miserable months, months for hunkering down and hibernating, for the lighting of fires – but it was now early March, and the weather was beginning to turn. There were days when I could feel spring in the air. Buds were forming on the branches of the trees, and crocuses pushed up through the fallen leaves on the cricket pitch in front of the house. I began to spend more time outside in the garden, watching the birds.

The pigeon racing calendar is divided into two seasons. Old bird racing, for yearlings and older, runs from April to July. The young bird season, for pigeons born after 1 January in the year they are raced, begins after the old bird season has finished, around the time our second child was due to be born. Young bird races are shorter than those for old birds: stopping around 300 miles, where old birds might fly up to 700. During the first year of their lives Eggy and Orange would be eligible to race only as young birds. It was then that they would build the experience that would allow them to compete as old birds the following year, when, I had tentatively decided, I would send them to Thurso. I had five months to get them ready for their first race. I would need to begin training them 'on the road' – taking them progressively further away from the loft to teach them to home from unfamiliar locations – at least six weeks before this. But before they'd be ready for their road training they would need to have been flying confidently on their own around the loft for a couple of months, building up their maps of what biologists call the 'familiar zone': the home territory immediately surrounding their loft.

Eggy and Orange were now flying well, but once their training began the possibility of losing them would be high. Losses – either while they are flying around the loft or during training and races – are common during the first year of a homing pigeon's life, and birds are more likely to be lost when flying in small groups or on their own than when flying as part of a larger flock. If I wanted to be sure of finishing the season with any pigeons left for the following year's old bird races, I would need to get hold of a few more.

Though it's hard to believe, there is a thriving online marketplace for pigeons. Specialist auction sites list hundreds of birds a week during the season, bred by enthusiastic amateurs in their garden sheds, or on the large stud farms which buy up famous birds to trade on their pedigrees. Offspring from well-known lines can be very expensive (in 2013 a bird named 'Bolt' from the loft of Leo Herremans, one of the most famous Belgian flyers, sold to a Chinese businessman for £260,000), but it's easy to find cheaper birds online, too.

I began to trawl the websites, looking for pigeons with which to expand my flock. I asked Ian for advice and he sent links to likely looking bloodlines. I liked the names of the lines – Jan Aarden, Janssen, Vinkenborg – and the way that, unlike in horse studding, strains were named after famous breeders rather than for individual winning birds. Late one night I put in a drunken bid for six dark chequered long-distance birds from a breeder in Cornwall. They turned up three days later, blinking and squeaking in the cardboard box in which they'd been sent, with 'LIVE PIGEONS' written on the side, and went into the loft to join Eggy and Orange. A week later I bought four more – dusky blue hens – from a stud in Yorkshire. Two more arrived a few days later from a fancier in Norfolk who, when I phoned him to check on delivery, praised the tenacity of his birds, their strength on the wing, their vigour.

I now had fourteen young birds in my loft, and before I could start their training I had to settle them. After Eggy and Orange's first flight I had attached a trap – a small box fitted with narrow bars through which they could enter but not leave – to the side of the loft, and built a wire settling cage which I could fit around the trap. For a few days I placed the new birds – six at a time – within this cage. They would stand on the landing board, looking around the garden and up at the sky. After I'd left them there for an hour I would open the trap and rattle my tin of corn. At first it took them a while to realise they were now free to enter the loft, and I had to gently usher them towards the bars until they dropped through. But after a few days they learned what the rattling signified, and would trap as soon as I called.

By early March the time had come to let the whole flock fly free for the first time. I waited until later in the day than I had when I'd first released Eggy and Orange, hoping that if they did decide to fly off they wouldn't venture far before night fell, when they would roost up until morning. I opened the trap at 4.00 p.m. The sky was overcast, the wind low. It was unseasonably cold. One by one the birds emerged. Eggy and Orange immediately took to the air, flying off over the trees. The others, the new birds, flew up to the roof, where they stood around pecking at the honeysuckle which grew up the wall behind. Every so often one would try to fly, stretching its wings and lifting itself a few inches above the ground, but never fully committing to the air. They seemed nervous to venture too far from the loft. Their home was an anchor, giving them a base from which to begin their explorations of the world.

After forty minutes or so Eggy and Orange came back to land on the roof. I opened the trap and rattled my tin and whistled. The younger birds seemed confused for a moment – they knew that the sound meant food was available, but quite where that food would come from was a mystery. Some fluttered in panic up into the air. One flew towards me and landed on my head. But after Eggy and Orange had come in to trap, four of the new birds followed them through the bars, and then the others realised what they were expected to do. Moments later they had all entered the loft through the trap and begun to feed.

For the next few weeks I flew the pigeons every morning and evening, and my life quickly fell into the rhythm provided by their comings and goings. When I got to the loft in the morning they would be waiting by the door of the trap, itching to be released. As soon as I opened it they would take off – laboriously at first, stirring the air beneath them with deep beats of their wings, then more easily, as they flew vertically up through the bare branches of the trees. When they got above the tree line the wind would hit and they would heel against it, like sailing boats catching a sudden gust, and arc off out of sight.

As they flew in the mornings I would work downstairs at the kitchen table, half watching them over the top of my computer screen as they flitted across my peripheral vision. Gradually their flight revealed things. On rainy days they would stay close to the house, their feathers having not yet developed the water-resistant chalky bloom which protects the plumage of older birds against the soddening rain. But on still days, when the sky was clear, they would climb higher and higher into the blue, rolling over each other with staccato feints and dodges. The sun caught their pale bellies and their beating wing tips as they turned into it, framing them with fire. Their shadows flickered across the wall at the back of the garden.

Their flight was joyous. Exuberant. Sometimes it looked as though they had lost control – that they were falling rather than flying – and I was afraid they would hit a building, or scalp themselves on the telephone wires that spidered across the street in front of the house. *Columbidae* take their name from the Greek *columba*, or 'diver', a name which describes the sculling way that they flap their wings, like swimmers, and when they flew together in a kit – the word fanciers use to describe a well-trained flock of pigeons – they seemed to expend hardly any energy at all in flight. When battling high winds, they would lift their shoulders high and form a V with their wings, the better to cut through the turbulent air. It looked like play, this flight, but really they were learning: learning to manoeuvre their bodies efficiently through the air's invisible eddies and currents, and learning too the lie of the land over which they flew.

After an hour or so they would begin to tire, their height diminishing on each circuit of the house. Eventually, after a few false approaches, they would come in to land, one after another, with a low, whistling flutter, on the roof of the loft. Their wings beat backwards as they approached; their tails spread wide, acting as air brakes. Usually they'd enter the trap within seconds, scrambling over each other in their keenness to eat, but if I'd misjudged the amount of feed I'd given them the night before they might stay out longer, dawdling on the roof and looking around, lingering in the sunshine and ignoring my increasingly frantic whistles and rattles. Occasionally, if I couldn't get them in before I had to leave to go to work, they stayed out all day, only coming back inside in the evening to feed. Once or twice they stayed out all night. When this happened I slept badly, fretful until I saw them the next morning lined up on the roof, waiting to be let back in.

Despite my childhood interest in pigeons, before Eggy and Orange entered my life I had never been much of a bird watcher, and my knowledge of avian life was limited. Still, as I watched them I came to notice things about the sky, and about the birds they shared it with. I began to study them, using my phone to video their landings and watching them back in slow motion, trying to work out the tricks of their movement, like Muybridge with his galloping horses. At half speed their agility was astonishing. Between plummeting off the roof of the house and landing on the loft they'd twist their bodies 180 degrees, grasping out with their feet to touch the ground before trusting it to take their inconsequential weight. Dora was fascinated by them, and wanted to know about the other birds that flew over our house, so I bought a pair of powerful binoculars and a book of bird identification from which we tried to learn the names. In watching, things were revealed to us. 'Attention', wrote the poet and bird watcher Mary Oliver, 'is the beginning of devotion.'

In my flight diary I noted the weather, wind direction and intensity, the time I let the birds out and how long they flew for. I listened. The garden was not a quiet place. Buses hummed along the High Road, machinery clunked in the distance, scaffolders shouted to each other, a roofer's gas torch roared. High overhead, planes groaned as they came in to land at London City Airport. Underneath it all, with the regularity of clockwork, came the soft, mechanical whirring of the pigeons' wings as they passed overhead.

The sky, I came to realise, was composed of several different layers, the inhabitants of which rarely interacted with each other. At ground level, as the spring sun began to warm the air, tiny flies blew around in clouds, looking like television interference, or the black spots you see before you faint. Higher up, in the trees, the bees and hoverflies buzzed, feeding from the blossoms that were emerging on the cherry tree. Small birds skimmed along the top of the fence at the back of the garden. Magpies flitted in each morning and cawed from the top of the trees, scattering the starlings and blue tits that gathered on the feeder in the neighbour's garden. I watched a pair of sparrows build a nest in the gutter of the house next door, and hoped they wouldn't be washed away when the spring rains came.

In the layer above, just over the rooftops but still close to the ground, lived the pigeons. The feral colony roosted on the houses opposite, flying across in the afternoons to eat the grain that had fallen to the floor under the feeder in my neighbour's garden. They flew with a cocky efficiency, swooping in through the trees with barely a wingbeat wasted. Sometimes I'd see another flock of racing pigeons far above, which I would later learn belonged to a fancier named Terry, a tall and quiet man with the air of a country vet, who had raced in most of the clubs in East London at one time or another, and flew his birds from his loft behind the bus garage on the High Road. Terry's birds looked like him: neat and trim, and they flew far higher and faster than mine.

Every evening a flock of brilliant green parakeets would swoop in a salvo over the house, making for the poplar trees on the marshes, screeching their Phaser-gun chirrups as they went. Ring-necked parakeets are relatively new to London but, like pigeons, they have come to thrive in the city, especially in the last few decades, as global warming has allowed them to breed. A persistent rumour – too wonderful to fact-check – is that the original pair were released by Jimi Hendrix from Carnaby Street as a publicity stunt, or an act of strangely tender Rock 'n' Roll rebellion. Others say that they escaped from the set of Humphrey Bogart's *The African Queen*, parts of which were filmed at Isleworth Studios in 1951. Wherever they originated, they first got a foothold in West London in the 1960s, and have been making their slow progress eastwards across the city, following the prevailing winds, ever since.

Far above, in a zone of their own, were the soarers and the seers: the gulls and geese and cormorants, flying with purpose on their migratory journeys, or to the reservoirs in the east to fish or roost. Above them flew the hawks. Once I watched as a pair of sparrowhawks broke for my flock high above the block of flats on the High Road. As they came nearer the feral birds took off from the roof opposite in panic. The hawks spent the next five minutes harrying the flock, wheeling and plunging towards them, hoping to pick off a straggler. Eventually they gave up and flew away to the north, but my birds wouldn't come back inside for hours, and one never came home at all.

After a few weeks my pigeons began to explore further afield. They'd head east over the scrubland of the old industrial estate behind our house, which was earmarked for development but currently lay fallow, providing a home for the foxes which my neighbour fed each night with hunks of bone that I'd find, half-chewed, scattered around my garden in the mornings. Or they would fly west over the cricket ground, soaring high above the plane trees along its edge as it bent round to the west. Sometimes they would travel north, following the railway line that picked its way between the houses towards Wanstead Flats. By wing they traced the layout of the streets below them, mapping the artificial canyons of the terraced houses, describing in the air the shapes of the roads beneath. As I watched I sometimes felt as though I was flying with them, learning this new territory alongside the birds.

I'd grown to trust them even when they flew far out of sight, and they seemed to be beginning to trust me, too, feeding from my hand when they trapped back in to the loft. But one day in the middle of March I let them out as usual and they took to the wing, flew up above the trees towards the railway line, and vanished over the roofs of the houses opposite. I kept watching, expecting them to pop back into view from the east, having followed the line of the High Road over to the cricket ground.

Minutes passed, then hours, and I began to wonder what had become of them.

The early stages of a pigeon's life are crucial in developing their ability to home from unknown locations when they grow up. While flying in the vicinity of home, pigeons navigate by what's called 'pilotage': following clear, established lines marked out by familiar landmarks. Within their home territory pigeons will often use roads or railways or other man-made markers to find their way, and once they have developed what they know to be a safe route they will tend to stick to it, even if it isn't the most efficient approach back to the loft. Biologists call this phenomenon 'route loyalty', and studies involving the GPS tracking of pigeons have shown just how 'stereotyped' and predictable their homing routes can be. Over time, pigeon fanciers learn the lines their birds favour when they return from certain race points, and know where to look for them in the sky when they are due back.

When they are a few months old, a group of birds will often take to the wing and fly far off, out of sight, in the way my young birds had. They will explore for hours, sometimes staying out all day. This behaviour is called 'ranging', or 'routing', or 'running', and it is a nervous time for any pigeon flyer. Though the birds sometimes get lost, ranging is an important part of a pigeon's navigational development, for it is during these early flights that they learn the landmarks they will refer to for the rest of their lives. It is only when they have been ranging well for several months that you can take them away from the loft and begin to train them from the road.

Quite how pigeons find their way home when they are released from unknown locations has proved to be one of the most disputed questions within the field of animal navigation. Charles Darwin's friend and correspondent, the pigeon fancier William Tegetmeier, believed that homing could be explained by vision alone. 'The idea of instinct is absurd,' he argued in his book *The*

*Homing or Carrier Pigeon* (*Le Pigeon Voyageur*): rather than being drawn home by some unknowable instinctive mechanism, a bird 'thrown in a new locality' would, he thought, typically fly around 'in gradually increasing circles, until at length it descries some familiar object, and then, and only then, dart off on its homeward flight.' A good intelligent bird thrown from the same place a second time would, Tegetmeier thought, waste no time ranging. 'There is no wheeling round,' he observed, 'but the road being known, he is off instantly.'

In the nineteenth century most biologists believed, along with Tegetmeier, that pigeons navigated either by using sight-based pilotage or by employing a form of dead reckoning: what biologists now call 'path integration'. By keeping track of the twists and turns of a journey away from home, it was thought, a pigeon could calculate the direction it needed to head in to find its way back. Think of the way in which some people are able, when wandering around an unfamiliar city, to keep track of the direction of their hotel despite the twists and turns they may take on the journey away from it. This is how ants navigate when they leave their colonies to search for food (a thesis that has been proved by attaching tiny stilts to ants' legs, causing them to miscalculate the length of their stride, and thus making them unable to home), and it might also, many nineteenth-century biologists believed, explain other forms of animal navigation.

In a letter written to the journal *Nature* in 1873, Charles Darwin recounted a story told by Ferdinand Von Wrangell, the Russian explorer, which he thought might show how animals used dead reckoning to navigate. In Northern Siberia Von Wrangell had noted the 'wonderful manner' in which Siberians were able to keep a true course towards their destinations despite 'passing for a long distance through hummocky ice, with incessant changes of direction, and with no guide in the heavens or on the frozen sea'. The Siberians' ability to navigate without map or compass didn't depend on any special sensory ability, Darwin argued, but could be explained through vision combined with proprioception – the body's sense of its own position in space – and memory alone. They didn't possess 'any special sense which is quite absent in us', said Darwin. Instead, they simply kept track of the deviations and distances of their outward journeys, and used this knowledge to plot a course for home when they wanted to get back to it. 'All men are able to do this in a greater or less degree,' Darwin concluded, 'and the natives of Siberia apparently to a wonderful extent, though probably in an unconscious manner.' It was this mechanism, he thought, that accounted for how animals homed, too.

Yet despite Darwin's support, the idea that pigeons navigated by dead reckoning was disproved fairly quickly. Birds placed in darkened revolving drums on their outward journeys were able to find their way back home from unfamiliar release sites without trouble. Others were anaesthetised for the outward journey before being released, but again no decline in homing efficiency was observed. It soon became apparent that something else, something far more mysterious, must be going on.

One thing that was clear, however, was that when flying around their home lofts pigeons navigated by memory, using the visual maps they had developed as young birds to locate themselves. In 1956 the German zoologist Gustav Kramer decided to test whether pigeons which were never allowed to fly free would be able to home successfully from distant release points. He conducted a series of experiments in which pigeons were kept, from their fledging onwards, in an aviary which allowed them to exercise but never to fly outside the loft. By observing the direction these birds headed when they were first released from a new liberation site, noting their 'vanishing bearings' and keeping records of where they were reported by other fanciers when they went missing, Kramer discovered that his aviary-bred pigeons were no worse at navigating over long distances than were their free-flying companions. But they *were* much worse at getting back inside their lofts once they'd returned to their familiar territory, as they had no idea what they looked like from above. To

know home, he concluded, a pigeon had to have been allowed to
see it from the air at a young age. Birds that were not allowed to
range would never be good at homing, therefore. They had to be
given their freedom: allowed to leave home in order to learn how
to get back to it. They would use the maps they built when
ranging to navigate for the rest of their lives.

For most of my life home meant the place in which I was born:
the Victorian terraced house – scruffy and cold but filled with
love and books – in which my parents still lived. It was not a
comfortable house: not a place you would typically describe as
homely. But it was there that I first learned what a home could
be. My mother, who was from the Netherlands, was obsessed
with the idea of what is called in Dutch *gezelligheid*: a species of
intense cosiness which, the Dutch claim, is untranslatable into
English. After my siblings and I had all flown the nest – to go to
university, to travel and live abroad – it was this house, and the
home my mother had made for us there, which continued to
draw us back.

Home is our original point of departure: the centre around
which we all orbit. In *The Poetics of Space*, the philosopher Gaston
Bachelard described homing as a feeling, a primitive one that, he
argued, is shared by all creatures. Home, he wrote, is 'our first
universe, a real cosmos in every sense of the word'; it is 'our
corner of the world' in which and through which we create our
first idea of ourselves as people. The theologian Mircea Eliade
thought of home as a point of view from which the world is first
brought into existence, the place from which, as he said, the real
'could be *founded*'. For Eliade home was a starting point, like the
piece of grit which allows a pearl to form in the shell of an oyster.
Without it nothing else can exist.

The pigeons could only learn to home if they were given the
opportunity to fly free, and potentially to get lost or even to die
in the process. It felt like a risky business, though it was also a
necessary one. In Henry Green's novel *Living*, the flight of a kit

of pigeons over a house becomes a metaphor for the way in which a home can anchor the mind, and for the way in which learning to love and be loved in turn can teach us what it means to stay in one place. The narrative of Green's novel flits between minds like a bird in flight, but one of the book's central consciousnesses is that of Lily Gates, a young woman who wants to escape the constraints of her life as a factory worker in Birmingham. Gates is acutely aware of the tension between her desire to run away and her need to put down roots. When she tries to escape from her old life with her lover, taking a train to Liverpool, she compares herself to the birds she has watched flying around her neighbours' houses back home. 'For as racing pigeon fly in the sky,' writes Green in his incantatory, sparsely articled prose,

> always they go round above house which provides for them or, if loosed at a distance from that house then they fly straight there, so her thoughts would not point away long from house which had provided for her. With us it is not only food, as possibly it is for pigeon, but if we are for any length of time among those who love us and whom we love too, then those people become part of ourselves.

Homes, like love, Green's image invites us to think, provide the still, stable point around which our thoughts and lives can orbit. But they are also thresholds: places we must depart from before we can fully understand what they mean.

A few weeks after the birds had begun to range, Natalya and I had gone to the hospital for a scan. She was beginning to show, and we could feel the baby move – there was new life fluttering under her skin, delicately but insistently present. It was a different hospital from the one in which Dora had been born but it felt familiar: the clinical smells, the ad-hoc sprawl of the buildings, the mystifying complexity of the signs. At the reception of the maternity wing pregnant women sat with their partners, waiting

to be scanned. I was nervous. We hadn't brought Dora with us
because we didn't know what had caused the previous miscarriages, and we didn't want her to be upset if it turned out that
something was wrong this time, too. But Natalya was calm. She
said things felt different this time; as though this pregnancy was
meant to be. She said she felt whole.

We were called by a smiling technician who managed to maintain a façade of excitement even though she must have welcomed
prospective parents into her cubicle many times each day. There
was a large screen on the wall, next to some vague watercolours
of female bodies. There was a sign saying 'NO PHOTOS'. The
technician asked Natalya to lie down, lubricating her probe
before applying it to Natalya's stomach. The baby, which had up
until then still felt largely theoretical – an idea rather than a person
– swam into focus on the screen. It was facing away from us, its
hands clasped close to its face, its delicate backbone traced across
the middle of the image. Its legs were furled over themselves, as
if it was curled up inside an egg. The technician manipulated her
probe, drawing yellow lines over the images she'd captured,
making maps of the inside of Natalya's body, measuring imper-
ceptible differences in organ dimensions, checking for anomalies,
making sure that all was as it should be. She asked if we wanted
to know the sex, and we said we wanted to keep it a surprise. We
could hear the muffled heartbeat pulsing like a wingbeat.

As we left she gave us a few photographs of the baby and told
us to pay £4 to the receptionist. You couldn't make out much in
the images, but we were enchanted by what we saw. They looked
like photos of the moon, or the bottom of a deep-sea trench.
There was the delicate white blob of a head and some ghostly
lines, which we took to be arms or legs. The photos, which we
pinned to our fridge until they faded in the spring sunshine, felt
to me like maps of our shared future.

That spring, as the birds began to range, we joined them below.
I would cycle out each morning with Dora to the nursery, or to

the supermarket, or to the marshes to sit by the river. The world, seen through Dora's eyes, was small, and contained, and safe. She talked about the area in which we lived as 'the planet': the orbit her attention encompassed. 'Do we live on that planet?' she asked about things she saw on the television, faraway places she had never visited. 'Are they on our planet?' she'd ask when we spoke about a new shop that had opened, or friends who had moved in nearby. The limits of her language mapped the limits of her world.

When Natalya and I had first moved here, before we had Dora, Leyton had felt grey and unfamiliar. At first it seemed to be a land of muscle gyms and betting shops. But, we soon began to discover, there was life here too. Charismatic churches with grandstanding names – 'The Church of the Everlasting Path'; 'The Church of the Holy and Eternal Tabernacle', with its symbol of a white dove bearing the good news – touted for business, tucked away in the middle of nondescript industrial estates. Fly-by-night enterprises that could no longer get a foothold in the increasingly upmarket areas of Clapton and London Fields had been pushed out here. Down the High Road there was a café called The Mogadishu outside which Somali cab drivers congregated to chew khat and drink coffee from small silver cups. Roma women wearing bright dresses and gold earrings walked their children to school, passing tired men coming home from their night shifts in the factories and warehouses which lined the river. Unable to afford to drink in pubs, working men congregated to drink on street corners, clasping cans wrapped in brown paper bags.

Other people like us were moving to the area. Together we colonised it with our bicycles and children and love of ruination and minimalist Scandinavian design. Every so often a new coffee shop – bare polished floors, naked light bulbs, repurposed scaffold-plank shelving – would spring up on the High Road, convinced that the area was on the cusp of gentrification. It was the last place in London from which you could still commute cheaply into the city centre by bus, and those who had been pushed out here through poverty lived in an uneasy truce with the new incomers like us, who saw in the Edwardian housing stock and wide green spaces limitless potential.

When we first arrived Natalya and I had gone on long walks, following water, to try to locate ourselves. The land immediately around our house was low-lying, damp and waterlogged: criss-crossed with streams and ancient agricultural ditches that snaked their way through the rows of terraced houses. To the west lay the marshes. To the east, the green span of Epping Forest, with its twisted trees and its black, depthless ponds, its undergrowth littered with crisp packets and condom wrappers.

After Dora was born we had begun to explore together. Our daily walk took us past the Polish delicatessen, the discount tool shop with its perpetual closing down sale; past Drumbeat, 'The Hart of Afrika and her Diaspora', a shop stocked with trinkets and withered plantain; past innumerable barber shops and chicken outlets and closed-down pubs. During the day, when Natalya was at work, Dora and I walked to the railway bridge where the feral pigeons roosted and watched them make their homes under the rusting iron. The trains rumbled above over their heads. The birds paid no heed to the anti-pigeon measures – plastic spikes and stretched netting – put in place by Network Rail, and sat quite contentedly on their nests, shitting all over the cars below. It was a small world, but it was one we came to be fascinated by.

In his poem 'Innocence', Patrick Kavanagh described the way that attending closely to the world on your doorstep, however constraining it might at first feel, could provide access to truths that were at once both specific and universal. Rather than being 'bounded' by the hedges and fields of the 'little farm' on which he grew up, as he grew he realised he was instead liberated by that very boundedness. To focus on the local provided access to general truths, truths which persisted beyond its borders. 'Love's doorway to life', he wrote, 'Is the same doorway everywhere.' Writing and thinking about the

small places he knew so intimately as a child allowed Kavanagh
to think about the world at large more deeply than he might
otherwise have been able to. 'To know fully even one field or
one land is a lifetime's experience', he wrote elsewhere. 'In the
world of poetic experience it is depth that counts, not width.
A gap in a hedge, a smooth rock surfacing a narrow lane, a
view of a woody meadow, the stream at the junction of four
small fields – these are as much as a man can fully experience.'

There can be, as Kavanagh knew, dangers lurking behind any
celebration of the local, however. In an essay entitled 'Parochialism
and Provincialism' he differentiated between what he saw as two
distinct ways of engaging with the world. The provincial, he
argued, valued smallness because it was familiar, and this familiarity often led to exclusion: of new experiences, but also of other
people. The parochial mind, on the other hand, embraced what
was on the doorstep because, as Kavanagh said, such a mind 'deals
in universals'. However far we travel from our origins, he
concluded, something always draws us back. 'Far have I travelled
from the warm womb', his essay concluded, 'Far have I travelled
from home.'

Childhood is a time for ranging, and for world-making: it is
the time when we form our understanding of what a home is,
but it is also when we place that home in relation to the wider
world. The landscape we learn as children – the landscape Natalya
and I were learning to inhabit through Dora's eyes – has hard
borders, and the places in which we grow up have an elemental
solidity that nowhere else will ever possess. Neuroscientists tell us
that it is through movement that we form our first memories,
memories which are place-bound: anchored in the world even as
we ourselves learn to navigate through it. Homes are the maps
we make as children, then, and we carry them with us for the rest
of our lives.

There is water everywhere round here, and the birds can smell it. There is water to the east, reaching far off into the distance, towards Norway and Denmark; water to the north, fingering the straits of Bergen and, not far beyond that, water stretching up to the wastes of the Arctic Circle. There is water to the south and to the west: the Firth of Forth cutting into the country, the sea penetrating deep into the dry, parched land.

As the birds pass the shoulder of Scotland they catch the first scent of home. They are familiar with this land: this known and measured ground. Most have flown from races this far north before.

Just after 11.00 a.m. the flock passes over the mouth of the River Tay, a short hop between two spits of land, only a few miles across. Visibility is good: they can clearly see to the other side. Even when they get to the wider estuary of the Firth of Forth, five miles further south, they have no trouble seeing over the water. They head straight over, crossing the seven miles of sea in minutes.

The air heats up as they get further south, and the birds, which cannot sweat, begin to pant as they fly. For some the heat is too much. On the outskirts of Edinburgh one of my pigeons – an unnamed blue hen with the ring number NWHUS6345 – catches sight of water and swoops down to it. She lands on the muddy bank of a small pond by the side of the A199 and drinks thirstily, dipping her beak deep into the water and using it as a straw, as pigeons, uniquely among all birds, do. After she's satiated she looks up and walks back towards the road.

Maybe she doesn't see it coming, or maybe she is too distracted by fatigue to avoid it, but on that road, by the village of East Calder, 180 miles from Thurso, and four hours after she began her race, she is hit by a car and killed. Three days later a man will call me to say he's found her body.

'I flew doos for sixty-five years,' he says, 'and I'd have wanted to know what happened to one of mine if it got lost. So I thought I should tell you.'

The rest of the birds fly on, still following the coast, before turning south again. They're flying with purpose now. In no time at all they will arrive at the Scottish border. After that England will lie before them, a patchwork of greens and browns stretching further than even they can see.

# 5

## Homegoing

The birds had been ranging well for a month when I went to meet Steve Chalkley, secretary, bookkeeper, chief timekeeper, administrator, and general factotum of the East London North Road Pigeon Racing Club. Steve lived in a neat terraced house a twenty-minute cycle ride away from me, down the High Road in Stratford. I knew I had come to the right place when I saw a kit of pigeons flying high above his house in tight formation. They were his team of old birds, Steve said when he opened the door, out for their afternoon exercise.

Steve was a big man with a short stubbly beard and a round face, and he walked with a slow, lolloping gait, like a hesitant bear. He wore a flat cap and a rugby shirt, and spoke in a cockney falsetto. His hand, when I shook it, was warm, and surprisingly soft.

Steve lived with his family in the house next door to his father, George. When they'd moved here Steve and George had knocked their gardens together, lining the space with pigeon lofts on three sides. Together they kept hundreds of birds. Steve had a sideline breeding finches, which flitted and sang in their small cages as we talked.

George had grown up in Bow, in East London, and had kept pigeons all his life, as his father had before him. He had left school at fourteen.

'I went to one, and it got bombed,' he said, 'then I went to another, and that got bombed and all. After that they wouldn't let me go any more.'

He remembered being evacuated from London during the war, but he ran away from the house in Cornwall where he had been placed because he hated the woman who looked after him there, and because he missed his pigeons.

'I never left home again after that,' he said.

Back in London he joined his father working on the markets: Roman Road, Leather Lane, Chapel. He worked for a long time in the old Billingsgate Fish Market on Lower Thames Street.

'When they moved out,' he said, 'they thought the building would collapse, because it was held together by the ice in the cellars. Ice as thick as you are tall.'

Later he moved to New Spitalfields, selling fruit and veg wholesale. It was a job that suited pigeon flying: after you were finished at 9.00 a.m. you could go home and spend all day with your birds.

Steve had continued working in the family trade, and now, like George had, worked night shifts at New Spitalfields, down the road on the banks of the River Lea. At night the market was lit by the orange glow of sodium-vapour lamps. What he liked most of all was to sit in his garden, he said, listening to his finches sing and watching his pigeons fly about the house. He found them endlessly fascinating. His eyes lit up when he spoke about their speed and agility, their performances in famous races, and the mystery of their homing instinct.

The first section of Steve's loft – which was large and well made, and painted dark green – contained his racing team: twelve hand-selected cocks that had performed well enough throughout the previous season to be kept for the next. Steve had been keeping this line of birds – which were originally Hartogs, an English variety bred for sprint and middle-distance racing – since the early 1990s, and by now, thanks to diligent inbreeding and backcrossing, he had established a line he could almost call his own. Each year he'd breed twenty to thirty young birds, some of which might, if they performed well, make it onto his racing team the following year.

Steve did most of the admin but George was honorary presi-
dent and race controller of the club. On race days it was his job
to use his network of spotters around the country to ascertain
weather conditions along the route, before giving the word to
liberate the birds. He was proud of his son. He was proud of the
efficiency of his racing and the loyalty displayed by his pigeons,
which would, he said, 'always work for him'.

'He's a real pigeon man,' George said. 'Most people send off
twenty, thirty birds to each race. Steve only races twelve. How
many d'you end the season with last year, Steve? Ten?'

'Eleven,' Steve replied, quietly pleased.

On their perches, Steve's pigeons looked immaculate. They
were bigger than those in my loft, and sleeker, too. Steve flew
them for two hours every day, morning and afternoon, unless the
wind was blowing too hard or it was foggy. In the run-up to the
racing season he would train them on the road every other day,
taking them up to fifty miles away, along the race line, before
releasing them to fly home. They always beat him back. When
they were young he trained them even harder. He never needed
to flag them – scaring his pigeons with a flag to keep them on the
wing around the house – for his birds were healthy and fit, and,
he said, they enjoyed flying for him.

Next to Steve's racing loft was an aviary holding his 'prisoners':
stock birds which had grown up in different lofts, or were too
valuable to race, and which were used solely for breeding. At the
back of the garden were two other lofts in which he housed his
young birds, separately from his old bird team, for the first year of
their life. These lofts could be completely darkened during the
summer months, which inhibited the pigeons' moult and encouraged them to keep their flight feathers until later in the season,
and thus compete for longer.

Like many fanciers Steve had a deep enmity for birds of prey.

'It's not so bad over the flats and the forest,' he said. 'It's
more if they're coming the other way, over the city, that they
get hit.'

He blamed the increasing regularity of hawk attacks on conser-vationists, and the meddling interventions of the RSPB.

'They put nest boxes for peregrines on top of tower blocks, rig up cameras so people can watch them breed. It's not natural.'

I didn't say that perhaps some people might feel that pigeon racing was unnatural, too, because Steve was in full flow now, railing against the absurdity of managed rewilding, the cheek of interfering with the natural order.

'They bought an island off the coast of Scotland,' he said, 'filled it full of equipment. And all the birds fucked off – there was nothing left to study. So they decided to do it in the cities instead. They want to wind their necks in a bit.'

Steve and George were luckier than most. At the back of their garden there was a line of tall poplars in which a large colony of crows lived. These would mob any birds of prey that came round looking to hunt, and so kept their pigeons reasonably safe. A fellow fancier who kept his loft only 800 feet away wasn't so fortunate.

'They're plaguing him,' Steve said. 'Once they know where the loft is they come back every few days and hit it. It frightens the birds. It's not so much that they get killed, it's more the fear. They won't home to the loft if they get spooked on the way in. They just run. You get so many losses.'

George came over with a cup of tea he'd made for me, and then they both began to explain the intricacies and difficulties of pigeon racing. To have any success as a flyer, Steve said, you had to play the long game. Breeding took time, training was labori-ous, and selecting which birds to enter in each race depended on careful observation and close familiarity with your team. A bad 'toss' – a training flight in which you take your birds away from their loft to release them – could ruin your racing for a year. Hawk attacks could undo months of road-work at a stroke, making even the best birds 'trap shy': unwilling to enter the loft on their return from a race.

Even flying around the house things can go wrong. Occasionally a group of young pigeons will, like swarming bees, leave their home loft, set a direction and fly into a clear sky, never to be seen again. Such 'flyaways' are rare, but they are not unheard of. Alf Baker, a famous fancier who raced in London from the 1950s to the '90s, ascribed flyaways to astrological conditions, and never let his birds out when the sun and the moon were in the sky at the same time. But most flyers put the behaviour down to the fact that pigeons live in colonies, and when a new round of young birds are born it might be evolutionarily beneficial for some to strike off to establish their own nests elsewhere.

Sickness can be devastating, too. If the loft is hit with illness you can lose most of your birds overnight, so quickly does it rip through a colony. Despite their reputation, pigeons aren't particularly prone to infection, but it's true that the diseases they end up dying of sound particularly unpleasant – chlamydia, herpes, E-coli – evocative, terrible-sounding pathogens that are more frightening for the fact that they exist in the realm of the human. It's perhaps for this reason that fanciers are so keen on magical cures and dubious health tonics.

Part of the skill of pigeon racing, Steve explained – perhaps most of it – was in the breeding, which took time. A true line could take twenty-five years to develop.

'You've got to know what you're looking for,' he said, 'and you've got to breed pigeons that suit the racing you're asking them to do. They've got to learn what's expected of them.'

Improving the line meant culling birds that hadn't performed well during the season. Steve spoke of the eugenicist struggles inside his loft with a hard-hearted clarity.

'There's no point carrying weak birds,' he said, 'they just cost you grain.'

Steve told me he believed in ley lines, in the power of the land, with its geomagnetic disturbances and dead zones, to disrupt the flow of pigeons as they flew over it. He believed they navigated by detecting electromagnetism: the earth, he said, gave off lines of force which were shaped 'like a doughnut', and the different lines had different frequencies. From far away pigeons followed the line that resonated with the frequency closest to that which they could detect at home. Steve believed that over time, as generation after generation of birds raced over the same land to the same loft, they came to know the territory over which they flew not just in their brains but in their wings and in their bones. Parents would pass the lines down to their offspring, and after a few generations the community would learn ever more efficient routes home. After years of careful selection a strain would develop, birds of proven fitness but also, Steve thought, born with some innate knowledge of home, a kind of inherited collective memory of the places their parents and grandparents had once flown over before them.

In 2003 the French artist Matali Crasset was commissioned by the Beauvois Pigeon Fanciers' Association to build them a loft. The result, *Capsule*, was a tall, orange, dome-like structure, based on the curving organic forms of ancient Egyptian pigeon lofts. The idea of the piece, said Crasset, was to preserve not just an environment but a relationship: a kinship between birds and people that had been maintained in the area for hundreds of years, but which was now at risk of dying out. '[W]ithout the lover of pigeons,' she said,

> without the knowledge and know-how of men and birds, without selection, apprenticeship, without transmission of practices, what then would remain would be pigeons, but not homing pigeons, not *voyageurs* [. . .] What is brought into existence are the relations by which pigeons transform men into talented pigeon fanciers and by which the fanciers transform the pigeons into reliable racing pigeons.

Pigeons have always lived closely with people. They are probably our oldest companion species, the relationship mirroring the development of human civilisation. They were first domesticated by the Sumerians – the people who invented writing – five to ten thousand years before the birth of Christ. In ancient Sumer, a fertile region in southern Mesopotamia, now Iraq, pigeons were housed in great temples and used as sacrificial animals and messengers, but they also became symbols of love and knowledge. They flew out from Noah's Ark over the flooded world, looking for a sign of home. They flew through ancient Egypt, bringing news of the deaths of kings. They flew over the Roman Empire, bearing messages from colonial outposts to the metropolitan centre. Hannibal used pigeons to stay in contact with his spies across Europe. In his *Natural History* Pliny describes how Decimus Brutus broke Mark Anthony's siege of Mutina by sending letters to the consuls via pigeon. 'What service', Pliny asked, 'did Anthony derive from his trenches, and his vigilant blockade, and even from his nets stretched across the river, while the winged messenger was traversing the air?'

In Europe during the Middle Ages only aristocrats were allowed to keep pigeons, and most large houses would have had a coop in which they were farmed for food, their droppings providing valuable fertiliser. After the discovery of gunpowder in the West, pigeon shit became an important source of saltpetre.

But it is as messengers that they have come to be most celebrated. For most of human history, information could travel only as fast as physical objects could, and until the Industrial Revolution the most efficient and dependable way of sending a message over long distances was to use a pigeon. During the nineteenth and early twentieth centuries they became important supplements to the technological communications networks which were then springing up across Europe. The Reuters news agency was founded in 1850 by Paul Julius Reuter, who established a flock of forty-five pigeons and used them to plug a gap in the fledgling telegraph network between Brussels and Aachen. In the few brief years he held his monopoly over information travelling between Belgium and Germany he made his fortune. The five sons of Mayer Amschel Rothschild consolidated their father's banking dynasty by using pigeons to stay in touch with one another as they travelled throughout Europe, and it's said that using this network they received news of the result of the Battle of Waterloo before the British Government did.

During the Siege of Paris in 1870–1, pigeons were carried out of the besieged city by balloon so that people as far afield as London could write letters to their loved ones trapped behind the walls. Letters were delivered to Tours, where they were photographed and reduced to microfiche. These were then sewn into the pigeons' tail feathers before they were released to fly back into Paris. Once they had arrived the messages would be projected onto a screen, then copied out on paper and hand-delivered. In this way, a single bird could carry up to 2,500 letters on each trip.

Until the early twentieth century, most newspapers would have kept a pigeon loft on the roof of their offices. Reporters used the birds to file breaking news stories, or to keep abreast of stock prices and the results of horse races. In France, journalists following the early bicycle racing tours carried baskets of pigeons on the front of their own bikes, using them to send updates on the race from the roadside. So important were these pigeon networks at providing scoops that newspapermen would sometimes hire falconers to intercept the birds of their rivals.

In war the reliability and privacy of pigeon post was particularly valuable. During the First World War pigeons were used by soldiers on the front to communicate with those behind the lines, and by tank commanders to send news of their movements when radios broke down. 'If it became necessary immediately to discard every line and method of communications used on the front, except one' wrote the British Army's Chief of Signals and Communications, Major General Fowler, after the First World War, 'and it were left to me to select that one method, I should unhesitatingly choose the pigeons. When the battle rages and everything gives way to barrage and machine gun fire, to say nothing of gas attacks and bombings, it is to the pigeon that we go for succour.'

*A pigeon is released from a tank.*

During the Second World War pigeons were carried by bomber crews who, if shot down, would release a bird with a message detailing their position so that they could be rescued. Between 1941 and the end of the war thousands of pigeons were attached to tiny parachutes and dropped over occupied France as part of 'Operation Columba'. They carried labels instructing those who found them to return the birds with news of enemy movements or weapons placements, and many civilians did, risking their lives in the process. Some of the last birds used in the war were sent with soldiers as they landed on the beaches of Normandy. In the end none were used for messaging – the radios carried by the troops worked well enough that day – but a few birds arrived back at their lofts in England covered in blood, having been released in the confusion when their handlers were shot dead on the French beaches.

The use – the exploitation – of the pigeon's extraordinary instincts and perceptual abilities reached its height during the

mid-twentieth century, just before they were made redundant
by technological progress, in the work of the psychologist
B. F. Skinner. Pigeons were beloved by behaviourist psychologists
like Skinner because they were biddable, because of their acuity
of vision and because, like us, they are primed to recognise
patterns. In 1942 Skinner was approached by the CIA to develop
an organically controlled homing system for ballistic missiles, and
he chose pigeons as his control subjects. He placed the birds in
small harnesses and fixed them in front of a screen onto which he
projected images of targets – ships at sea, or street intersections
seen from above. He then trained the birds to peck at the screen,
reinforcing this behaviour by feeding them when they successfully identified a target. A small capacitor mounted on the pigeons'
beaks translated their pecks into directional information, which
was then used to home the missile onto its target. In 1943, Skinner
gave a demonstration of the technique to his CIA handlers, but
although they were impressed by the efficiency of the training,
and by the pigeons' ability to identify targets, they could not take
the project seriously. 'It was a perfect performance,' Skinner
recalled, 'but the spectacle of a living pigeon carrying out its
assignment, no matter how beautifully, simply reminded the
committee of how utterly fantastic our proposal was.'

Skinner's 'Project Pigeon' was never used in anger, but the
birds' performances as messengers during the Second World War
had begun to change public perception of them. After the war
many British pigeons were awarded the Dickin Medal for animal
gallantry. They came to be thought of not as feral pests but as
heroes. In the post-war years, pigeon racing became a hugely
popular pastime. In the 1950s and '60s it was the most popular
sport, by participation, in Britain.

The closeness with which we used to share our lives with
pigeons seems very far away now, when they are at best ignored,
at worst reviled. But when I met Steve and George, whose lives
still revolved around their birds, I wondered if we could learn
something from them. There was an intimacy between them and

their pigeons which I admired. They were not sentimental men, but their flock seemed to be part of them, and they part of it. They knew all their birds individually, by sight, and could tell when any of them were sick or out of form without needing to go inside the loft. They watched their pigeons with profound attention, an attention that might best be described as love.

Throughout her career, the biologist and philosopher Donna Haraway has been interested in what it means to live in close proximity with animals. None of us, Haraway has said, should think of ourselves as individuals, isolated and alone. Whether we like it or not, our lives are inextricably entwined with the lives of others – both human and animal – and recognition of this entwining can teach us much about what it means to be rooted in the world.

Haraway began thinking about these things – kinship, empathy, identifying with the lives of others – in her 1986 essay 'A Cyborg Manifesto'. In that essay she argued that industrialisation and the rise of computer technology had led to a destruction of the local: a destruction of home. As jobs became automated and outsourced around the world, Haraway argued, so community was increasingly threatened. Under assault from the alienating effects of technology and capitalism, we were becoming ever more isolated.

Haraway developed these ideas in *When Species Meet*, a strange, provocative book about what it is that we are doing when we interact with non-human animals. Following Freud's suggestion, in his 1917 paper 'A Difficulty in the Path of Psycho-Analysis', Haraway described three conceptual 'wounds' which have stripped us of our individual sovereignty over the last 300 years. The first, 'the Copernican wound', 'removed Earth itself, man's home world, from the center of the cosmos'. The second, the 'Darwinian wound', made humans confront the fact that they were nothing more than another species of animal. Finally came the psychoanalytical wound, which 'posited an unconscious that undid the primacy of conscious processes, including the reason that comforted Man with his unique excellence'.

According to Freud these wounds had caused modern people to feel unhomed within themselves. As the Cartesian model of a person as a mind and body, separate and irreconcilable – a soul dwelling in its fleshy house – broke down, so too did our sense of ourselves as sovereign beings. But for Haraway our relationship with animals might provide a template for escape from this state of existential homelessness. As we have come to learn more about what our bodies actually consist of, we have been forced to recognise the innate communality of existence. Human genomes can only be found in '10 percent of all the cells that occupy the mundane space I call my body', she said: the other 90 per cent are filled with 'genomes of bacteria, fungi, protists, and such'. 'I am vastly outnumbered by my tiny companions,' Haraway concluded, 'better put, I become an adult human being in company with these tiny messmates. To be one is always to *become with* many.' Visiting Steve and George made me understand Haraway's ideas in a new way. I liked her insistence on the fact that to live well in the world we must 'become with' the beings we share it with. Life, for Haraway, and for the pigeon flyers I had met, is a communal endeavour: we are not islands, but archipelagos.

And, in the face of ecological catastrophe brought about by human action and inaction, her project is a hopeful one. In her most recent book, *Staying with the Trouble*, Haraway argues that attending to the world and 'staying close' to the organisms we share it with can produce a new way of thinking about what it is to have a home. Far from being removed from the world as its masters and controllers, we must think of ourselves as always and inevitably embedded in it. Haraway's vision is of what she calls the 'terrapolis': the shared environment created by animals and people in communion with one another. Pigeons, for Haraway, are the archetypal citizens of terrapolis. They are, she says, 'members of opportunistic social species who can and do live in myriad time and places. Highly diverse, they occupy many categories in many languages, sorted in English terms into wild and domestic worlds.' Pigeons are the perfect symbols of 'becoming with' because of their hybridity: not quite wild, they are also not quite *not* wild. Rather than being controlled by us they are 'codomesticated with their people'. As messengers they have always been powerful symbols of the conflict between nature and technology; and as organisms they occupy the contested ground that lies between the wild and the tame. Through them and with them, says Haraway, we too might learn to become good citizens of terrapolis.

Steve, like all the fanciers I'd met so far, seemed more attuned to what Haraway called 'becoming with' than are most pet owners. The key to being a successful flyer, he told me, was to attend both to the individual birds in your flock and to the colony of which they were a part. In this, pigeon fancying was more like beekeeping than it was like owning a dog or a cat. Though individual birds won races, it was the line – the continuity of the community – which allowed a racer to be successful over time.

Steve had paired up his old birds in February, after they had come through their winter moult, and his first round of eggs was just beginning to hatch. He showed me some of his squeakers, as pigeon squabs are called. They were still blind, a layer of skin covering their eyes, yellow down poking out between their just-fledged feathers. George brought over a bird that was only a few days old and put it in my hand. It was very warm, with wrinkly skin, and looked a bit like a hairy ballbag. Its oversized beak thrashed around, searching for food. He slipped an identification ring over three of its toes, then pushed the last one through. It would wear the ring for the rest of its life. I asked what sex it was and Steve got out a pendulum which he wafted over it.

'Back and forth: that means it's a boy,' he said.

A week after I met Steve and George, I was sitting with the men of the East London North Road Pigeon Racing Club, and the clocks were about to be struck. The ELNR has its home in the Leyton House Working Men's Club, a nondescript building in Stratford, just round the corner from Steve's house. From the outside it looks like a low-rise block of flats, but there is a car park to one side where feathers swirl around. Crates are piled up in one corner.

Inside the club was dark. There was a bar, stools and tables, a dartboard. The fruit machine in the corner was left mostly unplayed. On the large television screen, Formula 1 cars raced round their track in silence. On the noticeboard by the bar there were posters for charity fundraisers, horse racing away days, prize-givings and pigeon events. In the toilets was a sign which read 'PLEASE DO NOT VOMIT IN THE URINAL. USE WC PAN!'

Steve and George had told me to come to the club for the first meeting of the coming season. I wouldn't be racing yet, as I had no old birds and the young bird season wouldn't start until June, but I could meet the other flyers, they said, and get some training tips. I had been slightly nervous as I arrived, wearing my tastefully distressed artists' smock, carrying my fold-up bicycle, and wondering what the fanciers would make of me. I found them in a back room, sitting next to the pool table and the dance floor which saw action only on ladies' night. Each man had his allotted chair, and I took a stool from the stack by the door and perched on the end of one of the tables. I tastefully distressed my vowels and said hello.

'Is he a pigeon man?' asked Brian 'Woodo' Wodehouse, the chairman of the club, a well-known fancier who wrote a weekly column for the *Racing Pigeon* newspaper, and sold instructional DVDs in which he promised to reveal his secret winning methods.

'He will be,' said Steve.

Brian had white hair and a shrewd, friendly face. He was one of the most successful flyers in the club, said to be able to use the power of prayer to summon up a favourable wind during races.

There were a dozen other members of the ELNR in attendance that day, and all of them were men. Steve and George were there, along with two Johnnies – Big Johnny and Johnny Stockwell – an Alby and two Daves. I sat next to a man named Steve, who told me he had only got into pigeons last year, when he had retired. Like a lot of the flyers, he'd kept canaries for years but they kept dying, and the feed got too expensive, so he became a fancier instead. He had an air of resignation about his new hobby, as though it was inevitable that he would eventually take it up. He was still a novice, and like me he hovered round the edges of the group.

Johnny Stockwell and Alby were cousins. They had started flying because their uncles had kept pigeons before them. As boys they used to go to Trafalgar Square and catch feral birds, and when they started off they raced them to orange crates nailed to their garden wall.

Bob was tall and thin. He had sandy blond hair and wore thick glasses, and a jacket with a picture of a pigeon embroidered over the pocket. Bob bought British brands. He drove a Jaguar which had a leave.eu sticker in the back window. His neighbour, Smiley, was Moroccan. Smiley had just started racing. He had three pure white old birds, which he entered into every race, and which had always come back for him. Back in Morocco he flew in partnership with his brother, and he showed me a video on his phone of a recent liberation.

'They're much bigger races than here,' he said, 'much better organised, too. There're ten thousand birds flying there, and they always have good weather!'

The other members of the club mocked him gently, and grumbled when, during Ramadan, he wouldn't come down to the club to mark his own birds. Sometimes during the marking he would go off to find a quiet corner in which to pray.

Years ago there were dozens of racing clubs like this in East London, but the ELNR was one of the last remaining, composed of the few flyers who still lived in the area. The other clubs were either dwindling – some only had a couple of members left – or conglomerating, which forced the flyers to travel a long way to mark their birds.

'There used to be six clubs in Walthamstow alone,' said Steve, 'now it's just us. There's not really any new blood – the kids are all inside, playing computer games.'

As its name implies, the East London North Road races from the north of the country, the weekly liberation points following the line of the A1 up to Scotland. Most of the South London clubs race from the continent, 'on the south road', where there is more money and fame to be had. But racing from Europe is more expensive than it is from the north, as to train your birds you have to first take them across the sea. You get more losses, too: the North Road flyers called the Channel 'the moat' and 'the grave-yard', and said they would never risk their best birds on it. There were hushed mutterings of other goings-on on the south road: of fanciers using training runs as cover to smuggle contraband into the country. With 10 grams of cocaine attached to the leg of each, you could make a fortune with a flock of a hundred birds, even if you lost a few along the way.

Most of the flyers had worked in manual jobs until injury or ill health forced them to stop. They had been builders, labourers, market traders. They were all obsessed with their pigeons. Some had tattoos of birds on their arms: swallows on the skin between their fingers and thumbs; champion pigeons on their biceps, underneath which were inscribed the records of memorable race performances.

They ignored me at first, talking among themselves: about their birds, and about their ailments – their diabetes and arthritis, their gout. One man wore a mobile blood pressure monitor which purred softly every few minutes as it pumped air into the cuff on his arm. Most wore tracksuits and comfortable shoes. Dave showed off his socks, from which he'd removed the elastic so as to allow his ankles room to swell in the spring heat.

But after a few drinks they began to loosen up. Chris was moaning about the invader parakeets that flew over his garden each night as he trapped his birds in.

'They're non-native,' he said, 'absolute cunts. They make such a racket.'

The flyers agreed it was best to shoot them on sight. He went on a rant about his neighbour – 'a fucking cunt' – who had taken to flying a remote-controlled drone over his garden. 'It frightens all my birds.'

Alby recounted a hellish liberation he'd experienced the previous season.

'What kind of a cunt releases them at quarter to twelve, in the wind and the rain?' he asked. 'It's no wonder we lost so many.'

Alby asked what I was doing there, and I told him I'd bought some birds and wanted to race them.

'What do you want to get out of it?' he asked.

I told him I was fascinated by pigeons, and wanted to race them, but didn't really expect to win anything.

'Bullshit,' he said. 'That's how you start – pretty soon the lofts will have taken over your garden and your wife will have left you.'

Steve had calculated the location of my loft to register it with the RPRA, and he gave me a slip of paper recording its longitude and latitude. This would be the point from which my race distances would be measured, allowing for the average velocities of my pigeons to be calculated. All the flyers knew the precise location of each other's lofts, seemingly to within a few yards. They spoke in a shorthand, of liberation points and wind direction and the lineages of famous birds. They told me stories about pigeons – good pigeons – that had been sent off to races and lost, or had returned with huge wounds: their crops ripped open so that when they drank the water gushed and bubbled through the hole; the feathers of their wings ripped out, leaving the musculature on show. They told stories of birds which had gone missing for years before returning home to be immediately recognised by their owners. At the heart of their devotion was the mystery of how pigeons homed, and what it might mean.

It was time for the striking of the clocks, so Steve called us all to the back of the room where they sat on the green baize of the pool table. In the pre-quartz days pigeon racing clocks were often unreliable, and would lose or gain time against each other during races, and so they would need – at the beginning of the season and before and after every race – to be checked against a master clock. At the beginning of each race the time would be set on this master clock, and after the birds had been timed in at the end of the race the clocks would be struck again. Any difference in time between the two readings could be worked into the equations used to decide who had won. Now that the clocks are digital the striking is largely ritualistic: a way to signal the beginning and end of a race, and the moment the coming year's season formally begins.

Steve checked each clock in turn, emptied them of race rings, and then sealed them. He passed the clocks around so that we had one each.

'One minute, gents,' he said.

Silence fell. He counted down: 'Ten, nine, eight . . .'

When he counted to zero we pressed down the buttons on the top of our clocks, and they set with a loud thunk.

The first old bird race was a few weeks away, and three months after that the young bird races, in which my pigeons could compete, would begin. By mid-July I would need to have them ready for their first race, which would be from Peterborough. I put the date in my diary, said goodbye to the flyers and cycled off down the High Road.

## 12.03 p.m., Berwick-upon-Tweed, 302 miles from home

They have flown two hundred miles. There was a combine race from Berwick one month ago, and the memory is still fresh for the birds. Then the weather was cooler, the skies over the borders thick with high cloud, and Eggy and Orange made good time against the pack.

It doesn't take long for a pigeon to learn a new route – one flight is often all they need to map an unfamiliar landscape – but the land beneath them is almost unrecognisable now, yellowed as it is by weeks of drought. Rather than the fields, they follow the shape of the road, tracing the ribbon of the A1 over Haddington, over East Linton and Dunbar.

But when they hit the coast again they leave the land behind. The variable wind of the north has turned to a gentle north-westerly, and as they get to Berwick they head out to sea, flying low over the churning surf to avoid hawk attacks. They know that hawks do not like to swoop on birds flying over water in case they miss and end up in the sea. The pigeons fly low, only a few feet above the waves. If the wind stays in this direction the fastest birds will hug the coast and follow the line all the way to Norfolk, 250 miles to the south.

Does anyone notice them as they pass? Perhaps a fancier on the borders sees them, strung out in a raggedy line, coming over the sea from the north. But they are easy to miss. The thousand birds have fragmented by now. Just outside Berwick the leading pigeons hit a band of rain – I watch it roll in off the sea in real time on a satellite weather website, the sky briefly blackened – which drenches them. Some, the least experienced, the late breeds and the yearlings, are forced down by the weight of the water which clings to their feathers, to land in fields and trees along the route, where they will have to wait to dry out. But the shower is short, and most of them fly through it unscathed. Those that come through continue their journey, beating on for home.

# 6

## Homelands

The man I know only as Big Johnny Pigeon lives where he was born, in a neat 1930s semi-detached house – smelling muskily sweet, of animal – on the edge of the Olympic Park in East London. His house sits on a patch of marshy ground on an island formed by two tributaries of the River Lea. It's a hard place to get to – I cycled there through the newly landscaped park, along shiny bike lanes, over the maze of bridges which cross and re-cross the spruced-up ditches and canals, their borders planted with locally appropriate shrubs, checking the blue arrow on the map on my phone every few hundred yards to make sure I hadn't missed a turn – but Johnny likes it that way.

When I had met him at the club, Johnny told me he had a couple of young birds in his loft going spare, and that I should come and pick them up in a few weeks' time, once they'd been weaned from their parents.

'They're beautiful,' he said, 'they're so pale they look white. They're almost silver. You won't miss them in the air. You'll see them coming for miles.'

Johnny was not the most successful flyer in the club, but he struck me as one of the most attentive: one of the most devoted watchers of his birds. From his garden he pointed out a Victorian pumping station on which his pigeons sometimes settled during their loft flights, and Bazalgette's Northern Outfall, the huge overground sewer which runs from Hackney Wick to Beckton, carrying waste from the centre of town to the suburbs. Behind his house were some allotments next to which the council were putting up flats, but Johnny seemed to see through them to the land beyond.

'It's so flat you can see for miles around here,' he said. 'I used to watch the birds coming in after a race, all strung out in a line. You'd first see them ten minutes before they came in.'

It felt like an unloved patch of ground, but Johnny was content here. He had been born at home, and lived there with his mother until she died a few years ago. Now he lived alone. He had never spent more than three nights away from his house. Johnny didn't own a passport ('Why would I want one?' he said. 'Anyway, they cost too much, and they'll give 'em away to anyone these days') and had never in his life left the island of Great Britain. This house, and the landscape in which it sat, was his entire world.

Johnny shared his home with his dogs and some caged canaries, which sang in his kitchen while he made me a cup of tea. He told me he was given his first pair of pigeons – tipplers, renowned for their stamina and high-flying abilities – when he passed the eleven-plus exam, the first person in his family to do so. He left school at sixteen to work on the Overground and used to train his birds on the railway network, taking them, a pair at a time, to Cambridge, and to Peterborough, and releasing them from the station platforms before getting the train back home. The birds would always beat him back.

Nowadays he rarely left the house, as he found it hard to walk more than a few dozen yards at a time, and he couldn't drive. On race days he would get a taxi to the club, ten-minutes up the road, to mark his birds, but mostly he stayed at home, watching the skies.

'If it wasn't for the pigeons,' he said, 'I wouldn't see anyone.'

We went back to the garden, where Johnny showed me his birds. He told me what I should look for when selecting a pigeon to race or breed from. He noted damaged feathers, the tiny pinholes which formed when they had not grown out properly due to a lack of nutrition. He talked about body shape and something he called 'hand feel': the potential energy of the bird when held. Johnny showed me how you could tell when a bird had really been working in the air because of the line of dust which would form across the bottom of its flight feathers, the natural bloom of the pigeon having been rubbed off its body by the repetitive beating of its wings. These marks are like the tideline on a beach, he said: temporary records of otherwise invisible labour.

Johnny went into one of his lofts and picked up the two young pigeons he'd bred for me, beautiful, silvery pigeons that looked ghostly, almost translucent in the darkness.

'If your girlfriend don't like them she's mad,' he said, as he passed them to me.

They were nestmates, twenty-eight days old, nervous but gentle as I held them. He gave me a big training basket he didn't use any more to take them home in.

Before I left, we sat for a long time in his garden in the spring sunshine, watching his birds fly around the house. The day was bright and the wind was blustery, and Johnny's pigeons flicked through the air like dolphins playing on the surface of the sea. They seemed barely to flap their wings as they passed over his house, drawing the sun as they turned into it.

Despite having lived there all his life, Johnny had only a very hazy sense of how his home fitted into the general geography of London. But his knowledge of the air was unrivalled. He knew the migratory routes of the birds which flew over his house each spring and autumn, and the location of the lofts of the other flyers in the club. He said he could often tell which flyer a kit belonged to from the lines they took on returning from a race. He asked me where I lived, and considered the winds which would make it difficult for my birds and which I should welcome.

'Never fly your birds when there's a hint of east in the wind,' he said.

He loved long-distance racing – 'I can't be fucked with sprinting' – and had got some good results over the years, winning club races from Berwick, and combine races from Thurso. But he had never timed a pigeon in from Lerwick, on the Shetland Islands, 700 hundred miles to his loft, because his birds did not like to cross the sea.

She had no name then, but in the summer of 1954, a pigeon from a loft in West Germany got lost during a race from Munich. As she tried to find the route, she flew over the Iron Curtain and into East Germany. An anonymous Czech couple found her a few days later. They fed and watered her before attaching a message addressed to Radio Free Europe to her leg and releasing her to fly home. 'We plead you', they wrote in their message, '[n]ot to slow down in the fight against Communism because Communism must be destroyed. We beg for a speedy liberation from the power of the Kremlin and the establishment of a United States of Europe.' They signed their letter 'Unbowed Pilsen'.

When she arrived back at her loft the message was passed on to the press, and the pigeon to the authorities, who gave her to the Americans. The newspapers named her 'Leaping Lena'. On her arrival at the US Army's Pigeon Service Headquarters in Fort Monmouth she was given a hero's welcome. One thousand homing pigeons were released in her honour.

Over the next few months questions began to be asked about Lena. None of the papers agreed on the details of where she had come from, and no one could track down her original owners. It now seems as though the story of Leaping Lena was a piece of propaganda invented to drum up interest in US war bonds. But that didn't seem to matter to many Americans, who saw in the story an idea to believe in. 'For many of us', writes Elena Passarello of the episode, 'an idea is a kind of home – to fly to, to roost in. And an idea built inside a comforting framework – a feathered friend, for example – can fly much further than a fact can.' It didn't matter if it was faked: after her flight Leaping Lena became a symbol of liberation from the human world of borders and boundaries which she had flown over.

In 1943, living in Ashford in Kent after having been exiled from France, the philosopher Simone Weil wrote a book about what it means to be forced to cross borders and leave one's homeland. Weil had left home with her parents for America the year before, and had moved back to England in the hope of returning to France as a member of the Resistance. Her book *The Need for Roots* had an unlikely origin, having originally been commissioned as a policy report on the establishment of political institutions in post-war France for the Free French Resistance Movement, for which she was working at the time as an analyst. It was published, like all her work, only after her death.

In *The Need for Roots* Weil outlined what she saw as the four 'needs of the soul', the most significant of which, she argued, was the need for a sense of home. 'To be rooted', she wrote, 'is perhaps the most important and least recognised need' of all. For Weil, the idea of the homeland, and what it meant to belong to a place, was inevitably complicated by the nationalistic forces that were then ripping Europe apart. Feeling like you belonged somewhere, she argued, should mean recognising the obligations you had to your community: homeland was as much a psychological as a geographic concept. The idea of rootedness was particularly acute for her because her home seemed so fragile. Her exile was also an escape, and she felt a moral obligation for the people she had left behind. When she was diagnosed with tuberculosis at the end of 1943, she refused all medical treatment in solidarity, she said, with the occupied people of France. She limited her food intake to what would be available to those she had left behind, and died only a few months later, in a sanatorium in Ashford. The coroner reported that 'the deceased did kill and slay herself by refusing to eat whilst the balance of her mind was disturbed', but in the words of her biographer, Richard Rees, really she 'died of love'.

I grew up with a deep sense of the importance of the need for roots, a sense that was complicated by a distrust of the ideals of national belonging and identity that sometimes accompany it. Partly, I think now, looking back, this was because both my parents were from elsewhere. My mother was an exile, or at least an émigré. She grew up in the Netherlands, in a large house in the middle of the wood which her grandfather, who owned a local textile factory, had planted on a patch of land near a tiny village in the east of Holland before the war. Nothing ever happened there, and the afternoons were long and empty. My father grew up in Lincolnshire, in an equally flat landscape. He had left as soon as he was able, going to university at seventeen and then on to a journalism training scheme in Devon, before taking his first job in Glasgow. Later he settled in London, where he and my mother made their home together.

They had met at a Quaker work camp in Bolton when they were both sixteen. My mother's first memory of my father is of seeing him sitting by a fire, poking the embers and practising his voice, trying to hone and polish it: to rid it of its origins. 'I'm in *charge* of the fire,' he was intoning. '*I'm* in charge of the fire. I'm in charge of the *fire*.' They wrote letters to each other for years, falling in love at a distance before she finally agreed to marry him and moved from the Netherlands to London.

My mother knew no one in the city, and to make herself feel at home she had to change. Like him she practised her accent, stripping it of those markers that flagged her as foreign. She went on to have four children, and when we were growing up it sometimes felt that for my mother, who had been uprooted by love, it was only the home she erected around herself that allowed her to be at peace in a strange land.

Her own mother, Gudrun, had also been a foreigner to her children. She was German, and had met her future husband, Willem, on a trip to London in the 1930s, when they were both twenty-one. She had come to England to learn English; Willem had come to visit the textile mills of Lancashire to learn the family trade. Some friends invited them on a driving tour of the English

Riviera. The initial dalliance was brief, but it was enough to spark a lasting correspondence. They wrote long letters to each other for the next few years, and visited each other when they were able to.

Like my mother, Gudrun wrote in a language that was not her own, but those letters of hers which survive are chatty and full of life: she wrote about what she was doing, her dreams for the future and her aspirations for her country. In only the second letter she wrote to my grandfather, Gudrun confessed that her 'highest ambition' was for 'a large crowd of children'. Still, the question of identity, of what it meant to have a homeland, was a persistent worry. She was concerned about her family, 'and whether in a different country one would not always feel a foreigner. Fortunately, the Dutch are at least a peace-loving nation, so it is unlikely that war will break out between our two countries.'

In 1934, a year after Hitler came to power, Gudrun wrote to Willem expressing her worries about the future of Germany. Her letters got darker, bombastically nationalistic, and now make for unsettling reading. 'I feel everything through and through,' she wrote to him later that year, 'and in my heart I will always retain a strong German feeling [. . .] Your whole being is nothing without your fatherland. It is what you live for, it is what you put children in the world for, and it is what all your efforts should strive towards.'

When they got engaged, near the end of that year, my grandparents began a conversation about what it meant to belong to a place. Gudrun wrote to say she had been given a copy of the *Deutsches Einheits-Familienstammbuch* – the *Rassenhygiene*, or 'race-hygiene' book issued by the Nazi government to all those registering for marriage. 'I can tell you it gets under one's skin when one thinks about leaving one's Fatherland just at the moment when it is going so badly,' she wrote just before their marriage, after which she planned to leave Germany forever:

That is after all an irreversible step, and one's own children won't be German, and in that respect will be strangers to their own mother. I keep telling myself that racially our people belong together, and political borders are more or less arbitrary, and could change every day. Who can tell whether perhaps one day the whole of Europe has to stand up together against greater enemies: against the yellows or the blacks.

They were married in 1935, in Bonn, under a Nazi flag. After the wedding Gudrun moved to Holland to live with my grandfather in the forest his father had planted. Her father Otto, a lawyer, had facilitated the conglomeration of the chemical company IG Farben, which would go on to produce Zyklon B, the gas used in the chambers at Auschwitz-Birkenau and Dachau. Four years after my grandparents were married war broke out, and Gudrun fell silent. The letters she wrote to her family in Germany, which were all opened and covered in marks from the censor's pen, were full of insignificant chatter. My mother, born after the end of the war, remembers her as a melancholy, reticent woman who would shut down any conversation that tended to the boisterous with a gentle shushing. She rarely spoke about her childhood, or her father, or the war, and died, aged sixty-seven, of an anti-immune deficiency. I often wonder if this story was one of the things my mother was running away from, too.

A week after I visited Johnny the swifts arrived, cruising the upper air, almost invisible they flew so high. I first noticed their presence from the high squeaks of their cries. 'They've made it again,' wrote Ted Hughes in his poem 'Swifts', 'Which means the globe's still working'. On still days of high pressure I watched them fly far above my pigeons, their flight as assured as a cat's stalk across a rickety wooden fence. When I flew them on sunny days, when the swifts darted high above, the pigeons seemed to notice them, and would climb higher and higher into the blue to compete, gaining a better position from which to survey the land below. I wondered what they could see from up there. The arc of the river to the south? The glint of the towers in the City? Could they perhaps make out the curvature of the earth?

Natalya's belly was growing. We made plans for the coming baby, which was due to arrive in a few months' time. We painted a room at the back of the house for Dora so that the new child could have her old room. We bought a cot and a larger pram with an extra seat. Natalya wanted a home birth, and we contacted midwives to discuss arrangements. She went to a hypnobirthing class where she was encouraged to think of birth not as an ordeal but as an experience. She was given a notebook on which was written: 'My job is to relax and allow birth to happen.' She did not go back.

In May the midwife, a warm West Indian woman named Irene, who exuded distracted competence, came round to give our house the once-over. She wanted to know if we intended to use a birthing pool, why we wanted a home birth, who would be present. She told Natalya to lie down on the sofa and got out her stethoscope, which she pressed against Natalya's stomach. Dora and I crouched over it, put our ears to the hole, and listened to the little heart beating beneath the surface of Natalya's skin.

We didn't discuss it, but Natalya and I both worried about the coming birth, and as we made our preparations the pigeons became a welcome distraction. The birds were taking over our garden and my imagination. By night I dreamt of flurries of wings beating in the dark, of feathers drifting down from the sky, of rushing quickly over unfamiliar landscapes. I was becoming increasingly conscious of their needs: of how much care and attention they demanded, of what I still needed to do to get them ready for their first race. I flew them each morning, and if I didn't get back from work in time to let them out in the afternoon, too, I would feel guilty when I went to feed them in the evening. The loft needed cleaning daily. But rather than feeling constrained by their demands I was beginning to like the idea of staying put. I thought of the pigeons as markers of our own desire to nest, and began to luxuriate in the smallness of our world – its clearly defined limits, its sharp edges.

Alby and Woodo had given me a few more birds, and along with Big Johnny's I now had twenty pigeons in my flock. They were flying well around the loft. Most had been ranging for two months. The racing season was approaching. It was time to start training them on the road.

During the intermediate stages of a pigeon's race training, the flyer must take them on a series of training tosses from all the compass points around the loft. The purpose of these tosses is twofold. First, they let the pigeons get used to being held in a basket, so that they are prepared for the experience before they are sent away for their first race, when they will be transported in crates with dozens of other strange birds. Second, the flights increase the scope of the birds' familiar territory so that they can learn approaches to their loft from different directions, which allows them to find their way home if they overfly the loft or get blown off course on the way back from a race.

Until 1976 most flyers trained their birds using the railways, but after the British Railways Board decided to stop running pigeon wagons they had been forced onto the roads. As I couldn't drive, my only option was to train my birds by bicycle, something the other fanciers in the club mocked me for. But I liked the idea of using my bike to explore the local terrain alongside the pigeons. As a cycle courier I'd loved discovering London by riding over its bumps and cobbles, learning the texture of its streets intimately, through leg and saddle. Now, I thought, I would encounter the city at one remove, through the projected perspective of a bird in flight.

Selecting the release point for the first training toss was tricky. Johnny and Steve had warned me of the abundance of birds of prey in the green spaces this side of the River Lea. There were, they said, hundreds of sparrowhawks in Epping Forest. Buzzards circled the grasses of Wanstead Flats. Even built-up areas weren't safe: peregrine falcons nested on church spires, on the top floors of high-rises and the chimneys of converted factories, the better to survey the land around. To get my birds used to flying from the basket against raptors I would need to start them off closer to home.

At the end of May I took the pigeons for their first toss. I had basketed them up the previous evening to get them used to spending a night in confinement, as they would have to do come racing season. They were calm as I approached that evening, arrayed on their perches like trophies in a cabinet, each a precise wing-strike's distance from the next. I picked them up one by one and placed them in the basket Johnny had given me, where they cooed and pecked at each other for a few minutes before calming down. After they had settled, I placed the basket on the floor of the loft and closed the door for the night.

I went back to the birds at dawn. I had not fed them the night before, hoping this would make them more likely to head straight home when released, and that they'd be keener to trap when they got back to the loft. The sun was rising as I set off, but the morning air was cold. There were few cars on the road. I cycled down the High Road, then turned north up a side street. I sweated on my way up the hill with the pigeons cooing and grizzling in the basket on the front of my bike. The sky was hazy, as though a thunderstorm was going to break. When I got to the top of the hill I turned east, heading for Epping Forest.

The place from which I'd decided to fly them for their first toss was named Hollow Ponds. It was on the edge of the forest, a mile or so away from my house. It was a large open area next to a ring of ponds that had been dug out for gravel by prisoners during the Second World War. Trees fringed the ponds – gnarled oak and dying ash – but the central area was open and free from obstructions, with good visibility in all directions. The ponds were a popular cruising spot, and the bushes were littered with condom wrappers. A year previously the decomposing body of a Tottenham mobster had been found by a dog walker in the undergrowth, wrapped in a carpet and alive with scuttling rats.

I cycled to the middle of the field and propped my bike up on its stand, waiting for a few minutes while the birds settled. Johnny had warned me not to release them too soon, as they would need time to tune in to whatever unknowable sensory streams they used to orient themselves.

A woman jogged past with her small dog, which sniffed at the basket. She asked what was inside.

'Pigeons,' I said.

'You're just taking them for a walk?'

'I'll let them out and they'll fly home, I hope.'

She found the idea very funny. She said she'd seen another pigeon, a white one with a message tied to its neck, at the ponds a week before, and asked if it was one of mine. She showed me a poster she'd found taped to a tree. 'I lost my Harris Hawk while flying her here last week,' it read. 'If you see her, please call.'

After a few minutes my birds seemed to wake from their trance, and started fussing and pecking at one another again, which Johnny had said was a sign they were ready to be released. At ten past seven I opened the flap at the front of the basket and the first pigeon stepped gingerly out into the morning air. The rest soon followed, flying hard out of the basket and quickly gaining height. The flock struck out in a south-easterly direction, on a bearing away from home, before wheeling round to follow the line of the trees by the side of the pond. They climbed higher and higher with each turn around the field, and my heart soared with them. I could clearly make out Johnny's brilliant white bird leading the pack.

I watched them range across the sky from left to right for a few more moments until they found their line. This close to home they would rely solely on sight to navigate, and when they got to a sufficient height to spot a familiar landmark the kit tightened together and flew straight off towards the horizon. Within half a minute they had vanished from view.

As soon as I lost sight of them I climbed onto my bike and set off in pursuit, through the forest, up over the hill, and down the High Road. When I got home twenty minutes later Dora and Natalya had woken up. They were sitting in the kitchen having breakfast, looking out at the roof of the loft where the pigeons stood, waiting to be let back inside.

The parents of the writer W. G. Sebald were married in 1936, the year after my grandparents. They had met in Wertach im Allgäu, a small mountain village in Southern Bavaria, when Sebald's father, Georg Sebald, a soldier in the *Wehrmacht*, visited for a skiing holiday. After their marriage the couple travelled all over Germany, following Georg's military placements, but in 1943 they moved back to the village in which his mother had grown up. There she gave birth to Max, as he preferred to be called, on 18 May 1944. He lived there until he was eight and had, he later recalled, a happy childhood.

In Wertach im Allgäu, Sebald was isolated from the effects of the war. His village had not been bombed and was far from the front line. It had no railway link to the rest of Germany, and few people ever visited. After the war his father spent two years in a French prisoner-of-war camp, and was largely absent from his childhood. Instead Sebald was brought up by his maternal grandfather, who took him on long country walks and taught him the names of plants and birds. This period in his life – its occlusions, its ellipses, its strong sense of the complicated status of the homeland – would inform everything he wrote.

Like my grandparents, and perhaps my mother also, Sebald was haunted by what he called Germany's 'conspiracy of silence' over the war, and by the nationalistic amnesia that had descended after it was over: the suppression of memory which, as he saw it, was such a feature of post-war German literature. The war was never mentioned during his childhood until, at school, he was shown newsreel footage taken in Belsen. There was no discussion of what he had seen. In order to escape, Sebald moved from

Germany to England in the 1960s, first to Manchester and later to Norfolk, where he lived with his wife Ute and his daughter Anna for the rest of his life.

It was while teaching German literature at the University of East Anglia that, frustrated by the constraints of academic writing, he began, in his forties, to write the strange, meandering books – neither novels nor travelogues, but something in between – which would make him famous. His finest novel, *Austerlitz*, the last to be published in English before his death, is an attempt to excavate lost memories of a homeland. At the beginning of the novel an unnamed narrator meets a man in a railway station in Antwerp in 1967, and begins to talk to him. The man is Jacques Austerlitz. Over the course of the book the two continue to meet periodically, often in the bar of the Great Eastern Hotel at Liverpool Street Station in London, and Austerlitz gives, along with his life story, potted lectures to his acquaintance: on architecture, on the nature of time, on the design of forts, and also on the history and habits of homing pigeons.

Austerlitz, like Sebald, and like my grandmother, too, had been displaced from his homeland by history. He was born in Prague. His mother was an opera singer and his father managed a slipper-making factory. After the Nazi invasion of Czechoslovakia, Austerlitz tells the narrator, his father fled to Paris and he was sent by his mother on the Kindertransport to Liverpool Street Station, where he was adopted by a nonconformist preacher and his wife who lived in Bala in North Wales. He was a teenager before he discovered that his name was not really Dafydd Elias but Jacques Austerlitz.

At school, Austerlitz recounts, he met a boy named Gerald who, he tells the narrator, 'had suffered from awful homesickness'. 'He often told me about his family on these occasions,' Austerlitz says, 'and most of all he liked talking about the three homing pigeons who would be expecting his return, he thought, as eagerly as he usually awaited theirs.' Once, Austerlitz continues, one of Gerald's birds got lost on the homeward flight from Dolgellau, up the valley from his house, before returning home on foot, walking up the drive with a broken wing the following day. 'I often thought later of this tale of the bird making her long journey home alone,' he says,

> Wondering how she had managed to reach her destination over the steep terrain, circumventing numerous obstacles, and that question, said Austerlitz, a question which still exercises my mind today when I see a pigeon in flight, is one that, against all reason, seems to me connected with the way Gerald finally lost his life.

When Gerald goes up to Cambridge, Austerlitz and he continue to see each other regularly until Gerald, obsessed with the idea of flight, buys a small plane, and is killed when he crashes it into the Savoy Alps.

In Sebald's writing, home became a refuge, both physically and psychologically, but he also recognised that it was a concept that could just as easily be used to exclude people – the alien, the unfamiliar, and the foreign – as to comfort them. His great achievement was to evoke with and through the texture of his prose the *Unheimliche Heimat* – the 'strange homeland' – of post-war Germany he knew as a child, without ever quite confronting it directly. In a lecture he gave near the end of his life, he said that Germany now felt unreal to him, 'like an endless *déjà vu*', and that the only real home that remained for him 'was on the page'. Birds provided another kind of continuity: in *The Rings of Saturn*, a book in which another nameless narrator walks the flat Suffolk landscape in a kind of psychic daze, Sebald described watching swallows fly during the summer evenings of his childhood, when he 'would imagine that the world was held together by the courses they flew through the air'.

He was killed in a car crash in 2001. According to his American editor, who accompanied him on a reading tour just before he died, the last book he read, on a plane flying over the Atlantic, was a study of homing pigeons. After his death, a cutting from the *New York Times* about pigeons in war was found inserted into the American edition of *Austerlitz*, from which he read on that final journey.

## 1.37 p.m., Sunderland, 235 miles from home

The pigeons are halfway home by now. Do they know it? They have been on the wing for over six hours, and some are beginning to tire. The main flock passes high over Berwick, unseen and unacknowledged, just after midday. Ten minutes behind the main bunch flies a group of stragglers – maybe a few dozen birds who have been separated from the pack as it made its way south along the coast.

As they follow the land they skip between headlands, out over the sea and then back over the cliffs: their rocky red sandstone, their layered, buried fossils. They fly over the isle of Lindisfarne, and on down the Northumberland coast. The wind is pushing from the east. It has picked up now, and as they get further south the temperature rises.

It is too much for some of them. As they pass Newcastle one of my birds, a blue hen with the ring number NWHU2017S6475, a bird that has done well in previous races – from Berwick, and from Whitley Bay – and who knows the land below well, breaks from the pack. Perhaps, having failed to drink enough in the crates on the transporter, she is struck by thirst and, spotting the glimmering sheen of a pond or canal, decides to swoop down to stop and refresh.

On the ground, she feels the fatigue of her wings more starkly. The pull of home has weakened. She has no eggs to return to: her two most recent chicks fledged weeks ago. She's hungry now, too. She drinks from a pool of oily water in the gutter by a park and then walks towards a group of feral pigeons feeding on crusts of bread thrown by passers-by for the ducks.

An hour later, rested and with her energy returned, she takes to the skies again. Less urgently than before, she coasts along. As she approaches Sunderland she encounters another kit of racing pigeons: a group heading north from a liberation point in the south. She joins them. Such clashes between groups of birds travelling to different parts of the country are common on race days, when tens of thousands of birds might be flying over Britain at once, making their secret journeys.

The hen falls in with a group of six birds on the edge of the group, and she follows them down as they swoop in low to a loft in the back garden of a fancier in Thornhill, to the south of the city centre. The garden is unfamiliar but the trap looks much like the one on her home loft. She follows the birds down to the landing board and traps with them, feeding hungrily from the grain she finds in the hopper on the floor.

Days later, long after the race is over, the loft's owner, a man named Glen, notices the stray pigeon in his loft. He calls the number on the ring on her leg, and when I answer he tells me he has found my lost bird. He says she's looking well, a 'fine, tame bird', and that I shouldn't let her hang around if I don't want to spoil her. He asks me what I want him to do with her. I tell him I'll send a courier to pick her up in the next few days.

Her race is over, but a week later, two weeks after the clocks have been struck, she will be delivered back home to her loft, no worse the wear for her interrupted journey.

# 7

## Liberation

There is a great deal of disagreement over how best to prepare a team of young pigeons for their first race. 'Many fanciers', I read in Osman's *Racing Pigeons*,

> make 2 miles their first toss, followed by a toss at 5 miles, then 10 miles, 15 miles, and in steps up to the first race point at about 60 miles [. . .] What can happen if the birds are not taken far enough away is that when they get out of their baskets they may over-fly their lofts and get into strange country without noticing it. Many fanciers for this reason give their birds at least one toss north, south, east and west from the loft.

Less scrupulous flyers train their birds only once from the road, maybe a mile away from home, flying them over land they are already familiar with, simply so that they can tell their club mates that they have done some training. 'Birds handled in this way', Osman warned, 'can and do win short races but only because they are brought over the distance by the rest of the birds and just happen to trap quickly.' Patient, slow training, with frequent liberations from different places, was, he advised, the best way to build up a team of pigeons that would do well through the whole season.

A well-trained team of pigeons would be used to the basket, and to being liberated from unfamiliar release sites. I liked the word liberation: the way it dignified the pigeons with a kind of individual autonomy, but also because it described a feeling I longed for. Having been released, the pigeons were free to go where they wished, and there was something compelling about the fact that, if they were trained carefully and given a reason to, they would usually decide, of their own accord, to come back home. But in order to get them ready for the races they would need to be taken beyond their home territory. The connection they had with home had to be stretched in order for it to become strong.

For the next few weeks, after that first toss from Hollow Ponds, I took my birds out with me whenever I could. When the weather was fine I would basket them, strap the basket onto my bicycle, and head out. If I had to go to work, I would take them in the early mornings, before Dora and Natalya had woken up. If I'd spent the day at home writing I would go out in the evening, before dusk, when it would get too dark for them to navigate and they'd be tempted to roost up for the night.

Dora had started going to nursery, and some mornings I would pack her and a basket of pigeons onto my bicycle before setting out. After I dropped her at the gates and waved goodbye, I would cycle on to release them from somewhere nearby before heading in to work. I cycled east and flew them from the middle of Wanstead Flats, where skylarks sang and kestrels shivered overhead. I flew them from the south, from the middle of the Olympic Park. One evening I cycled to the edge of the North Circular and released them from a wide, open field where lonely men congregated to fly their remote-controlled drones in the soft spring air.

Often, when making these forays into unfamiliar territory, I followed water. One day I cycled up the River Ching – now little more than a ditch but once an important tributary of the River Lea – through the villas and sweeping drives of Chingford, before releasing my pigeons from a scruffy park where rats scurried in the undergrowth, and in which I found the stream's source. I followed the Lea south through Stratford, to where it meets the Thames at Leamouth, and flew the birds from beside the basin, wondering if they could detect the estuarine tang of the sea drifting off the Thames as they took to the air.

As summer took hold and the air warmed up, I rarely travelled anywhere without taking a few pigeons with me, basketed at the front of my bike. I took them to King's Cross and released them from the courtyard of the British Library before I went inside to read. I liked to imagine the route they might have taken on their way back home – over the brow of the Pentonville ridge and down the other side, sweeping low towards Dalston and following the basin of the Lea through Hackney and on over the marshes. I took them to my friends' birthday parties, releasing them theatrically from the balconies of blocks of flats and suburban gardens. On one occasion I took them to work in Bloomsbury and flew them out of the window of my office, but I worried my colleagues would notice what I was doing, so I didn't bring them in again.

It felt the same each time I liberated them: a sense of soaring excitement quickly followed by an intense, gnawing fear, a fear I found it impossible to ignore, and which persisted until I knew they had made it back home safely. There was little I could do to influence their flight, or to make them more likely to return: I simply had to wait and trust and hope. I had to learn to let go, to give the birds enough freedom for them to learn to home without giving them so much that they would be lost.

Natalya and I had kept Dora close during the first years of her life. The trauma of her birth made us overly cautious, and she was three years old before we let her spend her first night away from us. We were, I suppose, typical first-time parents, trying to strike the right balance between freedom and protectiveness, but, looking back, often erring on the side of smothering. I was surprised to discover that I was a more anxious parent than Natalya. In the park, or at swimming pools, it was I who would begin to fret as soon as Dora went beyond arm's reach, worrying she might fall from the swings, or walk into deep water before I could react.

Nightmare scenarios played in my mind whenever we were separated. But that spring, after she started nursery and spent more time away from us, I began to learn to let her be free.

In the park outside our house, Dora liked to play a game. She would go to the swings and ask me to push her.

'I want to go as high as the trees,' she would say, 'as high as the pigeons.' And then she would say, 'Tell me to go away.' I would push her, and as she got up to speed I would shout at her: 'Go away!' and 'What are you doing back here?' when she swung back. She squealed with delight at this, which felt like a ritualised game of exile and return.

In *Beyond the Pleasure Principle*, Sigmund Freud described watching a similar game being played by his grandson Ernst when he was eighteen months old. Ernst was a well-behaved boy but, said Freud, rather meanly, 'in no respect forward in his intellectual development'. During the game he would pick up all his toys and fling them to the corner of his room. He would accompany this behaviour with a 'loud long-drawn-out oo-o-oh', which Freud decided was his attempt to say *Fort!* or 'Gone!' Later Freud observed him playing with a wooden reel and string. Ernst would dangle the reel over the side of his cot until he could no longer see it and say 'oo-o-oh'. Then he would pull the reel up again, greeting its reappearance with a joyful *Da!* ('There!').

Freud understood the *fort-da* game to represent his grandson's attempt to overcome the trauma of separation by taming it through repetition. Why do we confront ourselves with those things that have caused us pain, Freud wondered, in dreams or wishes or compulsions to repeat behaviour? Such things are necessary, and secretly desired, he concluded, because they allow us to process these traumas. For Ernst, being separated from the objects he loved before seeing them reappear was, according to Freud, a means of mastering his own fear of separation.

I thought of Ernst's game a lot as Dora grew, and as I began to train the pigeons. The anxiety of each liberation, with the birds taken incrementally further away from home, was an uncomfortable but necessary act of enforced separation. Both the pigeons and I needed it to learn from it. Sometimes, when they failed to arrive on the day I had released them, a gloom would descend on me, and I would worry distractedly about their fates, sleeping fretfully and waking early to go down to the garden to see if they had arrived. When I did manage to beat them home from a training run and was able to watch them come in, the birds would sometimes turn up separately (the flock having been broken up over unfamiliar land, or having scattered after being chased by a hawk), strung out in a line against the sky like aircraft queuing patiently to land. Once or twice a pigeon would come back with a wound across its back or breast, having been attacked by a hawk, or having struck some branches in its panicked flight.

As I flew the birds from these parks and towpaths and lay-bys I began plotting their likely routes home. By following their projected journeys on the map on my computer, zooming in on the satellite view so that I could fly with them over the streets and houses, I began to see how my home was connected with the rest of the city. The imaginary journeys we shared allowed me to travel without ever having to leave the house.

In order to find your way home across unfamiliar terrain two things are necessary. The first is a map, the second a compass. The compass provides directional information, but doesn't tell you where you are in relation to your destination. The map allows you to locate yourself on the surface of the earth, and to know in what direction your target lies, but doesn't allow you to maintain a course home once you set off. If you have a map but not a compass, you won't be able to work out where home is. If you have a compass but no map, you won't know where you are in relation to it.

This 'map and compass' model of navigation was first applied to animals by a French biologist named C. Viguier in 1882, but the mechanisms which might underpin it didn't receive sustained scientific attention until the twentieth century. In the 1940s Gustav Kramer, the biologist who first discovered that pigeons that had never been allowed to fly outside were unable to home successfully, had become interested in the problem of bird navigation when he noted how his caged starlings appeared to possess an internal compass. He coined the word *Zugunruhe* – 'migratory restlessness' – to describe the anxious fluttering behaviour that migratory birds displayed when it was time to move on, and observed that during this time they tended to congregate in the areas of their cages most closely aligned with their natural migratory routes.

Kramer decided that pigeons, with their unique homing abilities and lack of seasonal migratory impulse, would make the perfect test subjects with which to investigate the biological mechanisms underpinning homing behaviour. During the 1940s and '50s he conducted experiments on what became known as the 'sun azimuth compass' thesis. He put pigeons in large circular cages, around the edge of which he placed twelve pots. Only one of the pots contained food, and over time the birds were trained to expect to be fed from a particular compass point. When their cages were rotated, the birds did not alter the direction from which they sought food. Rather than responding visually to the individual pot which contained food, Kramer concluded, they must be using some other mechanism to work out where they should expect food to be presented from.

Kramer had discovered that pigeons possess an extremely accurate internal sun compass which allows them to discern directional information from the azimuthal position of the sun. Later studies would show that migratory birds which fly at night can use the stars to navigate in a similar way. But Kramer also noted that – though they might take slightly longer to orient themselves – pigeons released from unfamiliar sites on overcast days were in the end no worse at homing than they were if they could see the sun. Evidence from experiments on migratory birds suggested that many species are sensitive to geomagnetism – songbirds kept in cages surrounded by Helmholtz coils, which invert the polarity of the magnetic fields they are exposed to, perform *Zugunruhe* on the opposite side of the cage to the one you would otherwise expect them to – and pigeons, too, Kramer concluded, possess two compasses: one based on the sun, the other on geomagnetic sensitivity.

Kramer was killed a few years later when he fell from a cliff while collecting baby pigeons for his experiments, but his theories were developed by one of his students, Klaus Hoffman. Hoffman had noticed that when he kept starlings in cages lit by artificial light, and gradually altered the amount of light they received each day, he was able to 'clock-shift' them, making them think they were at a different latitude than they actually were. When the birds were then fed, Hoffman found, they searched for food in the direction which corresponded perfectly to the angle by which they had been clock-shifted.

Pigeons also display this dramatic, time-based spatial behaviour. If you clock-shift a group of pigeons and release them from an unfamiliar place, they will initially fly on a bearing which is offset by the degree to which the shifting has altered their perception of compass direction. The implication of these experiments is that pigeons don't just use the sun as a directional compass: like bees they are able to use their internal chronometers to compensate for its movement on the horizon.

After Kramer and Hoffman's work the problem of pigeon compasses seemed to have been solved, but understanding the nature of their maps proved far more difficult. It was not until 1971, when a group of scientists at the University of Pisa, led by a biologist named Floriano Papi, conducted a series of rather brutal experiments, that the beginnings of an answer emerged. If you sever the olfactory nerves of pigeons, or render them temporarily anosmic by dousing their nostrils with zinc sulphate solution, Papi found, they lose the ability to home altogether. More extraordinarily still, if you keep young pigeons from birth in a loft that is completely isolated from the atmosphere, even if they are allowed to see outside of it, they will be unable to find their way back to it once displaced to an unfamiliar place. Most surprising of all, if you keep young pigeons in a loft in which the air flow is inverted – so that the external wind direction is reversed, via a system of fans and ducts, so as to come from the opposite direction inside the loft – they will, when released, fly off on a bearing deflected 180 degrees on the same axis away from home.

Papi concluded that pigeons navigate by using an olfactory 'gradient map' of the world, using odours undetectable to human noses to work out where they are in relation to home. Most scientists now agree that it is the smell of the wind, combined with a pigeon's sun and magnetic compasses, which allow them to navigate home from distant places. Quite what they might be smelling remained inconclusive until relatively recently, when a German scientist named H. G. Wallraff conducted an experiment using 'virtual pigeons': computer algorithms coded to behave as pigeons might, which flew through digital space. Wallraff spent three years driving in a 200-kilometre radius of the site of his pigeon loft in Würzburg, Germany, collecting ninety-six air samples as he went. He analysed these using gas chromatography, which allowed their chemical make-up to be identified. Wallraff then fed this data into his computer model. He found that when he released his virtual pigeons from a variety of 'release sites', they were able to use the data he had provided from his air samples, along with information relating to wind direction, to find their way back to their virtual home.

It is not, apparently, that home possesses an odour which operates like a beacon that allows pigeons to use smell to navigate. Instead it seems as if winds that come from certain directions on the earth's surface have stable and unchanging odours which pigeons can use to build up their olfactory gradient maps of the world, and the location of their home within it. One implication of this olfactory map model of bird navigation is that although a displaced pigeon knows the direction in which it has to travel to get home, and can use a suite of other sensory abilities to keep itself on target once it has begun to fly, it might not have any sense of how far it must go to get there. A pigeon flying home might just have to keep going until it arrives, or finds itself too exhausted to continue.

At the end of May I took the pigeons for one final training toss from the west, from Leyton Marshes, a mile or so away from my house, before heading north. I'd chosen for their release point the place where, in 1909, an engineer named Alliott Verdon Roe had made the first powered flight of a British-built aircraft. Roe had built his plane – made from steamed wood tensioned with piano wire, the wings clad in yellow cotton-oiled paper, with an under-carriage constructed from the forks of his brother's bicycle – in some stables in Putney, but had nowhere to fly it, having been denied permission to practise on Salisbury Plain, Wimbledon Common and Wormwood Scrubs. In desperation he consulted a map of London and noticed the green expanse of the marshes, which were open to the public and had no bylaws preventing the flying of aircraft. Without asking permission from the council, and under cover of darkness, he transported his plane to a railway arch he'd rented next to the River Lea.

The initial flights were short, barely more than skips of a few dozen yards, during which the wooden wheels of the plane swished over the tips of the grass. 'A 50-yd. hop, a crash, and then two weeks' work' was how Roe summarised the frustra-tions of these early attempts. His plane was still earthbound, but the freedom of flight was tantalisingly close. Within a month the distance and height of his hops had increased, and the world had begun to take an interest in what he was doing on that field by the Lea. Newspapers sent journalists to the marshes; the local council, troubled by what they called Roe's 'antics', put a bailiff on his tail to try to decide whether he was doing anything illegal.

On the morning of 13 July 1909, six years after the Wright brothers had first flown a heavier than air craft over the dunes at Kitty Hawk, Roe rolled his aeroplane out of the arch, started its small motorcycle engine, tested the flex of its wings, and positioned it for take-off. A photographer from the *Daily Mail* was on hand to capture the moment. Slowly, Roe began to taxi across the grass. His plane was not powerful, but he quickly picked up speed, rolling down the slight incline which ran away from the railway arches towards the river. A few yards on and his wheels left the ground. He felt the precise moment the bumps and vibrations ceased. Slowly at first and then more quickly Roe gained height. He climbed above the trees, rising to the level of the houses on the other side of the river.

Roe's triumphant flight lasted less than ten minutes. From his rickety cockpit he saw the sweeping curve of the Lee Navigation stretching to the north, bisected by the glittering rails of the train line. He saw the hills of the Lea Valley rolling out to the west. He saw the marshes fall away from under him, and the houses, stretching out on all sides, marching to the distant horizon. He felt, he later said, exhilarated and vindicated, but he also felt free: of the bounds of the earth and of the weight of expectation that had dogged his single-minded project.

One hundred years after Roe, on a changeable spring day with high wisps of cloud, I placed my basket of birds near to the spot from which he took flight. It was unseasonably cold that day, but the skies were clear, and the sun nearly at its azimuth, glinting off the water and the roof of the ice-skating rink which squats next to the Lea Bridge Road to the south like a vast aircraft hangar. I let the birds settle in their basket as I scanned the field, checking for hawks. There were trees lining the river, and a raised walkway to the east, running down the middle of the meadow. Some horses neighed from the stables in the distance. On one of the railway arches I found a plaque recording Roe's first flight, next to which someone had scrawled a piece of graffiti that said, 'Smoke crack and fly!'

By now the pigeons had settled, so I went over to the basket and opened the flap. They flew out in an instant, their grey bodies pouring upwards into the sky like smoke, the kit unfurling around me before heading up over the railway line. After two circuits of the field they were high enough to see their home. Buffeted by the wind but flying keenly, they looked strong and confident: a world away from the young, nervous birds they had been just a few months previously. Now they flew with purpose, and seemed to have a sense of what was expected of them. Within a few moments they were out of sight. I wondered what they might see from up there, so far above the ground, so free.

Near the end of the eighteenth century, as they first began to take to the air, people became interested in what the world might look like from above. Before this moment the aerial gaze we are now so familiar with from our GPS and smartphone maps was almost inconceivable: the province of heroes, or Gods, or birds. Such views were presumptuous. Though they did exist – *vedute* of European cities were drawn from tall buildings, and during the sixteenth century extremely accurate bird's-eye view maps of many cities began to be produced – these aerial views were projected rather than real: metaphors of omnipotence and owner-ship rather than accurate portraits of home as seen from above. In 1909 fewer than a thousand living people had experienced what Roe felt that day on the marshes: not just the physical sensation of flight, but the new ways of seeing it provided.

The first aerial photographs of earth were taken by the balloon-ist Gaspard-Félix Tournachon – a cartoonist, portrait photogra-pher, inventor and consummate self-promoter, who nicknamed himself 'Nadar' – over a village outside Paris in 1858. His images from this ascent, taken on a clumsy and labour-intensive camera from the rickety basket of a tethered hydrogen balloon, do not survive, but Nadar knew that what he had captured with them was revelatory. Seen from above 'the earth unfolds into an enormous unbounded carpet', he later wrote, 'without beginning or end.'

The earliest surviving aerial photographs date from 13
October 1860, when James Wallace Black and Samuel Archer
King took flight over Boston Harbor in their balloon *Queen of
the Air* and captured in detail the toy-towned roofs of the houses
and the ships below. They called their photograph 'Boston, as
the Eagle and the Wild Goose See It', already imagining the
radical avian empathy enabled by combining photography with
flight.

Early aerial photography was difficult. Sensitive chemicals and
long exposure times conspired against these early pioneers. At
first balloons provided the most reliable means of capturing
images of earth from the air, but as technology improved so
cameras became small and resilient enough to be borne aloft by
unmanned aircraft. Smaller balloons floated cameras over battlefields, and over the new cities that were springing up across the
globe. In 1888 Amédée Denisse fired a camera up into the heavens on a rocket and watched as it was carried down gently on its
parachute, clicking its shutter as it fell. By the end of the century
cameras were routinely attached to kites fitted with timers made
from fuses that would slowly burn down as they went aloft, firing
off their shots when they reached their apex.

One of the most remarkable of these early aerial photography
systems was designed by the apothecary and amateur photographer Julius Neubronner a year or so before Roe made his flight
over Leyton Marshes. Julius's father, a pharmacist and keen
fancier named Wilhelm, had used his pigeons to carry prescriptions from doctors working in rural areas to his dispensary,
allowing him to prepare their medicines in advance. When
Julius took over the family business he perfected his father's
pigeon drug-delivery network, training his birds to carry not
just prescriptions but medicine, too, and using them to carry
drugs to local hospitals. When one of his pigeons got lost in fog,
only returning home a month later, Julius wondered if it would
be possible to find out what his birds got up to when they were
in the air. And so he designed an extremely light camera with a

*One of Julius Neubronner's pigeon photographers.*

timed shutter and attached it to one of his pigeons using a tiny harness.

Neubronner's first test flights took place in 1907, and in 1908 he patented his 'Method of and Means for taking Photographs of Landscapes from Above'. As he experimented, his system became more sophisticated. The cameras he had designed were heavy, and the birds that carried them soon learned that the more quickly they returned home the sooner they would be relieved of their burdens. Taking a pigeon's average flying height and wind direction into account Neubronner could, with some accuracy, set up his system so that his camera pigeons would take a photograph when they flew over a specific target. He developed a mobile pigeon loft with a built-in darkroom in order to take his birds on the road and record landscapes even when they were far away from their home.

The photographs he captured are haunting and beautiful records of a remarkable collaboration. Neubronner had hoped his pictures would reveal the truth about the world as it was seen from above, but in fact they estranged it, transforming familiar subjects – street scenes, grand houses, formal gardens – into abstractions of colour and line. One or two capture him standing on the roof of his loft, waiting for his birds to come in to land. The ones I love the most are those in which you can see some evidence of the presence of the pigeons themselves: a blur of wing-tips intruding at the edges of the frame, a cocked head looking inquisitively behind.

*The world seen from above.*

Neubronner spent the next few years trying to drum up interest in his invention. He took his mobile loft to trade fairs, where he sold postcards depicting the surrounding countryside. He thought his pigeon photography system might also have military applications, and after the outbreak of the First World War his pigeons were flown over the battlefields of the Somme and Verdun. But in order to take useful images of enemy fortifications they had to be taken beyond the opposing lines, and this proved to be too difficult. The German army quickly lost interest in Neubronner's project, and he never made any money from it at all. Nevertheless, his pigeons were among the first unmanned drones ever deployed in war.

They also, as the artist Joan Fontcuberta has observed, contributed to a revolution in seeing. In his 1928 essay 'The

New Vision', the Hungarian photographer László Moholy-Nagy described the way in which perceiving the world from above would soon allow for a 'full experience of space'. Aerial views were, he said 'space compressors' and would go on to 'alter the previous conception of architectural relations'. It is this perspective – disembodied, godlike and distant, like that of a bird in flight – that we inhabit when we navigate on our smartphones today.

Neubronner's photographs recorded a thrilling kind of empathy: an intimacy between person and animal which I came to feel more strongly as I continued to train my birds from the road. Like photographs of the earth taken from the moon, his images allowed people to realise just how small their world – their home – actually was. But they also posed a question that remains unanswerable: Who took these photographs? Was it Neubronner? Or was it his pigeons?

I had become interested in the possibility of knowing where they might go during their flights, and what they might see from the air as they travelled home. I wanted to try to recreate Neubronner's images, so I bought a small digital camera on the internet. Once I'd removed its plastic casing to reduce its weight, I mounted it on a harness my mum had made for me from pieces of knicker elastic and bra clips – a tiny rucksack which a bird could wear on its front, with loops to go over its neck and below its tail – and strapped it to the belly of one of my pigeons. After checking that she could move unhindered around the loft while wearing the harness, I turned on the camera and opened the trap.

It had been a warm, still day, and the city was cooling as the birds flew up over the trees. They had been inside the loft since morning, and took to the air with delight. They began to circle the house, soaring high in the sky as the sun glinted off the windows of the houses around them. Every so often they would settle on my roof for a moment before taking off again to renew their circuit. As they passed over my head I caught sight of the bird wearing the camera, and could just make out the glinting red light which meant it was still recording.

After flying for an hour, as the sun began to set, the birds came in to land. I opened the trap and rattled my tin, and they went inside to feed. The camera was still attached to the bird. I released her from her harness and, with hands now shaking with excitement, plugged it into my laptop. On the screen, an image of my face swam into view. The video – crude and grainy though it was – began to play.

First it showed the interior of the loft. The pigeons stood on their perches, fussing with each other. When I opened the door the camera showed them leaving the trap one after another, flying over the garden wall, and then doubling back over the house. For one brief moment I saw myself looking up at them from the garden. Then I was left behind. The flock rose higher and higher, and I caught snatches of the wider view, framed by the jerky movement of their wings. I could see far over the plane trees that line the cricket pitch at the front of the house, and on to the distant parts of the city, where towers twinkled in the sunshine. Seen from this first-person perspective the pigeons' agility was astonishing: seasickness-inducing. I felt as though I was flying with them.

Each time the birds changed direction a whole new vista opened up. I could see the horizon, rows of terraced houses, the sweeping S of the train line running to the north of our house and, in the distance, the flash of blue that marked the reservoirs. When they got high enough I could almost make out the bowl of London, the hills of Walthamstow to the north-east, the dip in the land as it rolled down towards the river in the west.

I watched the video play for twenty minutes before the battery of the camera ran out. Near the end of the footage I was amazed to see a person cycling down the road who looked familiar. It was my sister, who lived around the corner from us, heading home with her two children on her bicycle.

*My house as the pigeon sees it.*

There was something uncanny about the experience of seeing such familiar things from this heightened and estranged perspective. I'd had a similarly intense feeling of recognition only once before. When Google rolled out its Street View technology, which allows you to see aerial and street-level photographs of any city – any street or house – in the world, I'd immediately done what, I'm sure, most people had: looked up addresses familiar to me to see what their digital equivalents looked like. I typed in the address I was living in at the time to see if I could find myself. Then I typed in my parents' address. There, on the doorstep, sat a person fixing a puncture. Though the face had been blurred by Google's anonymising software protocols, it was, unmistakably, a photograph of me.

★

After my experiments with pigeon photography, I bought a set of expensive GPS tracker rings from a Taiwanese company and used them to plot the routes my birds took on their training flights. I'd attach the rings – which weighed only a few grams – to their legs before releasing them. After they'd returned home I would take off the rings and download the data onto a computer. On the screen the records of their journeys were drawn in blue and red lines, each plotted point – recordings were taken once every two seconds during flight – marking their speed, their direction and the height at which they flew.

Sometimes the birds seemed to know as soon as they were released what routes to take, flying in a straight line from the liberation point to the loft. At other times they meandered, following the curves of rivers, or the sweeping arcs of roads. When the sky was overcast or they were flying from a new place, it took them far longer to orient themselves, and I watched as the plotted lines made crazy backtracks and circles across the map. On one release, from a motorway service station fifteen miles from home, on an overcast day when the cloud was low and thick, and the fog had begun to settle in the valleys of the land, they flew for hours in circles before eventually finding the route. They covered 80 miles in aimless flight that day, and many didn't make it home before night fell.

But as I made my videos and tracked their flight via GPS, I began to feel as though I was missing the very thing that had attracted me to the pigeons in the first place: the unknowable mystery of their flight. What I had liked initially about the moment of liberation was the trust it entailed, the hope and faith of it. You never quite knew what was going to happen to them up there, in the skies, after they had been released. You simply had to wait and trust that they would make it back. Their flight was a rebuke to the known world, with its mapped and recorded limits.

The tyranny of technology means that, increasingly, we are able to know perfectly not just where we are but where we have been,

and when we have been there. Unfamiliar places are encountered
not on their own terms but as they are mediated through our maps
and screens. We know what they are like long before we experience
their reality. The philosopher Walter Benjamin argued in 1932 that
'not to find one's way in a city may well be uninteresting and banal.
It requires ignorance – nothing more. But to lose oneself in a city
– as one loses oneself in a forest – that calls for quite a different
schooling', and getting lost has only become more difficult since
then. As a bicycle courier I had prided myself on my navigational
abilities – on the hard-won knowledge I had acquired through years
of cycling around the city, which allowed me to find my way and
deliver packages as efficiently as anyone. But as I flew the birds and
mapped their flight that summer, I began to think there was a loss
implicit in this way of knowing a landscape.

In *A Field Guide to Getting Lost*, Rebecca Solnit described the
way in which losing oneself is an important part of one's childhood development. 'There's an art of being at home in the
unknown,' she wrote, 'so that being in its midst isn't cause for
panic or suffering, of being at home with being lost.' That sense
of being at home in the unknown – being liberated through
becoming lost – is, Solnit continues, being eroded by the ubiquity
of digital maps and GPS and smartphones. Nowadays, when
navigating to a new place, we refer not to street signs but to the
glowing blue arrow which tells us, turn by turn, move by move,
how to get from A to B.

Pigeon flying offered an antidote to the world's knowability.
When the birds were up I had no idea where they might be: I
simply had to trust that all would be well. After a while I came to
see each flight as a release: a liberation from the tyranny of known
places and of maps. The anxiety I felt each time I let them fly was
like that which I'd discovered playing with Dora in the park, that
which a parent experiences when watching their child make her
first independent journeys through the wide world. It was a
frightening freedom, but also necessary. There was liberation to
be found in those feelings, too.

## 2.28 p.m., Whitby, 204 miles from home

The afternoon sun has warmed the air. It is touching 30°C in Northumberland, and the pigeons that have chosen to fly over the land are suffering most. Their throats flutter as they pant, trying to cool down.

The main part of the flock has stayed out to sea where the air is cooler, following the coast down south from Sunderland, skipping over the waves a few hundred yards out. At Hartlepool they follow the headland which juts out into the sea, tracing the mouth of the River Tees away from the open ocean until they are sure they can cross it. Most then turn south again, to fly over the Victorian resorts below – Marske and Saltburn – where holiday-makers line the beaches and dig for fossils in the cliffs. But at the edge of the Tees a few of them, exhausted by the buffeting wind above the waves, head back inland to find shelter.

The land changes beneath them as they leave Saltburn behind. As the flock passes near Staithes, where the houses run down to the quay in multicoloured terraces, they catch the eye of a peregrine falcon far on the horizon. She has ventured a long way from her cliff somewhere deep in the moors in search of food. In late July the last of her chicks are still on the nest. She has taught them to hunt, often catching the pigeons that fly through the area on race days, but she still must supplement their diet with her own quarry. The heat has made food scarce, and the moors are parched beneath her as she cruises the thermals, looking for a kill.

The pigeons are wary as they fly over this open country. They tend to avoid thick forest and field, where they know birds of prey might be waiting in ambush, and where there is little cover. But there is no helping it round here – no way to avoid the looming mass of the moors to the east, or the forests which girdle the towns and cities they pass over on their way south.

She approaches high from the west, rising on the warm air to soar far above the line of birds, hoping to intercept one of them on her stoop. The pigeons notice her long before she arrives. Their visual acuity, like hers, is astounding. The battle is one of optics as well as of claw and wing. As soon as they see her they scatter – the kit breaks in panic and the birds fly higher and higher, hoping to get above her so that she is unable to drop down onto them from the open sky.

The peregrine chooses her moment carefully. She ignores the birds that have now climbed above her, knowing she has lost the element of surprise. But she notices one, an inexperienced yearling hen, exhausted by the demands placed on her by the race and the weather. The peregrine lines herself up, then dives with impassive inevitability: wings tucked, legs retracted, head extended. It is all over in seconds. A snatch of claw through soft feather, piercing pain, a final struggle and a neat gush of scarlet blood. She lands on a patch of grass by the coastal path with her prize and begins to pluck it. It will make a good meal for her chicks.

# 8

## Homebound

In a paper entitled 'Superstition in the Pigeon', the psychologist B. F. Skinner, chief architect of the pigeon-guided homing missile, described his attempts to condition birds to respond to predictable stimuli. For his experiment he starved his pigeons to 70 per cent of their normal weight, then placed them in cages and gave them small amounts of food at regular, predetermined intervals, irrespective of how they behaved. Very quickly most began to display what Skinner called 'ritualistic behaviours', which they associated, he surmised, with being fed. One developed the habit of turning in counter-clockwise circles between feedings; another displayed a 'tossing' response, 'as if placing its head beneath an invisible bar and lifting it repeatedly'.

Skinner took these behaviours to demonstrate 'a sort of superstition' in the pigeons which was, he thought, analogous to that of humans. 'The bird', he argued, 'behaves as if there were a causal relation between its behavior and the presentation of food, although such a relation is lacking.' Like us, Skinner concluded, pigeons are pattern-seeking creatures, primed to see connections in the world even when they are not there.

Skinner was the most prominent proponent of the school of psychology known as behaviourism. He argued that rather than trying to ascribe thoughts and feelings to organisms – rather than trying to understand their minds – scientists should instead limit themselves to observing their outward behaviours. For Skinner, interiority was a chimera: a ghost that dwelt in the machine of the body. Psychology, he thought, should deal only in observable, measurable facts.

As I spent more time at the club, with the flyers, I found that pigeon racing attracted – or perhaps it is better to say it generated – magical speculation and ritualistic behaviour of the kind Skinner had identified in his pigeons. Partly this was because it was an activity over which its human participants appeared to have so little control: a flock of birds could go missing on an apparently straightforward training flight, never to be seen again, or they could return, sometimes months or years after they went missing, out of a blue sky to their home loft, as if nothing had happened. And so it was perhaps not surprising that their flyers tended to be superstitious men who stuck closely to those rituals that had served them well in the past.

I'd first noticed it when Steve and George wafted pendulums over their young birds to determine their sex, and when, at the club, discussion turned to the food supplements some of the fanciers used to prepare their pigeons for a race. The logic of sympathetic magic seemed to inform the way they added organic cider vinegar to their drinking water 'to keep their insides acidic', or hemp oil to their seed to make their feathers shine glossily after the moult. Some fanciers swore you should never fly your birds during periods of high solar activity, or when the earth's geomagnetic field was in flux.

The more I learned about the fickleness of pigeons, the more I came to see these beliefs as responses to the fact that, despite the best efforts of Kramer and Papi, the phenomenon of pigeon homing remained deeply mysterious. Though we have come to know a great deal about pigeon physiology over the past century, this knowledge is partial, and has come to us in the third person: through the objectifying measurements of science. Many pigeon fanciers feel that such accounts inevitably leave something out.

This is not a new anxiety. In his essay 'Why Look at Animals?', the art critic John Berger argued that as we have come to know more about the processes underpinning animal life, so have we lost some of the wonder we once had for the natural world. Since the Enlightenment, he said, when they were reduced to mere machines devoid of interiority, animals have come to be thought of as objects to observe or to keep rather than creatures with which we might share our lives. This disenchantment has reduced the animal to pet, or mere matter for industrial exploitation or, as in the zoo, to museum exhibit. When in the past humans kept animals because they performed certain social or religious functions – killed mice, carried messages, guarded possessions, or provided meat – nowadays they are kept irrespective of their utility. The presence of pets in the home – tamed, humanised and diminished in the process – mirrors a more general retreat from the natural world, a retreat exemplified, said Berger, by the conditions of the modern home. 'The small family living unit', he argued,

> lacks space, earth, other animals, seasons, natural temperatures, and so on. The pet is either sterilized or sexually isolated, extremely limited in its exercise, deprived of almost all other animal contact, and fed with artificial foods. This is the material process which lies behind the truism that pets come to resemble their masters or mistresses. They are creatures of their owner's way of life.

In trying to understand the otherness of animals we have instead diminished it.

My experiments with pigeon photography and GPS tracking were clumsy attempts to answer a question implicit in Berger's story of disenchantment, a question first posed by the Swedish philosopher and biologist Jakob von Uexküll. In 1934 Uexküll published his *A Foray into the Worlds of Animals and Humans*, an exploration of animal physiology that became a founding text for the fledgling discipline of what is called 'biosemiotics': a field of study based on the idea that in order to understand what it might be like to be another animal we first need to try to understand the environment in which it lives. Uexküll referred to what he called an organism's *umwelt* (literally 'around-world' or 'environment' or, perhaps, 'home'): the perceptual mantle which, he said, constituted every animal's uniquely subjective experience of the world. Because of this, animals, including humans, do not dwell in any externally given 'objective' reality, because such a thing does not and cannot exist. Instead they inhabit the *umwelt* formed by the sensory information that is available to them. The external world is given significance only according to the particular needs of the organism perceiving it.

Uexküll went on to suggest that all organisms should be thought of as being accompanied by a 'soap bubble' of consciousness, which sets the limits of their experience and only occasionally overlaps with those 'bubbles' inhabited by other kinds of organism. We are isolated from one another, he concluded, not only because we cannot communicate, but because we inhabit different and incompatible sensory homes. Or, as Berger put it, humans and animals look at each other across a 'narrow abyss of non-comprehension'. No matter how hard we might try to understand them in scientific, third-person terms, animals have, he went on, 'secrets which, unlike the secrets of caves, mountains, seas, are specifically addressed to man'.

Though the pigeon flyers in the club were motivated to race by the glory of winning, most of them were interested in pigeons because of the mystery of how they homed, and what it felt like for them as they did so. They were not sentimental men, but they spoke of this mystery in tones of hushed awe.

Even the otherwise straightforward Colin Osman was not immune to a kind of speculative theorising about the homing instinct you might generously classify as outlandish. One of the strangest chapters of *Racing Pigeons* (and the one I loved best) provided an overview of the various theories that have been proposed over the years to explain the homing instinct. Osman summarised Kramer's sun azimuth theory and the idea of geomagnetic sensitivity, but he also discussed what he called the 'ESP' hypothesis, which he likened to water-divining. 'The theory behind these curiosities', Osman wrote, 'is that every living thing can be identified by its own unique wavelength [. . .] the pigeon loft has a compound wavelength which the pigeon can detect. This, in effect, is like a radar beam and the pigeon homes on this radar beam by flying down to its source. It is as simple and as easy as flying directly towards a light.'

Despite resistance from the orthodox scientific community, the idea that pigeons home not to a particular geographical location but to a loft with which they have some kind of psychic bond has proved to be a persistent one. For over thirty years the renegade biologist Rupert Sheldrake has been promoting just such an idea, refining his theory of 'morphogenetic resonance' which, he says, explains a host of unsolved problems in biology: how organisms develop, how crystals form, and also how pigeons home.

At the beginning of June I went to meet Sheldrake. I was interested in his ideas, which had a gonzo, eccentric appeal, and I wanted to discuss them with him. It was one of the hottest summers on record. Bloated bluebottles flew in through the windows from the garden and bumped their heads lazily against the windowpanes. During the days we left all the doors open to try to get a breeze circulating through the house, but the air was still and sluggish and the heat squatted over us, slicking our bodies with sweat. When they landed on the roof of the loft after their training flights, the pigeons panted like greyhounds.

I sweated all the way as I cycled from my house to Sheldrake's, down the Lea Bridge Road, past the sad shrines to motorcyclists who had been killed in furious night-time races, over the dry marshes and on through Stoke Newington, then up over the ridge until I got to the low hills of Kentish Town, and the run-up towards Hampstead.

I'd taken Eggy and Orange – the most experienced birds in my flock – to Sheldrake's, seven miles or so from home. I wanted to show them to him, but I also had a vague idea that in flying them from his home to mine, over the parts of the city I was now cycling through, they would connect the dots: stitch the story together in some way.

Sheldrake lives in a grand house in Hampstead, overlooking the Heath. I locked my bicycle up outside and rang the bell. He opened the door and peered out: a tall, thin man with hooded eyes which gave him the look of a stoned hawk peering through a telescope. In the hallway there was an aquarium in which goldfish flicked through yellow water. Plants and books were scattered about. In the kitchen things fermented in jars: asparagus tips, lined up like severed fingers in their greeny-blue brine; lemons like plump, gnarled hand-grenades. A copy of Sandor Ellix Katz's *The Art of Fermentation* lay open on a countertop. Sheldrake offered me tea. He was boyishly enthused by the presence of the pigeons, and excited to watch their release from the Heath. We gave them some water and put them out on the balcony to acclimatise before going upstairs to talk.

His study was cosy – part music studio, part chemistry lab, part library. In one corner he had installed a homemade laboratory in which things bubbled and test tubes dried on wooden racks. A low hum came from somewhere out of sight. An experiment was going on. It felt like the kind of house in which an experiment was always going on. We sat down, and he began to explain his theory.

Sheldrake believes that all living things possess a 'morphogenetic field' – akin to a magnetic field, or to gravity – which governs their development and behaviour. These fields connect creatures with one another, but also with the collective memory of their species. Rather than being located in the brain, he argues that memory is 'inherent in nature': in remembering things we do not consult anything inside ourselves, but instead 'tune in' to the resonance of these morphic fields, tapping into the collective memory of our species as we do so.

The origins of Sheldrake's theory lie in his childhood fascination with pigeons. As a boy, growing up in Newark-on-Trent, he kept a pair of racing homers, which he used to train by bicycle. On race days he would watch the pigeons being liberated from the local railway station. When he went to Cambridge to read biology he found that scientists had only a very hazy understanding of the phenomenon of pigeon homing. The problem became one of his abiding research interests and his most enduring scientific romance.

After his undergraduate degree he worked as a researcher at Cambridge and became interested in epigenetics – the idea that genetic material alone, then thought to provide the essential 'key' which would unlock all the workings of biological life, was not sufficient to account for the development of organisms. People thought he was mad to be investigating such things, 'but I've been proved right now,' he said. He also became interested in the writings of Henri Bergson and Carl Jung.

In 1974 he moved to India to work for an agricultural institute, where he fell under the wing of a charismatic Benedictine monk named Bede Griffiths and went to live in an ashram. It was there that he wrote his first book, *A New Science of Life*, an anti-materialist attack on the Neo-Darwinists – in particular Richard Dawkins and Daniel Dennett – who were, Sheldrake believed, taking over biology and subverting Darwin's legacy. It did not go down well within the mainstream scientific community. Sir John Maddox, then editor of *Nature*, wrote an editorial in which he called *A New Science of Life* 'the best candidate for burning there has been for many years'.

Sheldrake has shuttled round the counter-cultural lecture circuit ever since, conducting his own experiments on dog–human telepathy, on the sense people have of being stared at, and on pigeon homing. The suggestive fertility of his ideas has attracted a bewildering range of fellow-travellers: ley-line junkies, pagan mystics, Anglican radicals, New Age psychogeographers. The scientific community, however, has shunned him, and he wears their disapproval with some pride.

Sheldrake is dismissive of all extant explanations of pigeon homing. He is sceptical of the sun map hypothesis, and points out that pigeons can home when wearing opaque lenses, and also when the sun is not visible at all. Of Papi's model of an odour map, he says that the trauma induced by severing a pigeon's olfactory nerve might cause it to become lost whether or not it depends on smell to home. Instead, he proposes that pigeons have a psychic connection with their homes. Geography, according to Sheldrake's theory, is irrelevant: rather than navigating using a map and compass, pigeons are connected to their lofts and the other members of their colony by a 'kind of psychic elastic band' which allows them to travel to the ends of the earth while always allowing them to feel the pull of home.

To test his theory Sheldrake proposed an experiment: rather than take the pigeon away from the loft, he asked, what would happen if you took the loft away from the pigeon? First, you would need to establish a flock of pigeons and train them to return to a mobile loft. This is not difficult – people had done it successfully during the First World War, using lofts which were housed in modified double-decker buses. Then, said Sheldrake, you remove the birds from the loft and move it away. At first they are flummoxed. Though they can see their loft, rather than flying straight to it they confusedly circle the space where it used to be. Eventually, however, the pigeons get the idea, and will start to trap in to the old loft at the new location. You can train them to do this up to a few miles away, but this, he says, is unremarkable: the birds could well just be flying high enough to see the old loft in its new location. The real test comes when you move the loft a few hundred miles away and see if they can still find their way back.

There have been a number of attempts to test Sheldrake's thesis over the years, but none have been particularly conclusive. He first conducted the experiment in the 1970s, when he found that he was able to train his birds to home to a mobile loft, but had to abandon the project when his pigeon stockman developed a debilitating case of pigeon fancier's lung. Later, after returning from India, he tried again, this time in Northern Ireland. But here the weather was bad, and he lost many of his birds to hawk attacks.

In its most recent iteration, Sheldrake set up the experiment on a ship belonging to the Royal Dutch Navy. The ship sailed to the Caribbean and back, while the pigeons were flown daily. Though this proved that pigeons could home to a moving ship over long distances, in the end the experiment was cancelled when the captain decided he had to test some sonar equipment for the French Navy instead.

'I said, "You've got to do this, we've spent a year preparing,"' Sheldrake told me. 'He said, "Well, I'd love to, but unfortunately they're paying millions of dollars for this research, and you aren't." And that was that. But we did get quite a bit of information, and it would be possible to repeat this experiment. I've just been too busy with all my other research to arrange it, because it would involve finding someone with a boat. But if one could persuade some wealthy person with a super yacht . . .' At this he trailed off, wistfully imagining the possibility of further experiments.

After we finished talking, we collected Eggy and Orange from Sheldrake's garden and went across the road to a clearing between a clump of trees on the patch of Heath opposite his house. The sky was bright and clear, with only a few wispy clouds far on the horizon. The sun was hot. I put the basket down on a raised hummock in the middle of the clearing, pointing it towards the east. We waited for them to settle. I wondered if they were tuning in to the morphic field that would pull them home.

After a few minutes I opened the flap and Eggy and Orange stalked cautiously out of the basket. They stood looking around for a few seconds, and then launched themselves up into the warm summer air. They flew over the trees, heading in an easterly direction, before veering off towards the south. Moments later they disappeared behind a tower block.

I wasn't sure the birds would be able to find their way home. I thought it might be too hot: the air was thick and heavy, and they might be too inexperienced to fly from this distance, the furthest from home they had ever been taken. I said I didn't know if they'd make it, but Sheldrake kept the faith.

'Well, they've headed in a generally easterly direction, haven't they?' he said hopefully. 'They'll be fine. They know where they're going.'

I cycled home with part of my mind on Eggy and Orange's flight, the other occupied with Sheldrake's theories. The question of whether or not he was correct did not seem particularly important: it was as a metaphor that I was most interested in the notion of morphic resonance, and as a metaphor it had great power. His is essentially a romantic vision – a poet's vision – and going to see him had felt like a kind of miniature pilgrimage. The attractiveness of his theory stems from the fact that it suggests we are all connected: part of a web of memory linked by the morphic field. I liked the idea that landscapes and beings together write the story of migration, and the story of home. As I cycled along, I thought of myself as swept along by my own morphic field, which connected me with Natalya and Dora and the home we were building together in Leyton. When I arrived back an hour or so later, I was high on exercise and morphic reverie. In the garden, standing on the roof of the loft, were Eggy and Orange, waiting to be let back inside.

## 4.07 p.m., Grimsby, 144 miles from home

The fastest pigeons are getting close to home now, and they surely know it. The wind has swung round to come from the east, and the volatile organic compounds it brings with it – a hint of pitch given off by the pine forests of the Urals? Carbon monoxide emitted by some distant chain of volcanoes? The oily tang of fish-boiling seas? – is more noticeable now. The wind brings with it news of home.

The pigeons adjust their line accordingly. For now most of them stay out to sea, the leading birds flying confidently across the sweeping bays of the coast, between Scarborough and over the chalk tower of Flamborough Lighthouse, standing straight and white against the blue sky.

But behind the leading birds the pack has fragmented. Many have given up in the heat of the day, and have flown down to land on the parched earth to wait until the evening cools the air. Some will roost up in passing towns, sleeping fitfully on rooftops until the next morning before continuing their journeys. Others have given up completely and will live out the rest of their lives among the feral birds of the coastal towns.

Of those still racing, still gripped by the urgency of home, thirty miles separate the leading birds from the rest of the bunch. Small kits – some numbering only a dozen or so birds – are strung out in the sky in a line along the coast.

The fastest pigeons pass over Grimsby just after 4.00 p.m. They are flying well, but the wind is picking up. When they were released at Thurso it had been negligible, but as they get to the middle of England it begins to blow more gustily. They adjust the angle of their flight accordingly: the route they take will form a bow to the west of the racing line, and those flyers living in the east of the country will benefit most from it. Still the birds hug the coast, cruising the turbulence created by the buffeting wind as it blows against the shore.

# 9

## Homeless

By mid-June the pigeons and I were settled in our routine. I would fly them twice daily around the loft: once in the morning, when Dora, Natalya and I would sit at the kitchen table and watch them as we ate our breakfast, and once in the evening, after I got back from work.

Dora had become more and more interested in the birds, which she accepted, as children do, as an unremarkable part of family life. She liked to watch them fly. She laughed at the way they would vanish behind a rooftop and then pop back into view on the other side, like a magic trick. She giggled with surprise when they landed on the roof of the loft after exercising. She had named the new pigeons – we now had a Milky, a Crispy and a Spoony in our flock – and she liked helping me feed and water them each morning before we set off to nursery. A few weeks previously Woodo had given me a young hen he'd bred for me late in the season, and Dora had claimed this bird as her own, forgoing her traditional naming system and christening her 'Aurora'.

Natalya was eight months pregnant and was about to leave her job. She was excited by the prospect of us spending more time together as a family, but she was apprehensive, too, about the loss of identity that might accompany it. She had always enjoyed the pressure of work and she didn't want, she said sometimes, when we discussed our future, motherhood to define her. She had a life of her own, independent of Dora and me, and, though she loved being a mother, she wanted to preserve that independence. We both fretted about the coming birth. It felt as though we'd only recently emerged from the daze of early parenthood. We had learned to react to Dora's moods and to anticipate her needs. We wondered what effect the presence of another child might have on what still felt at times like a delicate equilibrium.

The first race of the young bird season was less than a month away, and so for the next few weeks I took the pigeons out every day. I tried to pick release points that held some significance for what I had begun to think of, rather grandly, and never out loud, as my 'homing project'. When I could, I would take Dora with me on these journeys, sitting her in the seat attached to the handlebars of my bicycle while the pigeons cooed and skittered in their box in front of us. In the heat, Natalya stayed at home to welcome them back in. I was still under the sway of Sheldrake's theories, and had secretly begun to think of the pigeons' training flights as a means of connecting us with each other, tying the knots of our family together. Sometimes I tied messages to Natalya to their feet before Dora and I released them. I liked the fact that no one would know, if they looked up as my pigeons flew overhead, where they had come from or where they were going; the secret burdens they carried.

In early June Dora and I cycled to Wennington Green Park in Bow to release the birds for one final toss from the west before heading north, up the River Lea, to complete their race-line training. The site I had chosen was on the edge of a small park next to a busy main road, squeezed in between terraced houses and thrusting blocks of flats, near the canal which runs along the southern edge of Victoria Park.

The day was bright, with a pollutant haze shimmering on the horizon. (I found myself, more and more, noting the weather whenever I flew the birds: registering potentially disruptive fronts as they rolled towards the city, and planning my release times accordingly.) We cycled slowly across the marshes, passing dog walkers and joggers, then followed the spur of the canal as it cut westwards along the edge of Victoria Park. From the towpath we

watched bullet-headed carp flick themselves through the clear
water like snub-nosed submarines. Anglers fished for perch and
pike in the margins with a monkish devotion.

We arrived at the park when the heat of the day had subsided.
Thunderstorms were forecast later that evening, and the atmosphere was close, but for now the skies were clear.

The park – a scrubby, anonymous piece of ground three miles
in a straight line to the west of my loft – felt like a suitable place
from which to launch the pigeons on their final compass orientation flight before heading north. It was not just that we
wouldn't be bothered there (the only people we shared it with
that day were a pair of professional dog walkers, pulled along by
their charges while they gazed distractedly at their phones). It
was also a symbolically appropriate location: the place where
the artist Rachel Whiteread's sculpture *House* had once stood,
a work which questioned the nature of home better than any I
knew.

Whiteread has made the idea of home – its fragility, and its
unexpected smallness – central to much of her work. In 1990 she
made *Ghost*, a white plaster cast of the interior of the sitting room
of a condemned house in Archway. *Ghost* drew attention to the
stark borders of the spaces in which most of us dwell, confronting
viewers with an uncanny, solid inversion of airy domesticity:
Whiteread said the project involved 'mummifying the air in a
room'. Next she wanted to make a house-sized version of the
piece, but it proved difficult to find a building that was suitable
for casting. Whiteread wanted people to be able to walk around
the entire thing – it had to be monumental – and so she needed
to find an existing building with three exposed walls. It also
needed to be empty.

After much searching she found somewhere that would do:
193 Grove Road, the sole surviving house in a Victorian terrace
that had once run along the eastern edge of the park. The terrace
had been bombed during the war, and more recently the building had been condemned by Bow Council. But the man who

lived there, a retired dock worker named Sydney Gale, fought the plans ferociously. He spoke to the newspapers, denouncing artists and council alike, and made a banner that he hung from an upstairs window saying, 'THIS IS MY HOME, I LIVE HERE'. The battle between the homed and the unhomed – between the rampant fever dreams of speculators and local councils, and the desires of the people they were increasingly displacing – seemed perfectly emblematised by the fight over *House*, and its legacy.

Time was pressing. Margaret Thatcher wanted to create a 'green corridor' running north from the Isle of Dogs (then undergoing its own speculative regeneration) to Victoria Park, and the council was busy annexing patches of land along this line for the purpose. 'I had my studio nearby and used to cycle past,' Whiteread recalled a few years later. 'I was very conscious of the fact it was all about to change.'

After Gale had been evicted, work could begin. A team of technicians stripped the inside of the house, removing cupboards and sinks and staircases – that interior geography which makes a building into a home – and lined the shell with steel reinforcing bars. Next they sprayed the interior with Locrete, a special white concrete typically used to patch up the crumbling cliffs of Dover, before chipping off the bricks of the exterior of the building floor by floor. Eventually *House* emerged, a glittering obelisk squatting in the park.

Windows and doors appeared in negative, their clean, abstract lines breaking up the uniformity of the plinth-like block. You could still make out the shape of the staircase, zigzagging its way up an outside wall, as if each storey of the building could be zipped apart.

Whiteread's piece was really a kind of anti-home. In rapidly gentrifying Hackney it soon came to be read as a statement about the kinds of dwellings that were being lost as London re-imagined itself. In its ghostliness, *House* seemed to embody the end of one kind of London: grubby, ad hoc and unpolished. Yet quickly the sculpture was subverted by others. Someone

*Mummifying the air in a room.*

threw a splodge of red paint at it. Someone else daubed it with graffiti reading 'WOT FOR?' A few days later another hand wrote 'WHY NOT!' underneath, and drew a picture of a shrugging man. Soon the pigeons moved in, too, colonising the cracks between the floors which the casting process had left behind with their nests. The local council, never particularly keen on the work, gave the structure planning permission to stand for eighty days, but did not extend it. *House* existed from 25 October 1993 to 11 January 1994, when the diggers moved in to demolish it.

On the day Dora and I visited, there was not much left to see. The park has changed a lot in the last twenty-five years, as have the streets surrounding it. The trees lining the road, planted when the park was laid out, have grown tall. The site on which *House* stood is now overlooked by looming high-rises clad in sober brick. Few children played on the streets beneath them, and the area felt weirdly inert. But in one corner of the park, opposite a bright yellow church, we found a small trace of what had once been there: a brick question mark hidden in the grass, tracing the foundations of 193 Grove Road.

When we had located the spot, I placed the basket of birds on the ground and let them settle. Five minutes later I opened the flap to release them. At first, they didn't seem to realise they now had their freedom, and a few minutes passed before the first of them walked down the ramp onto the grass. It was Eggy. She looked around warily before taking off, the clattering of her wings alerting the others to the fact that they were free to fly away. One after another they followed her out and off into the air.

The kit climbed quickly, cruising around the park several times to find their bearings before heading off to the east. With a following wind they were soon out of sight. Natalya called me ten minutes later to say that all but two of the birds had arrived home safely. The missing pigeons both returned before night fell.

A few days after the flight from Bow, Natalya, Dora and I went to a 'country fair' on the marshes, round the corner from our house. The vibe was performative urban rural – people wore Barbour jackets paired with pristine trainers, or carefully muddied wellington boots – and the aim of the fair, according to the marketing bumf, was to provide 'a flavour of country life in the city'. A blacksmith hammered out coat racks and pokers on his mobile forge; beekeepers displayed the inside of a hive and celebrated the healing properties of locally produced honey. In a pen in the middle of the fair bored-looking sheep stood waiting to be fondled. We watched a falconer give a demonstration, cowering as she sent her hawks soaring high over the crowd before they returned to her gloved hand.

At one stall I got talking to a woman from the RSPB. She was a keen gardener and bird watcher, she said, and lived locally. She loved the variety of bird life on the marshes. A week before she'd watched a little bunting – a rare migratory bird that spends its winters in subtropical Asia – from a hide in the middle of the old filter beds to the west of our house. She showed us some video footage of a peregrine hen feeding her chicks, taken from inside a nest on a church spire in the City. There was a stuffed pigeon – illustrating the peregrine's main food source – on the stall, which I pointed out to Dora.

'I hate them,' the woman said. 'They come to my garden every day and eat the food I leave out for other birds. They scare them all away. I'd shoot them if I could.'

The intensity of her hatred was striking, but it was not surprising. I had got used to this kind of response by now. When I had first told people I was planning to house a flock of pigeons in my garden, most of them looked at me as though I had told them I was proposing to share my life with a family of rats, or cockroaches. Weren't they filthy birds? people asked. Didn't they carry diseases? Didn't they walk about on their gnarled and lumpy feet, staring at you with crazed yellow eyes? They were indiscriminate in their tastes, I was told, eating human vomit and cannibalising their fellow birds as they picked at the carcasses of fried chicken they scavenged from rubbish bins. Why didn't I get doves instead? They would be more photogenic, and surely more acceptable to my neighbours.

In answer I rhapsodised about the mystery of the pigeon's homing instinct and the metaphorical power of the birds. What I didn't tell them was that the pigeon's feral nature – its ability to make a home wherever it found itself – was for me part of its fascination. The truth was that over the past few months I had come to *like* their mess and their dirt. I admired the way they could thrive in the indifferent city. I was captivated by the itinerancy of pigeon life: its cocky, parasitic chanciness, its communalism, its unloved grit. Sometimes I envied it, too.

One of the reasons pigeons are so hated by city dwellers is that it is difficult to know quite where they belong. They are unclassifiable, culturally homeless, the animal equivalents of the anthropologist Mary Douglas's definition of dirt as 'matter out of

place'. The juxtaposition of wildness and civilisation emblematised by salmon returning to urban rivers, or hawks nesting on
city buildings, is something we find easy to celebrate. But pigeons
don't fit into the stable categories of 'wild' and 'tame'. They fly
between two worlds – the natural and the man-made – thriving
in both but welcome in neither. Environmentalists dislike pigeons
for the way they muscle out other species; city dwellers despise
them for the way they represent a grubby intrusion into the order
of urban life. Pigeons are said to be filthy, infectious, vectors of
dirt and disease. But really, I had begun to think, we do not hate
those rats with wings because they are unattractive. We hate them
because they remind us too much of ourselves.

The word 'ecology' was coined by the German zoologist Ernst
Haeckel in 1873, from the Greek *oikos*, meaning 'house' or 'dwelling place', and the suffix *ology*, meaning 'study'. During the nineteenth century, as the world became ever smaller, so the planet
increasingly came to be viewed not as a land of limitless wildness,
its natural potential waiting to be exploited, but as a small and
fragile home for which we had a responsibility to care. But the
rise of the ecological movement had a darker side, too. In
differentiating between the natural and the unnatural it created
distinctions which often threatened to exclude. From Romanticism
onwards, rootedness, identity and the natural world have been
placed in opposition to the man-made, the rootless and the cosmo-
politan, a divide often promoted by writers and artists who argue
that urbanisation and the alienating effects of capitalism are making
us lose our ability to *belong*: to feel at home in the world.

Over the course of his career, the phenomenologist Martin
Heidegger, a man who would prove to be darkly obsessed with
the idea of the home, diagnosed a general sense of homelessness
which, he held, characterised the experience of modernity.
Heidegger was born in the Black Forest in south-west Germany
in 1889. He studied theology at Freiburg University, and considered training as a priest before defecting to philosophy. He would

often retire to his mountain hut in the Black Forest to consider the state of our spiritual homelessness. Was mankind part of the world, Heidegger asked – of a piece with its stones and trees and animals – or were we doomed forever to live apart from it?

In a lecture which came to be titled 'Building Dwelling Thinking', written during the housing crisis in the wake of the Second World War, Heidegger argued that sometime during the early twentieth century people had forgotten how to feel at home in the world. His argument was familiar to a post-war generation, but its urgency was new. Mobilisation, globalisation and the entrenchment of global forces had, he thought, severed the connections between people and the places they inhabited. A mobile, migratory world didn't just mean individuals could be physically displaced from their homes: it also meant they could be unhomed psychically. It is for this reason, Heidegger later wrote in *Pathmarks*, that 'Homelessness is coming to be the destiny of the world.'

Heidegger's essay on dwelling was not so much about architecture as it was about meanings: about how the way we speak about the world provides one of the structures in which we dwell. Bridges don't just connect two banks that already exist, he said: they bring those banks into existence. A house isn't just a material structure: it generates the possibility of dwelling, the possibility of feeling at home in the first place. In this sense homes are a bit like language, Heidegger thought. We think we are using them, but really they are using us.

There was a darker undercurrent to Heidegger's diagnosis of mankind's homelessness. With his interest in the link between land and belonging, blood and soil, he was an attractive thinker for fascist political ideologies which saw the home as the only true source of individual identity, and used the concept to exclude and dehumanise outsiders. Heidegger joined the Nazi Party in 1933 and did not leave until after the end of the war. During the late 1940s he was banned from teaching due to his support for the Nazis, but in 1951 he resumed lecturing and writing. The Party were inspired by his work, as well as by ecologists such as Friedrich

Ratzel, to conceive their policy of *lebensraum* – 'living space' –
which they used to justify their expansionist ambitions, and their
belief in the importance of racial purity. In Heidegger's hands,
home became an ideological weapon: a means of separating the
clean from the unclean, the homed from the homeless. It was not
such a step for a man who believed that animals were 'poor in
world' to believe that certain people could be less rich in world
than others.

Now that my loft was well established, the feral pigeons that
flew around the garden had registered its presence. Often they'd
come and look at what was going on inside. These street-savvy
birds flew with a sly grace, an efficient swagger. They seemed
far more manoeuvrable, as they swept down between the
branches of the trees, or when diving to snatch some dropped
grain, than my own pigeons were. Some had even mastered the
habit of dropping into the trap of my loft to feed on spilled seed
before jumping out again, a trick mine never learned.

As I acquired more pigeons, they began to take over the
garden. Alby bred me a few dark chequers from his champion
stock, and Johnny gave me a pair of pied Hartogs he didn't have
room for. I built an extension to the loft, adding another row of
nest boxes to house my growing flock. I came to relish their
sheer multitude as they flickered in flight above my house, or
broke from the basket on training tosses. I liked the way they
resolved into a streamlined flock when they took to the wing,
and how, in the loft, they would fragment back into a squab-
bling community, each hen claiming her own perch, each cock
his own nest box.

When they flew around the house you could see them from
the end of the road, looping hard and fast above the trees. When
they landed on the roof, ominously lined up in a row like a scene
from Hitchcock's *The Birds*, I wondered what my neighbours
thought of them. On the whole they had left me to it, seeming
to view the intrusion of a flock of pigeons into their lives as just

one more way in which the feral lived close to us in Leyton. My pigeons were of a piece with the foxes that howled in the gardens at night, the sparrows which had taken up residence in the gutters, the moths that swarmed up through the cracks between the floorboards of our houses as summer arrived.

Tony Coles, founder and owner-operator of Coles Pest Busters, knows more than most about the pigeon's ability to thrive in cities. Part urban theorist, part geographer, part biologist, Tony has been targeting London's pigeons for over twenty years, and in that time he has grown to appreciate their tenacity. He fell into pest control by mistake. He had been working as a labourer, he said when I met him one morning in June, and a foreman asked him to deal with a nest of rats.

'I borrowed a friend's air rifle and sat there night after night,' he told me, 'shooting rats. I got them all. Then someone asked me to come and do his grey squirrels. I got some traps and got rid of them. Then I bought a van, and that was that.'

Tony had agreed to let me join him for what he called a 'ride along' – as though he were a policeman or undercover agent. He was waiting for me outside Canning Town station, his red ex-Royal Mail van adorned with a magnetic sign which said 'COLES PEST BUSTERS: YOUR PESTS, BUSTED!'

They say pet owners come to resemble their pets, but Tony seemed, over the years, to have grown to look like his quarry. His hair was ratty brown, his eyes deep black and rodent-like. A sliver of moustache quivered on his top lip as he spoke. He was wearing army fatigues and military-looking boots, and a fleece which bore the image of a rat caught in the cross-hairs of a rifle scope, putting up its hands in surrender.

We were going to survey a small commercial building in Bow, just next to the A11 flyover, which had a persistent pigeon problem. Tony said it was a typical job for him.

'You get a lot of these,' he said. 'It's either this or home calls: some old woman rattling around a massive house, who can't handle the pigeons nesting in her gutters. Or it's foxes. They've got huge over the past ten years or so for us. I do the golf clubs quite a lot, stalking them at night. It's hard to trap foxes – I usually just shoot them from an upstairs window. But you've got to be careful not to scare the neighbours.'

Tony marvelled at London's wildlife. He didn't hate the animals he destroyed, but he knew that their deaths provided him with a living. Of all the pests he is paid to eradicate, he had most respect for the pigeons. Rats were just vermin, he said, 'really unpleasant'. He became serious when he spoke about rats.

'I've known them to grow as long as your arm. They'll gnaw through anything. They'll eat through cables and electrocute themselves to death. Then one of their mates will come along and try to eat the body. Then he's electrocuted and all.'

Once, Tony said, he'd been called to a job on the London Underground and had found the bodies of four electrocuted rats laid out all in a row, the jaws of each clamped around the animal in front like a daisy-chain. I didn't know if I believed him.

He didn't like working with rats (that's what he called it: 'working with', as though the arrangement was collaborative), but there was something pure about Tony's battles with pigeons. He had respect for his quarry.

'I wouldn't say I like them, but I do admire them. You've got to. They can make their nests in all sorts of places. You put up spikes and they go and collect leaves to block them up. You put up nets and they'll find a way through. And they're clever: after a while they recognise you coming and fly off.'

We stopped at some traffic lights, and just when I thought Tony's reverie was in danger of humanising his quarry, he broke the silence that had fallen.

'But they're fucking disgusting, too. They shit everywhere and their shit makes you ill.'

Tony liked best what he called the 'wrap jobs': the kind we were going along to today. Most landlords, when confronted with a pigeon problem, address it piecemeal.

'First they get those fake plastic owls,' said Tony. 'Useless. Won't scare a thing.'

Later they might hire a falconer to fly a bird of prey around a bit, but that's no good either.

'The hawk might chase the pigeons away for an hour, but they'll soon be back. The falconers just like posing – they think they're in fucking *Kes*.'

After a while most people realise that they have to get serious if they want pigeons to stay away permanently. Tony used to use poison.

'It's a horrible way to go. Besides, it doesn't really work.'

Shooting doesn't really work either: other birds will quickly come to replace the ones you've killed. No, said Tony, the only sure way to get rid of pigeons once they've established their colony on a building is to make it impossible for them to nest there: to make them homeless.

The building Tony had been asked to inspect was a squat low-rise 1970s office block on the edge of a car park. As we pulled up outside, he was already commenting on the setting and likely problems he would face.

'It's the perfect height for nesting,' he said, explaining that pigeons do not like to make their nests higher than the fourth or fifth floor of a building, so that they can keep an eye on their sources of food on the streets below. Usually pigeons favour older buildings for their nest sites – a census of the pigeon population of Milan conducted in the 1990s found that they thrived in areas with a high proportion of pre-war buildings, the baroque lintels and ledges of which are more amenable nesting sites than the smooth glass obelisks which dominate the city centre – but they also often find refuge in nondescript neo-modernist blocks like this one.

We got out of the car and Tony began his survey, making notes on a clipboard as the building manager explained where the birds were nesting, the havoc they were playing with the ventilation. Tony took some photographs.

'Yeah, we can sort that for you,' he said. 'We'll spike up those ledges and put netting in across the wider gaps.'

'Will you shoot them?' asked the manager. 'Please would you shoot them?'

Tony said it might not be the best option. 'But don't worry, I'll get rid of them for you.'

It was a straightforward job, and we were only there for fifteen minutes or so before he decided it was time to go. He took a few final photographs on his phone before we got in the van and drove away.

This was why he liked the job, Tony said as he drove me back to the station. It was intellectual – you had to think things through – and yet it was also practical. There is an art to installing anti-pigeon measures: plastic and metal spikes are glued onto every available ledge; netting has to be strung up tightly between projecting walls. If it's not tight enough the pigeons will simply nest on top of it.

'You have to ask yourself questions,' he said. 'Think like a pigeon. What'll happen if I move the birds on from here? Will they go and nest somewhere else?'

There was a creative satisfaction to be had, too. When Tony is given free rein with a building, it ends up looking like a Christo wrap. The key is to make the place inhospitable enough so that other nearby buildings become more attractive.

'And then *their* owners call you,' he said. 'Honestly, I sometimes feel I'm just chasing the same birds around the city every day.'

He dropped me back at the station, where, before I said goodbye, we watched some feral pigeons fuss in the gutter, fighting over a discarded crust of pizza.

At the end of June it was time to take the birds upriver, along the line they would take when flying into London from the north. I had the idea that I would use these final training flights to connect the dots, drawing a line down the Lea Valley towards my house.

I would follow the Lea by bicycle as it wound out of the city, as far north as I could, towards Waltham Abbey and Broxbourne and Ware, and then take the pigeons further by train, if I was allowed on with a basket of birds (the law on which seemed slightly unclear).

This was the line, I thought, that they would most likely use when they flew back into London from the north. It was open land with clear landmarks for the birds to use for pilotage: the silvery thread of the river and the electricity pylons plotted a course which would be visible for miles around. Whatever the prevailing winds, the Lea Valley would become for them a famil- iar corridor, and the better they knew it the more confidently they might fly the crucial final miles of their journey, where most races are won or lost.

One golden summer afternoon, when the dying sun licked the brickwork of the houses, I set out with Dora to cycle upriver. My sister Liz, who I'd captured cycling down the High Road on my pigeon cam a few months before, came with us, along with her two children. The air was thick with dust blown up in the Sahara, which had drifted over northern Europe, crossing the Channel and giving the horizon a tinge of apocalyptic red.

We cycled along the towpath in convoy, our children chatter- ing with each other as we went, the pigeons cooing on the front of my bike. Outside a pub a man noticed the birds.

'Training them, are you?' he asked. 'I used to race in the Debden club on the North Road. Had to pack it in, though, when I got pigeon lung.'

We cycled on. New flats were going up everywhere round here, hulking glass reefs that loomed over the water. We passed lines of narrowboats moored against the bank. There were smart widebeam barges with satellite dishes and herb gardens on their roofs, but also run-down narrowboats that looked as though they were about to sink, and ersatz creations in timber and plastic with improbable roof-extensions made from salvaged garden sheds. The smell of their coal fires – tangy and sulphurous – drifted over the water. For those who couldn't get a foothold in the London housing market the boats were an attractive proposition, and their itinerancy was part of their charm. But I wondered how long they'd survive on the water, because the authorities were clamping down on unlicensed boats. There was talk of impoundings and evictions.

We went through locks where men had gathered to drink and smoke in the sunshine, and who waved to us jauntily as we passed. Gradually the Lee Navigation, the once-natural branch of the river that had been canalised in the eighteenth century to allow goods to be more easily transported out of London, became grubbier, the water littered with traffic cones, shopping trolleys and discarded stolen mopeds.

Once we got past the North Circular, I began to notice the encampments in the undergrowth. People were living in the scrubland next to the reservoirs, in temporary huts made from tarpaulins spread between the trees. The boats and the tents were both symptoms of London's housing crisis, which everyone talks about but no one knows how to fix. Desperate people had been squeezed out by the dizzying climb of house prices, and the expense of renting, and the results of this were visible everywhere around here.

On the towpath we passed pylons on which graffiti was daubed – 'Flat Earth'; 'Fuck Boris'; 'Give us Homes!'. The area stank of rubbish, the smell drifting over from the processing plant to the west. There were horses in the fields under the pylons, tended by Travellers. Halfway towards the M25 we passed a sunken river cruiser, its cushions and furnishings bobbing about in its soaked interior. A pair of moorhens had set up home on its backboard, and their chicks were just beginning to leave the nest and explore.

After an hour and a half cycling, we arrived at Ramney Marsh, a meadow floodplain next to the canal, near Waltham Abbey, on the edge of London. It looked like a good launch site: far enough away from the pylons that had lined the valley all along our route to keep the birds from hitting them when they were first released, but still within sight of home. We were ten miles or so distant, with a clear run for the birds all the way back.

We parked our bikes and let the pigeons settle before opening the baskets. When we pulled down the flaps they took off perfectly, slapping their wings in unison. As they climbed, the individual birds soon formed up into a kit which nosed its way around in the edges of the sky, and within moments they were out of sight.

On the ride home, I realised that the wind was more blustery than it had been on the way out, when it was at our backs, and that the pigeons would now be flying headlong into it. The clouds had gathered, too, and turned darker. When we arrived back two hours later only four of the pigeons had returned – Milky, a pair of anonymous blues which had not yet been named, and Eggy. The rest of the flock – Crispy, Orange, Spoony, Aurora and the others – were still missing. As dusk began to fall a few more birds came in. By nightfall only eight had returned.

That night the thunderstorm broke and the rain lashed down. The sky was lit with threads of lightning, and you could feel the thunder crack in your skull. I slept badly, waking with worry, until the storm cleared.

The next morning I rose early and went down to the garden to see if any more birds had returned. I sat with a coffee watching the crows chase the magpies on the roofs of the houses opposite. The wind had stilled and the sky was clear, but there was no sign of the missing pigeons. I waited all morning, rattling my tin, calling forlornly for more to come in, but at midday I had to catch a train to Manchester, and so I left Natalya and Dora and asked them to call me if any more turned up. Natalya texted throughout the day as a few stragglers came in, but two days after the disastrous toss, four of my birds were still missing.

Three days later one final bird came back. It was Aurora. She had been out for days, and was in a sorry state. The wattle above her beak was oily, damp and yellowed, when it should be chalky white and dry. She was mad with hunger, and ignored me as I picked her up and placed her in a nest box to feed on her own. She felt as light as a piece of paper. She ate her bodyweight in seed, drank deeply, and fell asleep.

I wondered where she'd been in the days since I'd lost her. Did she simply circle the territory, trying to remember the way? Did she think of giving up? I told Ian about her return.

'She's got heart, that bird,' he said. 'She'll have learned a lot, too. Might make a champion.'

## 5.40 p.m., the Wash, 100 miles from home

The memory of this land is buried deep. All of the birds have raced from here as young birds; many have made the journey dozens of times. As they cross into the familiar zone the pigeons switch navigation systems, moving from the abstractions of their olfactory gradient map to the comforting certainty of visual cues.

But the wind is picking up now, sending them east of where they want to go, and the clouds are closing in. A storm is forming out to sea, and the birds can sense it. Before the race many of the flyers were concerned about losing birds over the Wash, and it's true that when, in the coming days, pigeons that have gone missing during the race are reported, many will be found around here, huddling in gardens or trying to make their way into garden sheds which they have mistaken for lofts.

North of the Wash, just by Skegness, the leading bunch splits in two. Half the birds – not necessarily the quickest, but those most familiar with the route – head inland. They can see almost as far as Peterborough, from where many of them first flew as yearlings eighteen months before. The other half – less experienced, or unwilling to leave the protection of the sea – fly across the bay to the Norfolk coast to join the land again on the other side, following its bulge around to the east, and then doglegging back down south. These birds will carry on flying over the sea until they realise they've gone too far south, and will head inland at Clacton. When Woodo was a boy, he once told me, he used to go on day trips to Clacton to watch the pigeons fly by: thousands of them, skimming along just above the waves. But today only a few dozen birds are taking that route, and within a few minutes they have all passed on to the south.

# Waiting

It was late June, and the first race of the young bird season – from Peterborough, 70 miles, as the pigeon flies, from my loft – was only a few weeks away. The birds would need to be homing well from 50 miles before they'd be ready. Natalya's due date was approaching, too, and she was becoming slightly fed up, both with her pregnancy, which was becoming uncomfortable in the hot, muggy summer, and with my obsession with the pigeons.

In the lead-up to the first race, thoughts of the pigeons consumed me. It was as though I'd displaced my anxieties over the coming birth with worry for the birds. I found I couldn't concentrate on my work. When I wasn't training them, I spent much of my time in the garden watching them fly. The men in the club talked about pigeons 'coming into form' in the lead-up to the season, and I had learned that half the skill of flying a successful team lay in being able to read their fitness in the brightness of their eyes, and in the wattle around their beaks, which would change colour from white to pink as they hit their peak.

After the disastrous toss from Ramney Marsh I'd given them time to recover, but a week later, at the beginning of July, I cycled back up the Lea on my own to fly them again. I'd kept them close in the intervening days, giving them only a few short tosses from which they'd all homed easily. Today I would take them further than they had ever flown from before. The sky was overcast, and spots of rain fell as I rode the now-familiar route: down Lea Bridge Road before turning north, up through Walthamstow Marshes and along the banks of the river.

The towpath was empty as I cycled out of the city, kicking up mud and pinging tiny pieces of gravel into the water with the tyres of my bicycle as I went. The boaters were still asleep, and the cycle commuters who lived further upriver had not yet begun to head in to the city. I passed a boat named *Wet Dream* which had a heron perching on its roof. It was still there when I cycled back a couple of hours later, standing so still I took it to be made of plastic until it unfurled its cumbersome wings and flapped away.

I cycled on past Ramney Marsh until the factories and rubbish-processing plants gave way to a landscape of manicured parks and fishing lakes and golf courses. After two hours' cycling I arrived in Broxbourne, a commuter town on the edge of London, twelve miles north of my loft. I found a steep artificial hill next to a sewage treatment plant and pushed my bike to the top of it. It provided a good vantage point: from the top I could see the edge of the blue Chiltern Hills in the west, the sparkling towers of Canary Wharf to the south. I placed the pigeons in their basket on the grass and waited for them to settle. While I waited a huge flock flew overhead: one hundred or so pigeons flying in tight formation towards the south. They were, I guessed, those of another fancier on a training flight from further up the valley.

The wind was calmer than it had been the week before. I could hear the distant rumble of a train and the low, throbbing hum of a nearby motorway. After letting them settle I opened the flap of the basket and lifted out a pigeon. I had decided this time to give the birds a 'single-up' toss, releasing them individually rather than letting them all fly home together. On race day they would most likely be flying in a bunch with unfamiliar birds, and, though they would all be heading in the same general direction, when they got near home they would have to break from the others to fly the final miles on their own. A single-up toss would prepare them for this most crucial stage of the race.

I opened my hand and threw the pigeon into the air. Its wings stretched, flapping laboriously as it climbed into the sky. It circled the field a few times to gain height, but when it spotted the pylons in the distance it flew higher, over the trees on a bearing for home. Once it had cleared the area I reached into the basket, picked up another bird, and released it. This one didn't hesitate, flying straight over the motorway to the south and on to follow the pylons running next to the river.

It was just after I had released the fifth bird that I spotted her. She emerged from behind the trees to the north, soaring high over the field: a sparrowhawk, searching for an easy kill. She moved swiftly towards the pigeon I had just released, which was still circling the edge of the field, following the treeline for cover. From beneath, the hawk's white mottled underbelly blent into the clouds, making her difficult to spot. She watched from a hundred feet or so above, waiting for her moment. When the pigeon turned at the eastern edge of the field, she took her opportunity and dropped from the sky in a fast, hard dive.

She seemed to fall more quickly than she should have, as though pulled by a force stronger than gravity. When she got to within twenty feet of it, the pigeon noticed her and broke in panic, flying madly off between the branches of the trees. The hawk pulled out of her stoop and turned to follow. Her pivot looked mechanical: preordained. Quickly she closed in on the pigeon. When she was within snatching distance she reached out her claws and clutched at the air. But she missed, and after the half-hearted dogfight seemed to lose interest, soaring off over the trees in search of easier prey.

I waited a long time to make sure she'd gone before releasing the rest of the birds, and over an hour had passed before I had liberated them all, one after another. Once I'd lost sight of the final pigeon over the horizon, I got back on my bike and started for home. Before I got there Natalya phoned to tell me the birds had begun to arrive back at the loft. By the time I arrived all of them had returned, but Lone Ranger had a huge open wound across his chest. I wondered if the hawk might have caught up with him, or if he might have hit the wires strung between the electricity pylons in his panic. I fed and watered him, isolating him in a nest box to allow him to recover, and within a few days he was flying well around the loft once again.

The pigeons' training continued over the next few weeks. Every other day I'd take them out on the road, each time slightly further away from home. If they beat me back I'd increase the distance the next time I took them out. When I'd gone beyond the range of my bicycle I took them on the train, anxiously clasping my basket and hoping that people wouldn't notice the cooing and shuffling coming from within. I press-ganged people I knew who could drive into taking them further afield. A friend made regular trips to Cambridge, and so one day I cycled to his house with a basket of birds, which he released from a field on the edge of the city. He had been warned by a porter not to liberate them from his college gardens because a pair of peregrine falcons had been seen nesting on the spire of the chapel.

The art of pigeon racing, I was coming to learn, is the art of watching, and of waiting. When you first get your birds, you must wait as they settle into their loft. As they range, you must wait for them to become familiar with their home territory before taking them out on the road. When training begins, you must wait for the right weather before tossing them, and once they've had a few basket tosses, you must wait until they are ready before you take them further away.

'You can ruin a young bird racing it too hard,' Big Johnny had warned me at the club one night. 'You want to take it easy with them so you've got enough left for your old bird team for next year.'

Natalya and I were waiting for our child to be born, too, and as we waited we made our final preparations for the coming birth. At the end of June, Irene the midwife had visited the house one last time to check that we had all we needed. She explained that we should call her if Natalya felt labour begin, or if her waters broke, but that we mustn't be alarmed if it took her a while to arrive.

'I have lots of mothers, they're all about to pop!' she said. 'And all just before I have to go on holiday.'

She checked we were ready. Did we have a supply of clean towels? Nappies and clothes for the baby? We performed our domesticity for her, pointing out the safety gates we had installed at the foot of the stairs, the plug guards we'd fitted in all the sockets.

When I had told friends, especially a few who were doctors, that we were planning to have our second child at home, many had pointed out what they perceived to be the dangers involved. Some pursed their lips, silently implying that we were taking a great risk. Others were more forthright, speaking openly about the complications they had experienced on the wards, the unforeseen disasters, the increased risks of intervention with a home birth. Giving birth was a medical procedure, they said, implying that only the foolhardy would choose to have a baby outside a hospital.

We wanted to have our second child at home in part because of our memories of Dora's birth, and the months of anxiety which had followed it. In the days after she was born, Dora wouldn't feed, and her weight fell dramatically. When the midwife had visited us and looked down gravely at her, struggling to stay awake as she drank pathetically, and told us we needed, as a matter of urgency, to take her in to A&E, it felt as though something – our homecoming – had been denied to us.

Back on the ward, Dora was placed in a rectangular plastic crib and a tube was inserted down her throat through which a nurse fed her every hour with a huge syringe. A brusque consultant who had written a book extolling the benefits of breastfeeding, which had been pressed into our hands by friends in the weeks before Dora's birth, popped by each day and told Natalya with a sunny voice that she just needed to keep trying. I sat in the armchair beside her bed watching her weep while she tried to feed her child and wondered where our idyll was. Never have I felt so lonely, so sick for a home which didn't then seem to exist.

The three of us sat in that room together for four days. When eventually we were allowed to leave, my parents came to pick us up. It was raining, and Natalya carried Dora – fragile, and sleepy, and still impossibly tiny – in a sling under her coat. The raindrops splashed on her face as we walked through the hospital car park.

In the weeks afterwards the three of us tried to nest, to discover what family life felt like, but still we struggled to settle. Dora was weak, and she rarely seemed at ease. She wouldn't feed from the breast, and it was difficult to make her take a bottle, too. She wouldn't wake herself from hunger during the night and so we had to set alarm clocks, rising mechanically every two hours to feed her. When we woke her up, she would cry her pitiful, thin cry, as though dazed by the life she had been born into.

Like all new parents, we worried about everything in those early days, and Dora became the unwitting go-between in our cross-purposed conversations, a token of our anxiety. In our desperation to get her to eat, a kind of madness descended on us which, looking back, had as much to do with our own exhaustion as anything else. We took her to consultants and quacks. A cranial osteopath recommended by our midwife said she could feel that Dora's bones were improperly aligned due to the trauma of her birth. She wafted her hands vaguely over Dora's body and gently manipulated her skull, saying she'd need to come back for another treatment a week later if we wanted to see any improvement. We did not go back. In the evenings we called breastfeeding advice lines but were never able to get through.

A week after we'd returned home, we called a lactation consultant named Jo who, friends said, could do wonderful things with latches and raised palates. I liked Jo. She had lived in a radical women's commune during the 1980s and now spent her time travelling around London helping desperate parents learn to breastfeed their children. She looked inside Dora's mouth and said she might be tongue-tied, and showed us some techniques that would, she said, allow her to feed more easily.

Natalya was exhausted by the effort and the worry. After the broken nights she would sleep in the mornings, when the rising dawn brought a sense of new hope. I'd take Dora out in the pram, walking with her to the park, or to the river. Once I remember trying to call someone – anyone – to tell them how lonely I felt. When no one answered I sat by a tree and cried.

After the birth of her first and only child, the American writer and political campaigner Charlotte Perkins Gilman began to suffer from what we would call, nowadays, a severe bout of post-natal depression. She connected her feelings of psychological distress with the idea of home, which she had come to view as a kind of prison. In her autobiography Gilman described how after giving birth she would weep in pain and frustration while trying to breastfeed her baby. 'Instead of love and happiness,' she wrote, '[I would] feel only pain. The tears ran down on my breast [. . .] Nothing was more utterly bitter than this, that even motherhood brought no joy.'

Diagnosed with hysteria – a condition once believed to be caused by the wanderings of the womb, and which covered a bewildering array of symptoms – Gilman was ordered to undergo the psychologist Silas Weir Mitchell's 'rest cure', which involved enforced bed rest and a special diet of fatty foods. Mitchell believed that hysterics should be shielded from all forms of stimulation, and in its insistence on sedentariness and isolation, his cure recreated all the worst aspects of the Victorian home. Rather than listening to his patients' stories – talking to them to try to ascertain what it was that they were thinking and feeling, as Freud was later to do – he treated their bodies, which he thought of as mere empty vessels in which their fragile minds dwelt, and could on occasion be lost within.

For Gilman, the rest cure was a disaster. She objected to being placed under house arrest, and she objected to the fact that in her isolation she wasn't allowed to write. A few years later she fiction-alised the experience of this isolation in her gothic horror story *The Yellow Wallpaper.*

In Gilman's story a physician imprisons his wife in a house in the countryside in order to allow her to recover from the birth of her first child. She is locked away in a room of her own at the top of the house, with barred windows and a bed screwed to the floor. There she becomes obsessed with the lurid yellow wallpa-per that surrounds her bed, and begins to see a figure moving within it. Gradually she goes mad, and longs to release the figure from the wallpaper. The ambiguous conclusion of the story, in which the narrator creeps around the walls of her room, stepping carefully over the collapsed body of her husband as she goes, is an unsettling portrayal of the way in which homes can become pris-ons, especially for women. *The Yellow Wallpaper* is a story about the physical isolation of home, and the way in which mothers in particular can be driven mad by society's homely expectations. Years later Gilman said that she had written the story as a sort of domestic feminist parable: a way to 'reach Dr S. Weir Mitchell and convince him of the error of his ways'. She hoped that in telling her story she would allow other women to avoid the devastating isolation she had experienced when she became a mother.

For Gilman, homes and madness were inextricably linked. Late in life she wrote an essay in which she argued that, as an idea and an institution, home had not kept pace with modernity. Homes, Gilman said, often forced women to become slaves to their husbands and their families. 'In all this long period of progress,' she argued, 'the moving world has carried with it the unmoving home; the man free, the woman still limited to her domestic functions. We have constantly believed that this was the true way to live, the natural way, the only way.' Anticipating the arguments of second wave feminists such as Selma James and Silvia Federici, who in the 1970s argued that women should be paid for the housework they, invariably, did, Gilman argued for a complete reappraisal of domestic life and of what it meant to dwell together. 'The home is a beautiful ideal,' she concluded, 'but have we no others?'

What I found so perceptive about Gilman's writing was her clear-eyed certainty about the doubled nature of parenthood. Gilman realised that becoming a parent could be traumatic as well as glorious; life-changing in more ways than one. Having children gives a great deal, but it also takes things from you, things that it often takes a while to realise you have lost. I worried about the implications of her argument, too. Was I, free as I was to indulge in my obsessions, to go out training my birds while Natalya stayed at home and waited for them to return, just another agent of the social structures Gilman had sought, over one hundred years ago, to do away with? One thing that gave me hope was that there was time to change. Gilman thought that the home was a human institution and that, as such, it could always be made and re-made by human hands, and one of her most radical acts was to show that we are not obliged to play the parts assigned to us.

During their road training I had lost six more pigeons. This, Osman warned in *Racing Pigeons*, was to be expected, especially for the novice fancier. Some of them had simply taken off from the roof of the loft, flown away and never come back. Others had been blown off course by high winds on their return from training tosses, or had been swept up by another team of racing birds and followed them into the wrong loft. Often these missing birds would return a few days later of their own accord, looking ruffled and slightly thin but otherwise no worse for the experience, but sometimes they were reported far from home, and I would have to go and collect them myself.

Once a woman in Twickenham phoned to tell me she'd found one of my pigeons in her garden: it was exhausted, she said, and had tried to get into her shed, having mistaken it for a loft. I went to collect it and carried it home on the Underground in a cardboard box. A fancier in Romford reported that Orange, who had gone missing during a training flight from Bishop's Stortford, had followed his young birds inside after he'd let them out for a loft fly. He worked nights in Canning Town, he said, and would be happy to take Orange there and release him from the station platform for me. He phoned the following evening to tell me that Orange had cleared the area well, and he arrived back at my loft a few minutes later.

One blustery day a mechanic who had his workshop in a railway arch behind my house called to tell me that two of my pigeons had crashed into his van in the strong winds. He said he had dropped them both off at a veterinary surgery around the corner, but that one of them did not look at all well, with a broken wing and a smashed eye. In the reception of the vets an LED candle was flickering next to a note which read, 'When the candle is burning someone is saying goodbye to their pet. Please be respectful.' I took both birds home, but the one with the broken wing died of his injuries in the night.

The pigeons that were left in my flock were flying well. I'd come to know their habits and behaviours: which of them would fly directly home from a toss and which would dawdle on the roof once they arrived, which perches and nest boxes they favoured in the loft, their particular tastes in seed. My fastest birds were Milky, Aurora and Lone Ranger. Eggy and Orange were reliable homers but bad trappers. Sometimes, when I let the flock out for their morning flight, Eggy and Orange would fly off and I wouldn't see them again until nightfall. I wondered if they had other, secret lives elsewhere.

By mid-July all of the birds had flown from Cambridge half a dozen times, and they were exercising around the loft for an hour twice a day. They looked fit: when at rest their eyes gleamed, and their wattles were chalky white. In the hand they felt muscular but also light, as though filled with air. They were, I thought, ready.

One Friday evening in the middle of July, two days after our child had been due to be born, I cycled to the club to mark the birds for their first race. I'd spent the previous days trying to decide which pigeons to enter. Eggy and Orange had the most experience in the basket, but they were also my worst trappers, and sprint races like Peterborough can be won or lost in the time it takes a reticent pigeon to fly down from the roof and into the loft. The others had all had fewer training tosses, and had spent less time on the wing around the loft.

In the end I decided to enter four pigeons: Eggy, Orange, Milky and Lone Ranger. If I lost them all, I'd have only twelve birds left for the rest of the season, but I'd trained them well, Ian assured me, the race was short, and the weather for the weekend was forecast to be fine.

The car park was busy when I arrived at the club. Baskets of birds were stacked up in rows, and from inside came a frantic cooing and shuffling. There didn't appear to be any order in the arrangement of the baskets, but the flyers were good at keeping track of whose birds were next in line to be marked.

They were keen for the young bird racing to begin because the old bird season had been a washout. Bad weather had caused several races to be cancelled, and even when the weather was fine returns were lower than usual.

One by one the flyers came up to the marking table holding their baskets and passed their race sheets, on which they'd noted the details of their entries – ring number, sex and description – to Johnny. Woodo was racing both cocks and hens, and as they waited to be marked they danced and called to each other from their baskets. One by one, he took the birds out and passed them over. The flyers knew their birds intimately, and the marking gave them an opportunity to celebrate their achievements. As he handed them over – wings pinned to their sides, heads held close to his chest – Woodo recounted the lineages of his pigeons. He pointed out old injuries and healed scars and told the stories behind them. He passed me a bird which had feathers sticking out at odd angles from its head. He said it had almost been killed when a jealous cock had scalped it as a baby, but had pulled through and now raced well.

I carried Brian's bird over to Johnny. Next to him sat Chris, who was pulling the rings, and next to him was a wooden board with a bent nail hammered into it. Chris placed a small elastic band with a unique number printed on it over the nail and stretched it open. I read out the pigeon's ring number, and Johnny checked it off on the list.

'GB17-65436,' I called out.

'65436?' said Johnny as he found the bird on the list. 'That's a dark chequered cock.' I pushed one of the bird's feet through the open rubber band and took him over to Bob.

'Cock?' asked Bob, who was standing beside the baskets holding a lump of chalk. 'Put him in there.' He held a flap open as I dropped the bird inside, before chalking a tally on the side.

After Brian had marked his birds it was Chris's turn, and after that my name was called. It didn't take long to retrieve my four pigeons from their basket and pass them over. Big Johnny spotted Lone Ranger instantly.

'That's a cockerel,' he said. 'I'd know that bird anywhere: he's the spitting image of his father.'

Seventeen flyers had entered 270 birds into the race, and after they had all been marked the pigeons were loaded onto a trailer to be driven to the pick-up point, where they would join birds from other clubs in the lorry. After seeing them off and sweeping the floor we went inside to strike the clocks. Inside the club Steve was filling in the paperwork. There had been a wake at the club earlier in the day, and we picked at the leftover sausage rolls and scotch eggs while we waited for the clocks to be struck.

'He wasn't into pigeons,' said George, 'but he was still a good man.'

The fanciers spoke quietly while we waited, but every now and then someone said something contentious and the conversation bubbled up until it distracted Steve, who called for order.

When he'd completed his paperwork, Steve turned to the master clock in front of him. At 7.29 p.m. he called out the time.

'One minute to go, gents,' he said. The conversation stopped as we checked that our own clocks were ready. Steve called again.

'Thirty seconds,' he said, then 'ten . . . five . . . get ready . . . now.'

The room echoed with the sound of seventeen plungers being pushed home.

'Check your clocks, everyone,' said Steve. 'They should say seven-thirty.' The race was officially underway.

In my pocket, my phone buzzed. It was a message from Natalya: 'Come home.' I picked up my clock and said goodbye to the others.

'Be lucky, Jon,' said Brian.

'Have a good race,' said Johnny. I wished them luck. I put my clock in my rucksack, fetched my bike from the car park and set off for home.


When I arrived Natalya was bent over the counter in the kitchen, moaning softly as the contractions hit. Dora was upstairs, emptying the contents of her dresser onto the floor. The baby was coming. The contractions passed in intense waves over Natalya's body, like storm fronts rolling in. They had begun an hour ago, she said, but they were coming closer together now, and she thought we might not have much time before the baby arrived. She had called Irene who was on her way.

I went upstairs to put Dora to bed and called my sister Anna. Irene arrived while I was upstairs. Anna got there a few minutes later. When I came back down Natalya was sitting on the floor in the front room, her back propped against the sofa. The contractions had increased in intensity, and the periods between them had shortened.

'Where do you want to have the baby?' Irene asked. Natalya said she was happy where she was. Irene told me to roll up the carpet and turn the central heating on. She said it was time to push. There was an edge to her voice. Something was wrong, she said. Natalya's waters had still not broken, and with each contraction the baby's heart rate dropped. Irene told Anna to order an ambulance.

'You have to do this now,' she said to Natalya, urgent but calm. 'It's happening.'

We'd been waiting for this moment for months, but the waiting was of a different kind now: an intense, terrifying kind of waiting; a waiting we wanted to be over. A blue light flashed through the windows and I went to the door to let in the paramedics. Back in the room Irene and my sister helped Natalya turn onto all fours.

'This is it,' Irene said. 'Baby's not happy: you need to get him out now.' Natalya pushed one final time. She made a noise as though she was lifting a heavy weight, and then Irene drew out a long, grey body which immediately began to writhe in her arms. His colour changed to pink in a matter of seconds as air and life were drawn into his lungs. We waited for him to cry, and then it came: long and clear and piercing.

I went upstairs to wake Dora, and while she was admiring her new brother Irene checked Natalya over. When she was satisfied, the paramedics, who had been sitting patiently in the kitchen in case they were needed, were sent away. Natalya sat in the middle of the room on the floor, holding her son, beaming with happiness.

It took us a while to come up with a name for him, but a month after he was born we went to the town hall to register his birth. The registrar was chatty. She was new to the job, she said, but she already knew she loved it: the stories she heard, the beginnings and ends of lives she witnessed. She wrote down the place of birth on the top of her form: 'Leyton'. Then she wrote his name: 'Ivo Dušan John Day'. She used an old dip pen and a special ink made from the nests of gall wasps. The ink would get darker and darker with age as the tannins bit into the paper, she said, staining it rusty orange.

★

That first night we all lay together in bed, watching Ivo blink his dark eyes and screw up his face as he cried. He had delicate white spots across his nose. His ears were scrunched up and his mouth puckered. He was stockier than Dora had been, and he ate with an angry gusto so that we didn't worry whether he was getting enough food. We were exhausted but happy. Natalya said she felt that Ivo's birth had fixed her in some way – fixed her body, but also her mind, as though the natural inevitability of his birth had allowed her to forget the traumas of Dora's.

The day after Ivo was born a stream of visitors came to the house, and I waited for news from Peterborough. The weather to the north of London was bad, with driving rainstorms outside Cambridge. At 5.00 p.m. Brian phoned to tell me the race had been held over until tomorrow, and not to expect any birds that evening.

He called again the following morning. The pigeons had been released at 9.00 a.m., he said, into a light west wind. It would probably take them about an hour and forty-five minutes to fly the 70 miles back home. The clocks would be struck at 2.00 p.m. 'Be lucky,' he said as he hung up. At 10.00 a.m. I went and sat outside in the garden with Ivo while Natalya slept upstairs. He lay in my arms as I looked up at the sky, and waited.

As I sat in the garden next to the loft, I divided my time between watching the sky and watching Ivo. At 10.30 a.m. I started peering into the sky in earnest, hoping to see some sign on the horizon. I checked that my clock was working and that the trap was set up correctly for the returning birds. I made sure there was seed in my tin to rattle when they arrived. Fifteen minutes later I saw what looked like a long line of racing pigeons, coming in over the rooftops to the north, and my heart leaped. But quickly the line fragmented back into a ragged flock, and I realised it was just a bunch of feral birds flying around the block.

Ten more minutes passed and doubt crept in. I began to wonder where my pigeons had got to.

At 11.05 a.m., twenty minutes after their expected time of arrival, I recalibrated my expectations. I told myself that the wind might not have been blowing so strongly over Peterborough as it was in London, or that perhaps it had swung round to become a headwind somewhere along the route. At 70 miles distance, every minute that passes accounts for 35 yards per minute in average velocity flown. In a sprint race the difference between first and tenth place can be a matter of a few dozen yards per minute. Every second is important: a race can be won or lost in the time it takes to remove a race rubber from a bird and place it in the clock.

As the minutes ticked by, I became a realist, and then a fatalist. Half an hour after they were due back I accepted the fact that I now probably would not get on the leader board. I would have been happy if my birds came back in respectable time, even if they were at the back of the pack. But still, I hoped, I might not come last. Eventually even this hope subsided. At 11.30 a.m. I resigned myself to failure. I knew now that I wouldn't get a bird on the clock. All I could hope for, now, was that they'd come home at all.

Five minutes later, two hours and thirty-five minutes after they had been released in Peterborough, I looked up to see a pigeon on the roof of my house. It was Lone Ranger. I hadn't noticed him come in: suddenly he was just there, silhouetted against the sky, like a visitation. He dropped off the roof into an elegant swooping dive and landed on the trap. Holding Ivo on one arm I rattled my tin of grain to encourage him to trap, but he wouldn't come in and instead flew back up to the roof. I had been too keen and had spooked him, so I waited with my heart beating, cursing my clumsiness, until a few moments later he flew down again to the trap. He turned once, looked carefully around, and finally dropped inside.

After putting Ivo down on his bouncer, I went over and opened the trap. I reached in and caught Lone Ranger, pinning his wings to his sides while I removed the rubber ring from his leg. When I let him go, he clattered through the wires of the trap and went straight to the drinker, where he gulped down water. I placed his race ring in the small hole at the top of the clock and pushed the plunger home. The time was 11.37 a.m. It had taken him two hours and thirty-seven minutes to fly home, giving him a velocity, I calculated, of 780 yards per minute, or around 26 mph. It was a slow time.

The next bird arrived four minutes later. It was Orange. This time I saw him as he came in, one of a long line of birds heading westwards towards their own lofts nearer the river. Orange broke from the flock when he got above the flats on the High Road. He flew down in a great swooping glide onto the landing board and trapped straight in to the loft. I sat in the garden for the rest of the afternoon, but by the time I had to leave for the club for the striking, no more of my birds had come in.

Back at the club the flyers congratulated me on Ivo's birth.

'You named him yet?' asked Johnny.

'First boy? He's got to be John, hasn't he?' said Alby.

'It reminds me of the time my wife fell down the stairs just before a race,' said Brian. 'I had to take her to hospital, but on the way there I bumped into our neighbours, who said they'd take her for me. Then I went home and still managed to clock the birds in. The pigeons always come first.'

The flyers were coy about their results. Some talked vaguely about it being a fast race, but most claimed to be unhappy with their birds' performances. While we waited for Steve and Alby to work out the velocities, people talked about their pigeons: how many had returned, how readily they had trapped.

'I saw two flying over, and thought: they're heading over to Johnny's,' said Chris. There was a discussion about the weather, and whether the convoyer had released the birds at the right time. Johnny felt he should have waited for the squally rain to pass; Bob thought he'd done all right.

'The birds did look beaten, though,' he said.

'Mine came back all broken up,' Alby said. 'I knew that would happen. They must have hit a patch of weather.'

Steve called us to order to announce the results. I listened as he read out the names. Three of Brian's birds had come first, second and third – the fastest with an average velocity of 1,450 yards per minute – a solid but not exceptional speed for a short race like this. Johnny had come next, then Steve and George. The velocities were all within a few dozen yards per minute of each other. By the time Steve got to the end of the list, it was clear I had come dead last.

'Don't worry about it,' said Bob, 'it's only your first race. You're a novice flying a small team. I'd say you're doing alright.'

When I got home Ivo was asleep, and Natalya and Dora were watching over him. One of the other missing pigeons, Aurora, had turned up; she stood wearily on her perch. There was still no sign of Eggy but, two weeks after the race had finished, she came home, too, still wearing her race rubber, which was cracked and bleached by the sun.

## 6.55 p.m., Cambridge, 44 miles from home

At Skegness the leading birds, flying together in a bunch, swing round to the south-west to follow the coast. Their line takes them away from the open water in the middle of the Wash, past Gibraltar Point, and on across the final mile of sea they will cover on this journey. When they get to the corner of the Wash, the birds turn for the south, heading inland over the muddy estuary.

As long as they can, they continue to follow water. They find the mouth of the River Ouse and bend south with it, passing over King's Lynn and Stowbridge and Downham Market. Below them the Fens are wide and open, and they feel uncomfortable flying over the endless flatness. There is nowhere to hide around here if they catch the eye of another hawk.

At Ely some of the birds are able to make out the first landmarks they know by sight are near their homes. They can see in great detail on clear days: can recognise the jut of a spire, or the glint of a railway line, from 70 miles away. They read the angles of the landscape. The recognition of place is a like a key settling in a lock.

A third of the pigeons released in Thurso this morning have made it this far south by now. The last few hundred are still flying hard and, barring disaster, they will make it home before night.

On the outskirts of London, in Essex and Kent, flyers have taken to their gardens. They look up to the skies, watching for returns. They sit in their deckchairs, their clocks on their laps, their tins of grain nearby. Most have kept half an eye out all after-noon, just in case some exceptional bird has flown the course at record speed, but none of them really expects anything until now. The waiting has begun in earnest.

The first birds fly over Cambridge just after half past six. They have been on the wing for over eleven hours by now, and they feel fatigue deep in their muscles. They all know the route: they know the roads they must follow, the hedge-lines and pylon runs which will most efficiently lead them in on their final approaches.

By 7.30 p.m. the fastest birds have hit the edges of Epping Forest. The trees spread out below them, clinging to the last of their greenness against the parched fields and meadows. The forest is dangerous territory. Sparrowhawks roost high on the tallest of the oaks. This forest has always provided a home for outlaws: Queen Boudicca is said to have camped here the night before she marched on London and the outlaw Dick Turpin had his hideout somewhere in the wood's dark interior.

In 1841 the poet John Clare escaped from the asylum near here in the forest in which he had been incarcerated for four years. He set off to walk to Helpston in Northamptonshire, 80 miles to the north, in search of the woman he believed to be his wife. The journey took him four days, and when he arrived he was told that Mary, his childhood love, had died. He described himself then as 'homeless at home and half gratified to feel that I can be happy anywhere'. He died, having never found another home, fifteen years later.

# Homesick

We lived in the days after Ivo was born ignorant of weeks and months. Time passed in vague amounts, marked only by his changes. Gradually he learned to open his eyes, unclench his fists, roll over. He raked our faces with lovingly jagged fingernails. I liked to smell his enormous head, still rich with its new-baby musk; to kiss his fat cheeks and his plump lips. His eyes – deep and dark and old, like wells – were unable to focus, but he would turn towards sounds when he heard them, and gurgle back at us as we sang to him. The summer was hot and clammy, broken by the occasional thunderstorms which rolled in off the marshes and astonished us with their power.

As the young bird season continued, the distances of the races increased, the liberation points moving north along the A1 up the spine of the country. I spent the days before each race watching the birds fly around the loft, trying to decide which of them were coming into form. I studied weather forecasts with the obsessive intensity of a farmer waiting to harvest his crops or a fisherman about to put to sea.

The pigeons were now exercising for hours each day. Sometimes they'd stay close to the house, orbiting at the height of the roof-tops, dipping and weaving between one another within the kit as they turned together. But at other times, when the weather was fine, and some unknowable impulse seized them, they'd go out ranging far from home, so that I wouldn't see them until they got back hours later. This was less nerve-racking than it had been when they were young, and, even when they were away for hours, they always returned in the end. I was learning to trust them, to be at peace with their absences, and I hoped they were coming to trust me, too.

The second race of the season was from Newark on Trent, 110 miles from home. I entered six birds: the four that had raced from Peterborough on the weekend of Ivo's birth and another two which Dora hadn't yet named – one blue-barred hen and one dark chequered cock – both of which had been coming well from their weekly training flights. I wanted to give all the birds at least one race during their first season so that they'd be better prepared to race as old birds the following spring, but I didn't want to send the whole flock in any single week in case disaster struck and I lost them all.

The morning after the Newark marking I was sitting in the kitchen with Ivo, who had woken early after a fretful night, when Brian called to tell me the birds had been liberated at dawn and flown into perfect skies. In London the clouds were high and soft, backlit by the orange sun. The air was still. It was a quick race, and my first pair of pigeons arrived home two hours after they had been released. They appeared initially as dark points on the horizon, pinpricks of black against the blue, before flying straight down to the roof of the house. Orange was in front with Milky, her pied head stark white against the sky, following close behind. When they landed they stood on the roof for a few minutes, ignoring me as I rattled my tin and tried to coax them down. As the minutes passed I became agitated, but they finally dropped off the roof into lazy swooping glides, trapped, and went inside the loft to feed. There was no sign of the other four birds. They must, I thought, have overflown the loft, drawn along in their enthusiasm with another kit. But they worked their way back one by one over the course of the day, and by late afternoon all six had returned.

At the club that evening Alby announced that Orange and Milky had come 19th and 22nd out of 26 birds. When I told the other flyers about their unwillingness to trap, they said I needed to take them in hand if I wanted my results to improve.

'You mustn't ever let them sit around on the roof like that,' said Brian. 'They'll mingle with the feral birds and pick up all sorts of diseases. They should only ever be in the basket, in the air, or in the loft. Never anywhere else. If you want to win races you'll need to get them under control.'

Did I want to win races? Six months before, when I had first bought Eggy and Orange in Blackpool, I had told myself that I had no interest in racing for its own sake: all I really wanted to do was to try and train my flock to home. But after I had joined the club and begun to race, I felt a slight twinge of competitiveness awaken in me. Alby had been right when he had warned me that I should be careful with the birds – that I would quickly become addicted – but I still wasn't quite sure what it was I was becoming addicted to.

The following week the weather was poor, with squally rainstorms breaking out along the route of the race, which was back at Newark, so the liberation was delayed until late afternoon. Conditions made for a hard, slow race. I lost two of the six birds I had entered, and the four that did make it home returned singly, their feathers ruffled after flying through the storm, their ceres, the fleshy skin around their eyes, red raw from the driving wind. The race had been a smash, and no one really knew why. At the club the flyers grumbled about their losses and the state their pigeons had returned in. They blamed the convoyer who, they said, should never have liberated the birds into such brutal skies.

My weeks came to revolve around the races once again: the anticipation in the days leading up to them, the marking on Fridays, and the striking on Saturdays took up most of the time I didn't spend at home. Before each race I would consult maps, measuring distances and trying to work out the route the birds were likely to take. I liked the way the races gave a shape to my weeks, just as the locations of the liberation points gave a shape to my mental map of Britain.

Pigeon racing isn't much of a spectator sport, but as the distance of the races increased during that first season, I came to love the anticipation of waiting for the birds to arrive: my intense, fevered hope turning to anxiety as the hours passed, which was broken in a moment when I finally saw them strung out in a line on the horizon. Sometimes they came in high and fast from the north, on a straight bearing from the race point, before circling down and taking a celebratory lap around the house. But often I wouldn't see them arrive at all, and they would simply appear on the roof before swooping lazily down to trap. Once or twice, after hard races, they would return so exhausted that I would have to pick them up and place them inside the loft myself, feeding them by hand until their strength returned.

At the club the flyers tried to reconstruct the flights of their birds. They taught me how to interpret the story of a race: to read the conditions the pigeons had flown through on their bodies. After a while I was able to anticipate the lines they favoured when the wind came from the east or the west. I learned to check their feet for mud after they'd homed, to know if they had landed on the banks of a river or pond to drink on the way home, which might mean they were not yet strong enough to be sent further; how to tell if a pigeon had flown through a rainstorm or through high winds, and to decide which were in good enough condition to race the following week. I learned to check their flight feathers before each race, too, to see what stage of the moult they were at and whether they were still fit to fly.

I was coming to know the pigeons individually, even at a distance. Lone Ranger, Milky, Aurora and Crispy were my fastest and most consistent birds. Eggy and Orange were dependable but slow. They'd often come in an hour or so behind the others, but they would always return eventually. The other pigeons had not distinguished themselves in the races. They were flying well on their exercise flights, but many of them were still trapping badly, and they would often sit on the roof of the house for hours on their return from races or from a training toss before coming inside to feed.

★

Near the end of July, halfway through the young bird season, Alby took me aside one evening at the club and suggested I do something to improve my standings. I had been coming last fairly consistently each week, and if I wanted to do better, he said, I needed to get my birds under control.

Pigeon flyers make a distinction between a pigeon's fitness – its physical readiness to fly a certain distance – and its 'motivation': its innate desire to home. Both must be strong in order to produce a winning bird.

'Your birds are fit enough,' said Alby, 'you know that 'cause they're coming well for you. But you need to do something to motivate them. You need to make them *want* to home more quickly.'

During the first year of their lives young pigeons are generally flown 'to the perch'. Before they pair up, mate, build a nest and raise young in the loft, they are motivated only by the fact that they know home to be a safe, secure place where they will be provided with food, water and shelter. At this stage in their lives the only control their flyer has over them is hunger. If I cut down on feed on the day of the basketing, Alby said, then they might be inclined to trap more readily when they returned. The danger of this was that if I withheld too much food before a race the pigeons wouldn't have sufficient energy to fly home quickly in the first place.

When flying to the perch, getting this balance – between hunger and satiation, desire and capability – right is the key to successful racing, and some flyers go so far as to weigh their birds before important races to ensure that they are at the correct flying weight before sending them. But there were other ways of motivating pigeons to home quickly, said Alby, most of which involved manipulating their psychological relationship with their loft. In order to get the most out of my birds, he said, I would have to allow them to start to breed.

As the races continued into July, the birds began to pair up. Each of the cocks had claimed a nest box, and they protected them aggressively from all comers. Whenever a rival cock tried to invade another bird's territory, the resident pigeon would puff up his neck, growl and attack. When I put a hand inside to clean out a drinker or feeder, they would raise themselves up haughtily, batting my hand away with their wings like outraged maiden aunts.

In Osman's *Racing Pigeons* I was introduced to the earthy argot of pigeon sex. A hen in heat, I discovered, was said to be 'rank'; mating was referred to as 'the treading of the hen', and when a cock harries his hen to sit on the nest after he has trod her he was said to 'drive' her. In my loft, as the hens became rank, their cocks began to dance for them, performing figure-of-eight waggles and foot shuffles with their chests puffed out, stroking the floor of the loft with their tail feathers as they pranced about like tiny matadors. If a hen was keen she would approach the cock and peck at his neck and beak, gently ruffling his feathers. The cock would then open his beak and the hen would place her own inside it, as though they were kissing. During these kisses the cock would regurgitate a small amount of pigeon milk into his potential mate's beak from his crop, which proved to her that he would be able to feed their offspring.

If she was still amenable, the hen would crouch down low to the ground, pushing her wings aside to expose her cloaca, the small sexual opening hidden under the feathers beneath her tail. The treading took a matter of seconds. Afterwards the pair would be mated for life.

In the days after treading, the pigeons, like us, began to nest. The cocks returned from their daily exercise flights carrying wisps of straw, feathers and twigs which were often too large to fit through the entrance of the trap, and they would place this material carefully in their nest boxes before cementing them together with a fine coating of shit. Then they would sit on their nests and call for their hens with a low, throaty, gurgling rumble, a sound quite unlike their usual cooing. If this didn't work they would chase their hens around the loft, wrestling them into the boxes by force. Sometimes they would drive their mates so hard that the hens found it difficult to feed, so I had to separate the pairs until the cocks calmed down again.

On the tenth day after treading, the hens laid their first eggs: pale white and delicate, their shells almost luminescent, like pearls, or the semi-transparent skin of cave-dwelling fish. Exactly fifty-two hours afterwards they laid their second egg. The pair then took turns to incubate the eggs, sitting for twelve hours each until they hatched two weeks later. Once a pigeon was sitting, very little could induce it to leave its nest.

I checked on the eggs twice a day, anxious that in their inexperience my pigeons might not be able to incubate their first clutch successfully. But all of them sat tight, growling at me but not moving when I felt the astonishing heat beneath them, and eighteen days after laying, the first of the eggs began to hatch.

Most hatched in the evening. The chicks used their beaks to cut perfect circles around the edge of their shells, which their parents then threw from the nest, and which I'd find on the floor of the loft the next morning. The baby pigeons were tiny, covered in a brilliant yellow down, with skin stretched over their eyelids. Their skin was translucent: you could see the X-ray shadows of their organs beneath it, the milk in their crops, the ghostly outline of their nascent feathers.

The squeakers grew quickly. Fed on the rich pigeon milk provided by their parents, they doubled in size every few days. When I reached inside their boxes to clean them out, they rose up and clacked their beaks angrily at me, looking like miniature pterodactyls. Five days after they'd hatched they opened their eyes. I attached rings to their legs that they would wear for the rest of their lives.

Ten days after they'd hatched, small quills began to emerge from their skin, first lining the bottom of their wings, then protruding from all over their heads and bodies. Soon feathers began to push out, quickly covering them. After two weeks they began to look like pigeons, and after thirty days they were fully fledged and ready to leave their nests.

It is only once they have established their own territory within the loft, paired up, and bred a clutch of young that pigeons finally and permanently solidify their connection with home. After they have bred there, pigeons come to regard their loft, wrote Edgar Chamberlain in *The Homing Pigeon*, 'in exactly the same way as mothers regard their cradles. [It is] a lode-star which guides the wanderer and stimulates her energy, thus ensuring her safe return.' After they've raised a round of young, pigeons will fly further and faster to get back home, and their relationship with their loft can then be manipulated in various ways in order to motivate them to return from races more quickly. This is what Alby advised me to start doing.

The simplest way to motivate a pigeon, he said, was to wait until it was sitting on ten-day-old eggs before sending it to a race. Then, knowing its eggs might be about to hatch, it would fly home more quickly to sit on them again. Another method, which Osman called 'spoofing' or 'fooling', involved substituting an unhatched egg for a young bird from another nest on the eve of a race, which made the pigeon believe its eggs had just hatched, compelling it to return as quickly as it could.

But the most popular method used by fanciers to motivate their birds was called 'the widowhood system'. It sounded ominous. A few weeks after the young birds had fledged and been taken away from their parents, a flyer would separate his cocks and hens, keeping them in different sections of the loft where they couldn't see or hear each other. Before the race the cocks would be 'shown' to the hens: paraded in front of them in a basket without letting the pairs physically interact. When the cocks had returned from their race, they would be allowed to share their nest boxes with their mates for the evening. The rest of the time the couples were kept apart. The cocks soon learned that the faster they returned home the more time they would be allowed to spend with their mates, which, the theory went, would make them race harder to get home in the first place, and trap more quickly when they arrived.

It was homesickness, said Alby, that drew the widowhood birds on, making them fly harder and faster than they would ever do of their own accord. And if I wanted to win a pigeon race, he advised, I would have to be willing to manipulate my pigeons' feelings of homesickness in this way. Only by separating my cocks from their nests and mates would I start to do better in the races. It felt like a stark decision, one I wasn't sure I wanted to make.

Before having children I'd never thought of myself as particularly prone to homesickness. I had sometimes felt lonely – on school trips, and during the first weeks of university, when the misery of isolation and unfamiliarity felt overpowering – but these had turned out to be fleeting moments of slightly self-indulgent melancholy which I had secretly rather enjoyed, and which had soon passed. After Dora had been born, however, I began to experience homesickness of an intensity I had not known before.

The feeling was most strong when I was further away, as though the morphic elastic band that Rupert Sheldrake believed connected all organisms with their homes and families had been stretched to breaking point. A few months after Dora was born, I had travelled to America for what my publisher referred to, as it transpired rather optimistically, as a 'book tour', but which really amounted to a few readings in tiny venues to ever-diminishing crowds. During the days, the friends I was staying with went to work and lived their busy, New York lives. I had nothing to do, so I browsed in bookshops and sat in parks, watching the feral pigeons, waiting until it was late enough in England to call home. One day I rode the subway to the north of Manhattan where I sat in the brilliant sunshine overlooking the Hudson and wallowed in my loneliness.

Nostalgia is a neologism taken from the Greek words *nostos* – 'to return' or 'to journey home' – and *algos*: 'pain' or 'suffering'. The term wasn't coined until 1688, when a young medical student named Johannes Hofer described a new illness he had observed in Swiss mercenaries serving abroad. Separated from their homeland, these soldiers became anxious. They couldn't sleep. They suffered from heart palpitations, lesions on their skin, an aversion to food, and what Hofer called 'slow hectic fevers'. Eventually, some of them died.

Their symptoms were exacerbated by contact with those things that reminded them of home – a picture of their old village; the 'Ranz des Vaches', a traditional melody played by Swiss herdsmen as they drove their cattle to pasture; the smell of an alpine meadow – and they were also, Hofer observed, often temporarily alleviated by exposure to those very same things. But the only permanent cure for homesickness, he believed, was for the patient to return home.

Before Hofer, homesickness was referred to in German as *heimweh*, meaning 'home-woe', or *sehnsucht*, which means 'longing', or 'pining'. It has a cousin in the Welsh word *hiraeth*, which describes grief for a lost and un-reclaimable past and place, and the bittersweet Portuguese *saudade*. In his *Anatomy of Melancholy* Robert Burton described homesickness as 'banishment', which he defined as a 'childish humour to hone after home'. Burton was dismissive of the feeling, arguing that banishment was an unintelligible, irrational emotion, one which led its sufferers to 'prefer, as base Icelanders and Norwegians do, their own ragged island before Italy or Greece'.

*Heimweh* was only translated as 'homesickness' one hundred years after Hofer had written his thesis, in a European travel guide written by the German writer Johann Keyssler and first published in English in 1756. In a chapter entitled 'Observations on Switzerland and the Alps', Keyssler described what he called an 'exotic disease' which he associated with the people of Bern. 'The Swissers,' he wrote, 'however bold and hardy, when abroad, feel a kind of anxiety and uneasy longing after the fresh air to which they were accustomed from their infancy, without being able to account for such disquietude.' Homesickness meant a longing for a place, but it masked a longing for a time, too: a longing for childhood.

Nostalgia soon became known as the 'Swiss disease' in English, but not everyone agreed with Hofer that it was caused by the psychic strain of being removed from one's homeland. One contemporary of Hofer's, a doctor named J. J. Scheuchzer, argued that the high incidence of nostalgia among Swiss mercenaries derived primarily from the fact that they were exposed to huge variations in atmospheric pressure when they came down from the Alps to fight on the plains. Another doctor argued that the nostalgic Swiss had been driven mad by the 'unremitting clanging of cowbells', which had damaged their nerves and minds.

During the eighteenth century, nostalgia began to shift its meaning, coming to describe not just a geographical but a psychological displacement. For Immanuel Kant the nostalgia of the Swiss had little to do with geography, being instead the result 'of a longing that is aroused by the recollection of a carefree and neighbourly company in their youth, a longing for the places where they enjoyed the very simple pleasures of life.' When these soldiers returned home, Kant believed, they were cured of their homesickness not because the sight of home alleviated their symptoms, but because they came to realise that the homes of their childhood were fictions that no longer existed. 'They think that everything has drastically changed,' he wrote, 'but it is that they cannot bring back their youth.'

By the mid-nineteenth century, as population groups became more mobile, nostalgia became an increasingly popular medical condition. It was experienced particularly acutely by soldiers in the American Civil War: displaced men who were fighting, and dying, for a home which was as much an idea as it was a reality. During the war Silas Weir Mitchell – the neurologist who had prescribed Charlotte Perkins Gilman her 'rest cure' after the birth of her child – described hundreds of cases of homesickness amongst Union soldiers which, he said, 'were serious additions to the perils of wounds and disease'. Music was thought to be a particularly dangerous trigger of nostalgia, and Army bands were forbidden, wrote an infantryman named S. Millett Thompson, from playing 'pathetic or plaintive tunes, such as *Home, Sweet Home* [. . .] *Auld Lang Syne*, etc., lest they serve to dispirit, and unnerve, our suffering men.' Soon nostalgia came to describe not only the feelings engendered by the loss of one's home, but a generalised wistful yearning for the past. By the twentieth century, in a world of easy and fast travel, when those who felt they had lost touch with home were able to return to it more easily than ever before, the memories people had of their own childhood homes often bore no relation to the reality of those places when they returned to them. Nostalgia became doubly alienating when those afflicted realised that they could never go back because the homes of their youth no longer existed.

For the second half of the young bird season I tried to follow Alby's advice. After the squeakers had fledged, I split up my cocks and hens. The cocks stayed in the nest boxes they had claimed for themselves and the hens roosted on their perches in another section of the loft. I flew them separately in the morning and afternoon, but when I took them on training tosses I released them all together so that they would fly alongside each other, and on returning home would enter the loft together.

Gradually I started to do better in the races. Two weeks after I split them up, I came 18th from Newark. The following race was from Wetherby, and I came 17th. Week by week I was moving up the table. But I was uncomfortable flying my pigeons using the widowhood method. It felt unnecessarily cruel to manipulate what I took to be their homing feelings in this way: to separate them from their offspring, and from each other, only letting them run together when they'd done what I wanted of them. It felt as if the balance between us, the co-domestication of me and my birds, had been tipped too far in my favour. I thought of Darwin, and the question he asked of fanciers: do they control their pigeons, or do their pigeons control them?

There is a danger to anthropomorphising animals, who live in their own ways and in their own worlds. Their otherness is something we should not try to tame. Nevertheless, as the races continued, I decided that flying widowhood, though it might make my birds home more quickly, was not for me. When I'd first got Eggy and Orange, Ian had told me that there was nothing unethical about pigeon racing. Didn't the flyers love their birds? And weren't the pigeons always free to fly away at any time if they wanted to, whenever they were liberated from the loft? But, I began to think, this couldn't be the case if their connection with home had been intensified through nesting or widowhood. If the loft was the only home they had, wasn't it cruel to force them to choose between it and the wide world? By the end of August, I found I had lost the desire to manipulate my birds in this way. I opened the doors between the two sections of the loft and let them all run together. If they wanted to come home, I thought, they would have to come of their own accord. If this meant that I wouldn't ever win a pigeon race then that was something I could accept.

My first season as a pigeon racer finished as it had begun. In the final race, a short sprint of 70 miles from Peterborough, my first bird back, Lone Ranger, came dead last. I wasn't disappointed. I knew I couldn't really compete with the best flyers in the club, men who had been racing pigeons all their lives: Woodo and Steve and George, who topped the results board most weeks, or Alby and Big Johnny and Bob, who, with their smaller teams, often triumphed in the longer, less predictable races. The thrill of the pigeons' homecoming, and the mystery of where they had been between liberation and return, still enthralled me. Each time they returned from an unfamiliar race point, they strengthened their own connection with home, and with the routes they had taken to get back to it.

I realised then that it wasn't my pigeons' success I cared about so much as their presence, and their journeys themselves. The races, I began to see, were just an excuse to indulge in a kind of speculative, armchair cartography. By the end of their first season I had come to think of my birds as emissaries, mapping the land they flew over on my behalf, beating its bounds with each flap of their wings. I was happy at home. My dreams of adventure had retreated. Partly, I began to think, this was because the birds were now out there, journeying on my behalf. I had no need to travel: I could stay at home with Natalya and Dora and Ivo while we waited together for them to return.

## 7.49 p.m., Romford, 8 miles from home

Twelve hours after they have been liberated in Thurso, the first of the birds are approaching London. They are exhausted, but they are heartened by the proximity of home, and the familiarity of the places they now fly over. This part of the route is scored into their brains like paths worn across a muddy field. When they get within the orbit of their lofts, instinct takes over. They've flown through this sky thousands of times before now. Soon, they know, they will be home.

At 7.15 p.m. I call Bob.

'You're going to tell me you've got one,' he says as he answers the phone. But I haven't, and neither has he. Bob has spoken to Alby and Woodo, he says, but 'they haven't seen a feather yet either'.

'It's still all to play for,' Bob says. 'Don't give up yet. Even if you don't get one back tonight you might tomorrow morning. Make sure you clock it in if you do.'

The fastest of the birds arrive at their lofts half an hour after we speak. A fancier in Romford, eight miles from my loft, reports the first return. They come in a flurry after that: Alby gets two, Woodo gets one and then another one fifteen minutes later. The fancier in Romford reports three more on the night. The phone lines buzz in expectation.

Everyone says their birds look beaten by the heat. They have lost a lot of weight, and when they trap they fall straight on their drinkers, ignoring their nests and their mates. The fastest bird has flown the 498 miles to her home in twelve hours and thirty-two minutes, given her a winning velocity of 1,217 yards per minute. It isn't a particularly fast time, but this is to be expected: the day has been hotter than any Thurso race on record.

After speaking to Bob, I go outside to sit in the garden and watch the sky. The air begins to cool as dusk falls. Soon I will have to go to the club to strike the clocks. But there is still time for one of my birds to come in before then. I sit, still and hopeful, in the gathering gloom. The last of the swifts scream overhead, not yet having departed on their journey south. In the distance, I can hear the rumble of a train. I watch as it passes through the gaps between the houses.

# 12

# Homecoming

By September, as my first racing season reached its end, the pigeons had begun to moult. Birds in good health should shed all their primary flight feathers – the ten feathers running from their wingtips along the edge of their wings, those responsible for their power in flight – in the first year of their life if they are to race well the following season. The feathers dropped off one by one, like dominoes. When the fourth or fifth feather fell, the birds began to lose the downy feathers on their bodies, too. They do not like to fly far when they are deep in the moult, so after the season ended I stopped training them, only letting them out when the weather was fine. By the end of autumn they were beginning to look ragged around their necks and heads.

In November winter set in and the land froze hard. The trees along the cricket pitch were barren; their leaves stripped overnight in one fierce storm. Snow fell, and settled. The geese flew south to their winter homes from the marshes, honking bleakly as they left. I still let the pigeons out to fly whenever I could, but when the weather was foul they stood on their perches, picking at their loose feathers and letting them float to the floor of the loft. They blew around the garden, lying under bushes with the snow, white against the hard black ground.

In the old days, fanciers used to allow their birds to go 'fielding' in winter. They would chase them out from the loft, shut it up, and let them take their chances in the wild until spring arrived, and it would be time to breed again. Nowadays winter for a pigeon fancier is a time for taking stock, for letting your birds moult in peace, giving them gentle exercise and plenty of baths while you plan the following year's racing. It is also the time, I was told, to cull unwanted birds. Only the best pigeons should be allowed to breed the following year: it would only damage the team to carry the weak.

Though they loved their birds, most of the flyers I had met were unsentimental about unproved individual pigeons. Culling, they said, was part of the sport. If I didn't want to do it – a quick tug of the head in a dark sack, a splash of crimson against hessian, the sharp iron smell of blood – they would come and do it for me. Osman, too, was clear on the need to cull. 'It does not matter what pure strain they belong to or how much was paid for their grandparents,' he advised, 'if they have not shown themselves worth their keep in racing, they must go.' But I didn't have enough birds to need to cull any, and anyway, though I didn't like to admit it to the other flyers, neither did I have the stomach for it. If this meant that the genetic stock of my loft would be impaired, I thought, I was happy to live with that.

As the pigeons moulted, Natalya and I turned inward, too. In January, a year after I had first brought Eggy and Orange back home from Blackpool, I went on sabbatical from my job. Natalya was still off work, and so the four of us spent most of our time together as a family. Home became small, our needs local and immediate. We stopped going out as much. Only rarely did we cross the River Lea. Days went by when we never ventured more than half a mile from our house. Sometimes, if the skies were clear, I would take the pigeons upriver, or fly them from the marshes to keep them sharp. The rest of the time, we nested. The smallness of our lives began to feel like a comfort rather than a constraint.

Though I had tried to hide it, when I had first visited the other flyers, the proximity of their birds – the closeness of those lives so intertwined – had slightly disgusted me. I was surprised that they could ignore the smell, the mess and dirt of the animals with which they shared their lives. But by Christmas I, too, had given myself over to my pigeons. Not needing to leave the house, I stopped washing as much, luxuriating in my hot animal stink. Once I went into the library and a friend pointed out the long streak of pigeon shit down my arm, which I hadn't noticed. I flicked it off and saw the look of disgust in his eyes. I felt as if I was becoming feral.

I had been prejudiced against staying put. Going on journeys always seems more exciting than remaining in one place. The story of the lone figure going out into the world to battle the elements and overcome hardship on the road, discovering something about himself – because he usually is a he – in the process is a timelessly attractive one. But my year with the pigeons had taught me that there could be pleasure to be had in *not* travelling. Instead it was the return that mattered: journeys, I began to see, were often just excuses to come back home.

That winter I assembled a library of anti-travel writing: books that didn't recount heroic adventures taking their protagonists far from home, but instead described what it felt like to stay in one place, and what could be learned from doing so. I read *Ancrene Wisse*, the thirteenth-century guidebook for anchoresses written for three sisters of noble birth who had elected to retire from the world to live a life of quiet prayer and contemplation. 'True anchoresses are called birds,' observed the anonymous author, 'for they leave the earth – that is, love of all worldly things – and through yearning in heart for heavenly things fly upwards towards heaven.' I liked the simplicity of the image, however misleading it might have been. Though their bodies were willingly confined to their cells, the anchoresses' minds were free to range where they liked.

I read the Oulipian author Georges Perec's sedentary travelogue, *An Attempt at Exhausting a Place in Paris*, in which he describes, in flat, observational prose, the experience of sitting for days outside a café in the square of Saint-Sulpice in Paris. Much had already been written about Saint-Sulpice, Perec wrote in his introduction, before he began his experiment, but with his essay he wanted, he said, 'to describe that which is generally not taken note of, that which is not noticed, that which has no importance: what happens when nothing happens other than the weather, people, cars, and clouds.' One of the things he recorded most obsessively was the pigeons: how they sat on the edges of the stone basins in the middle of the square, how they flew 'in splendid unity' around it. They were background noise, urban familiars, and Perec only noticed them when he gave himself time to do so.

In his essay 'Of Idleness' Michel de Montaigne described how, after an adventurous life as a diplomat, he had retired to a garret on his estate to write, inventing a new literary form – the essay – in the process. In his isolation he had determined, he said, 'to spend in privacy and repose the little remainder of time I have to live,' but he found that though his body was still, his consciousness could not be. Staying put, Montaigne realised, didn't necessarily mean stupefying, and to travel in the mind could be just as liberating as going on some great adventure. 'Do not go far away,' he urged in another essay, 'you have plenty to do at home!'

Montaigne's account of his self-imposed incarceration antici-pated another strange book I had read, by the eighteenth-century Italian soldier and nobleman Xavier de Maistre. In 1790, when he was twenty-seven years old, de Maistre had been sentenced to forty-two days of house arrest for killing a fellow officer in a duel. In *Voyage Around My Room* de Maistre described his imprison-ment as a kind of liberation. Accompanied by his dog Rosine, he spent his sentence journeying round his bedroom, moving between his bed and his armchair, his sofa and his window, noting the particular quality of the light as it shone in at different times of day, the smells and sounds he experienced as he travelled around his home. Staying put allowed him to concentrate on what was on his doorstep.

De Maistre's book reminded me of a painting I had once seen by Giorgio de Chirico. *Ulysses' Return* portrays Ulysses rowing around a room in a puddle of water which looks a bit like a rug. The room is indifferently furnished: there is a high, sweeping red armchair propped against the left-hand wall and a white kitchen chair on the opposite side of the room. Above the armchair there is a painting, also by de Chirico, and opposite that an open window showing a view of some ruins. Ulysses sits alone in his boat. The door of the room, leading to the outside world, stands open. But he remains where he is, rowing to nowhere in the middle of his room.

When I'd first seen this painting I had thought it was about the loneliness of heroism: about the tribulations of leaving the comforts of home behind to nobly take on the great burdens of adventure. Now I saw in Ulysses' rowing a sort of hubris, or self-indulgence, one, I thought, I might have been guilty of indulging in during the past few years. Maybe, the painting seemed to suggest, leaving home isn't a heroic act at all. Maybe leaving home isn't even possible. Maybe once we have learned what home is we bring it with us wherever we go. Or maybe we leave part of ourselves at home whenever we depart from it.

With the young birds I had bred over winter there were now thirty pigeons in my flock. By the end of January my second round of squeakers had fledged and left their nests, so I started swapping the eggs the birds continued to lay for plastic ones in order to prevent them from breeding any more. Cold winds were blowing in from Siberia. Every few days a flurry of snow would dust the garden and the roof of the loft. But when the weather was fine I let the pigeons out as usual and they would land on the roof in an evenly spaced row, stark black against the white snow.

The old bird season, my second season as a fully fledged pigeon racer, would begin in April, and there would be races each week from then until July. This year I planned to send pigeons to every race. The furthest any bird in my flock had flown before was from Wetherby, 174 miles to me, but the old bird races would take them much further from home: to Whitley Bay, 250 miles to the north, and to Berwick-upon-Tweed, on the borders of Scotland. Many of the race points were places I had never been to. I knew them only as names on a map, or whispered into my ear by the shipping forecast which I'd lie and listen to at night after Ivo had woken me and I couldn't sleep.

The final race of the season, which would take place at the beginning of July, was also the longest in the calendar. Thurso is the northernmost town in the British Isles, and from there, if they flew in a straight line, my pigeons would have to fly 504 miles to get back home. Their flight would take them over the entire length of Britain. There are longer pigeon races on the North Road – some clubs race from Lerwick, on the Shetland Islands, a distance of six or seven hundred miles to flyers in the south of the country – but none are more prestigious. Besides, Lerwick, with its island release, was a fickle race, increasingly so in recent years, when bad weather and hawk attacks and the misleading microwaves given off by mobile phone masts were, many flyers believed, causing more and more pigeons to get lost as they flew over the water. From Lerwick good birds could vanish into clear skies for no apparent reason, Alby and Woodo said. There was little point risking them over the sea.

The south roaders had their own marathon races: from Tarbes and Barcelona and Rome. But on the north road Thurso was the high point of the season. A win from that far away would make a bird famous and its flyer rich. A Thurso winning pigeon would immediately be worth thousands of pounds as a stud bird, and its name would live forever on the pages of the fancy press.

Still, it might be too much for my relatively inexperienced birds. At the club the flyers frowned when I told them I planned to send to Thurso. They warned me that it would be hard to get returns from yearlings over that distance.

'Why don't you wait another year,' they said, 'when they'll have had more experience?'

Only Bob was encouraging.

'What you've got to remember,' he said to me one evening in February after the club AGM, when the season's liberation points were decided and the niceties of rules were argued about, 'is that you're racing against the premier league. These lot keep hundreds of birds, and they send dozens to each race. You're never going to beat them in the sprints with such a small team.'

He told me about a flyer he used to race against who was desperate to win from Peterborough.

'You know what he did?' he said. 'He drove his birds to Peterborough, every day, for two weeks before the race. He flew them in all weathers – through rain and wind and fog. And when the race came round he won it easy. How are you going to compete with that? You can't even drive.'

Rather than try and beat the mob flyers on the sprint races, Bob said, I should concentrate on getting a few of my birds experienced enough to fly the distance and enter them in the longer races, like Thurso, in which weather and luck and tenacity might win out over numbers.

'Then it's anyone's race,' he said with a smile. 'All you need is one game bird.'

I wanted to send to Thurso not because I was under any illusions that my pigeons would win, but because I had the idea that getting a bird back from so far away would represent the end of something. It was a whimsical idea, but I couldn't shake it off. I thought that if I could get one of my pigeons to fly 504 miles from the edge of the country down the length of Britain, over its drab motorways, its rivers and nestled towns and along its savage coastline – then it might confirm the sense of rootedness I had been feeling since Ivo had been born. If I could get a pigeon back from Thurso, I thought, then I might finally feel properly homed in turn.

I had three months to prepare the birds for their first race of the old bird season, after which the weekly races and daily loft flights would be enough to keep them sharp. But winter stretched long into February and March, and there were only a few days when the weather was good enough to take them out on the road. By February the pigeons had been sitting fatly on their perches for months, and when I let them out for their daily flights they were sluggish as they flapped through the cold, damp air. On rainy days, their wings sodden with water, they flew with the sound of a damp newspaper slapping onto the palm of a hand.

But as the weather finally began to turn I started training them from the basket once again. I started them off slowly, flying them close, revisiting the places they'd first learned to home from the year before, when I'd trained them as young birds. At the beginning of March I took them back to Hollow Ponds. Clouds hung billowingly on the horizon that day and the birds broke from the basket like greyhounds bolting from the trap. They returned home long before I did.

After I had flown them from Hollow Ponds a few times, I took them back to Wanstead Flats and Leyton Marshes, and then upriver again. Though it had been six months since they were last released from these places, they seemed to know the routes intuitively. As soon as I opened the basket they would fly up and vanish over the horizon on a straight bearing for home.

Now that Natalya was off work, we often set out all together, as a family, to train the birds. We took them to the Olympic Park and ate picnics while the pigeons settled, before releasing them and racing them home. We cycled up the Lea to explore the land at the edges of Hertfordshire. It was a strange sight – a caravan of bicycles festooned with children and pigeons rolling along the footpath – but I secretly rather liked the eccentricity. I knew that soon Dora and Ivo would be deeply embarrassed by the idea that their father was pigeon fancier, but for now it was simply a normal part of family and life.

It was comforting to re-encounter the places we visited alongside the birds. The ponds, the railway arch from which Alliott Roe had made his powered flight, the site of Rachel Whiteread's *House*, the long, grubby stretch of the Lea up which we cycled had, in the year since I had become a pigeon fancier, become familiar to us, too. They were now places with stories and memories attached to them rather than abstract locations on the map. They had come to form our familiar territory.

Homes are places, but they are stories, too: both the narratives of how we got to be where we are, and the tales we tell about the places we find ourselves in. Near the end of her life, the anthropologist Mary Douglas wrote a strange, obsessive book about what she called 'ring cycles': the invisible structures that, she believed, permeated most classical and biblical literature, representing an older form of narrative shaping than that which we are now used to. Buried deep in these ancient texts were, she found, structures that enact something of the homeward movement their stories often described. 'Homing', she wrote:

is another of our fundamental mental resources, like making analogies and parallelisms. [. . .] The traveller sets out with a destination in mind, reaches it, turns around, and travels back the same route to the beginning [. . .] We know what homing means; we do it all the time, we can recognize a return to the beginning when we see it, and we can transpose it to a literary form.

Douglas went on to identify the endings of long ring compositions as the inevitable outcome of those stories' own beginnings. We know how most narratives will finish long before we get to the end of them, she thought, because we can recognise their shapes even when the incidents they recount are unfamiliar to us. The greatest stories both describe and bring about a sense of homecoming, therefore, and in doing so they have provided the maps by which we home ourselves.

Homer's *Odyssey* is the best known of a group of poems called the *nostoi* – the returns – which describe the homecoming of various heroes after the Trojan War had scattered them. Many of these works have been lost, but the story of Odysseus' wanderings has found a home deep within western culture. Throughout the poem Odysseus fears not only that he will suffer hardship or die, but that if he fails to return he will be denied his 'nostos': his homecoming. It is not simply the physical reality of returning to his wife and son in Ithaca that he is driven by on his journey back to them; nor is it the psychological comfort of home which pulls him on. Running deep through the poem is the idea that in returning to Ithaca his story will finally be complete.

In book 13 Odysseus arrives back in Ithaca disguised as a homeless beggar. Five moments of recognition follow. The first happens when Odysseus' old dog Argos, whom he had known only as a puppy before setting forth to the Trojan War twenty years before, pricks up his ears on hearing his master's voice, dying soon afterwards, his destiny fulfilled. The second happens when Odysseus' old nurse Eurycleia washes his feet and recognises him by the scar on his thigh, which he received on a hunting trip when he was a boy.

After Odysseus kills the suitors who have been competing for his wife's hand, he starts a mighty fire to cleanse the marital home. It is only after he has done this that Eurycleia tells Penelope that her husband has returned. At first Penelope won't believe the stranger is him. 'My Odysseus has lost his home,' she says, in Emily Wilson's translation, 'and far away from Greece, he lost his life.' When Odysseus sheds his disguise she is almost convinced her husband has returned, but she has one final test for him. Penelope asks Eurycleia to make up their old bed, which, she says, has been moved outside the marital chamber since he built it there. 'She spoke to test him,' the poem says, and he becomes angry because he knows that he is being tested.

Odysseus tells Penelope that he made the bed himself, using an ancient olive tree for one of its bedposts. Lying at the centre of the home, he knows it can never be moved. It is only after he has described the bed and its construction that Penelope is finally willing to recognise that the wandering stranger before her truly is Odysseus. 'The bed is yours,' she says. 'The gods have brought you home. Back to your well-built house.'

Penelope is not often thought to be the hero of the poem. While Odysseus is out gallivanting she stays behind. By day she weaves the tapestry which, once complete, will mark the end of her self-imposed period of mourning. But by night, unbeknownst to her suitors, she unpicks it again. This is the one freedom she has within the poem: a domestic freedom, one that is itself rooted in the house. Does this mean she is to be read as a victim? 'Penelope's marriage,' writes Marina Benjamin, 'like so many templates handed down to us, written in stone, [. . .] skews unequally.' While her husband gets to 'fight wars, travel the world, bed nymphs', Penelope stays at home and 'simply frets'. You might say that Penelope is utterly dependent on her husband, both for her material comfort and for her identity. And yet this would be to misread, says Benjamin, her character, and the long years she spends holding her suitors at bay with her wit and charm and skill. It takes more than one person to make a home, the poem suggests, and Penelope's heroism is of a quieter sort than that of her husband. Perhaps this is because her life isn't there to be written about at all, but to be lived. Perhaps it is because her life really takes place off the page.

My homecoming that spring was less dramatic than that of Odysseus. There was no moment of clarity: no sudden thunderbolt of recognition. But during the first year of Ivo's life I realised that something had changed in my relationship with home. When I'd had my crisis of domestication in B&Q, I had thought that having children, with all its joy, also represented the end of something. But that spring, as Ivo grew and the birds flew and Natalya and I learned to know each other again, I realised that the change we had experienced was actually more of a beginning.

Maybe we had just become more experienced parents, and learned what it meant to work together to look after another person, but it was also the case that Ivo's arrival seemed to banish those feelings of homesickness which had dogged us since we had first moved to Leyton. Dora had started at school. We had made friends in the area. We started a community garden on a scrap of land opposite our house. We met our neighbours and joined local committees. We knew the names of shopkeepers; our neighbours who fed the foxes looked after the pigeons when we went on holiday. We saw my sister Liz regularly, and my other sister Anna moved nearby to start her own family. Natalya and I had learned to be together, and to help each other when things were difficult. I had learned to be more patient. I had thought that in order to understand what home was, I needed to depart from it. But as Ivo grew, I realised I had been at home for a long time already, even if I had never quite realised it until then.

The 2018 old bird season started disastrously. Bad weather in March meant that none of the other flyers had been able to give their pigeons sufficient training and so the first race, from Newark, was cancelled. The next race was from Laceby, a small town to the west of Grimsby, near the mouth of the Humber Estuary. This was a washout, too. I had entered four birds: Eggy, Orange, Lone Ranger and Milky. Eggy and Orange were still bad trappers, but they were my most consistent racers, and they also had the most experience. Lone Ranger and Milky were sitting on eggs and would, I hoped, home faster because of this.

At the club that Friday the flyers were apprehensive. Laceby was a new race point, and Alby didn't like the look of its topography.

'It's in a car park just above the town,' he said. 'It's high ground, and when the sea mist rolls in it settles on either side of the hill. If the birds get liberated and fly into that they're fucked.'

The day after the marking the rain lashed down across the length of the route, and Brian called in the morning to say the pigeons had been held in the lorry overnight. This happened again for the next two days, until the convoyer gave up and drove his load back down south. The pigeons were eventually released from Ware in Hertfordshire, no more than 10 miles from the lofts of most of the flyers. They should have made it back home easily, but the losses were unaccountably large. Woodo lost nearly all his hens – 'good birds, experienced birds', he said mournfully in the club the following week – and he was wary of losing more. Steve, who only kept a small team of cocks, had lost half of them. Woodo thought they must have bolted into the mist and in their confusion flown too fast to realise where they were going. They might not have stopped before they crossed the Channel, he said. Many of the flyers had lost their best pigeons before the season had even begun. I was secretly gleeful when all four of the birds I had sent returned on the day.

'You've got a chance now,' said Bob gleefully when we gathered for the marking the following week.

After Laceby the weather improved and the races became more predictable. The following week, the birds flew through sun and a light westerly from Wetherby. My fastest pigeon was Crispy. She came 21st out of 31. Orange, Eggy, Aurora and Lone Ranger followed close behind. The week after they flew from Newark again, and Milky came 31st of 46. The week after that, Orange came 6th of 12. They were getting faster.

As the racing continued, the birds began to find their form. I was never higher than two thirds down the results, but I was, Steve said when he took me aside at the club one day, doing OK.

'You're racing in the most competitive club in London and you're not coming last,' he said. 'I'd say it's going well.'

The next race was from Whitley Bay, on the east coast just north of Newcastle. The distance was 250 miles to me: the furthest my birds had ever flown. The marking was busier than I'd ever seen it. The baskets were piled up high in the car park, and the sun glinted between them, glancing off motes of dust which floated through the air. It felt like all the members of the club had sent birds to the race, and many other flyers I didn't recognise were there, too. Inside, the club was packed and expectations were high.

'It's like the good old days,' said Bob.

We crowded around the table in the back room and Steve called for silence as we waited to strike the clocks.

The pigeons were liberated two days later, at 7.00 a.m., into variable winds. The weather looked good along the route, and at midday I went outside to wait for them. My first arrival was Lone Ranger, who returned home an hour later. He had flown 250 miles in five hours and twenty minutes – a competitive time – and came 31st out of 46 clocked birds.

'Special round of applause for this one,' said Alby, who was looking at me as he read out the results, 'I know you've worked hard for it.' The men applauded, and I felt proud, despite the fact that I'd done little to make my birds fly home any faster.

The following week the pigeons were back at Newark. I sent eight, but halfway through the race a storm hit, and the wind picked up in London. I waited nervously for the pigeons to return, but by the evening only two of them had. A few more made it back in the following days, but a week after the race I was still three birds short. One of the missing birds was Milky, and I wondered what had become of her.

At the beginning of June they flew from Berwick. It was another hard race. When Brian called to tell me the birds were up, he said I should expect them to be quick. He predicted that with the following wind they'd do 55 mph, and so should cover the 300 miles to me in five and a half hours. They had been released at 10.00 a.m., and I waited in the garden for them all afternoon. At ten past four I got my first bird. It was Aurora, and she was exhausted by her journey. She sat on the roof of the loft and wouldn't trap, so I picked her up and placed her inside. Forty minutes later Lone Ranger came back, looking fine and fit, with barely a feather out of place. Over the next few hours Crispy, Orange and Eggy all turned up, too.

Preparations for Thurso began two weeks before the race. Big Johnny had advised me to pair my birds up eighteen days before basketing. That way, he said, the cocks would tread the hens in good time, and the hens would lay their eggs seven days later. By the time of the basketing, the pigeons would have been sitting on their eggs for ten days. In the days after I had re-paired the birds I dosed them with various tonics, vaccinated them against the commonest pigeon illnesses, and cleaned and disinfected the loft so that they wouldn't pick up any colds.

I missed the next race, from Perth, because the forecast was bad and I was scared I'd lose the birds I hoped to send to Thurso. So my penultimate race was back at Newark. The weather looked promising and I decided to enter four pigeons I hadn't raced before, giving them a chance to prove themselves before letting them rest for the autumn. It was the day after the summer solstice. As I waited for the birds the swifts screamed high overhead.

The pigeons had been released at 7.15 a.m. and I had no idea how long they would take to return. I sat in the garden looking up. The sky was completely empty of clouds, as it had been all week. Against the blue, the only marks were the contrails of aeroplanes heading to Europe. All four of the pigeons came home within race time, which I took to be a good omen.

In the week leading up to Thurso I watched the weather obsessively. It had been hot for weeks. Low pressure had moved in over the land. The water in the reservoirs fell. Fires broke out on the moors. There was talk of a hosepipe ban. Archaeological sites were revealed in the fields.

The sun beat down on the day of the marking. In the evening I went to the loft to select the birds I planned on sending to Thurso. The pigeons stood patiently on their perches. One by one I picked up six birds – Eggy, Orange, Crispy, Aurora and two unnamed chequered hens – and placed them in the basket. They had all flown from Berwick, and had been coming well from the shorter races and their training flights. They looked fit, and I hoped they'd all be able to fly the distance. They cooed angrily at first, falling silent as they settled. I carried the basket through the house and loaded it onto my bicycle. Natalya, Dora and Ivo waved me off. The pigeons were calm as I cycled down the High Road through the soft evening air.

# Home

I waited a long time for the birds to return that evening. As the sun went down and the flies began to dance, I sat in my deckchair and scanned the skies until it was too dark to see.

None of my birds made it home that night. They weren't there the next morning either, though I woke early and went downstairs with Ivo as soon as the sun rose, sitting there from first light until the midday heat drove us back inside. In the evening I had to go out, so I left the trap of the loft open, hoping they'd let themselves back inside, but when I arrived back at the loft later that night and shone my torch inside, there were still six empty perches.

I had to wait three days before I saw the first of them. I would like to say that I saw him fly in high from the north, dropping out of the clear blue sky and onto the roof of the loft, but it didn't happen like that. I was upstairs in my study when Natalya called. There was a pigeon walking around the kitchen, she said. It looked familiar, and was wearing a blue rubber race ring on its leg.

I ran downstairs as quickly as I could. There, strutting around as if he owned the place, was Orange. I went out to the garden, opened the trap and rattled my tin, and he flew up to the loft and trapped. I opened the door of the trap and gently grasped him around his wings. Orange felt calm in my hands, and lighter than when I had sent him north the previous week. But his wings still felt strong beneath my fingers. His heartbeat, a solid whump-whump in his chest, slowed as it marked out the dying effort of his flight. I gripped his feet between my fingers, took the ring off his leg, and placed it into the opening on the clock before pressing the plunger home. In the evening I would take the clock to the club to work out what velocity he had made in the race. I opened the loft and let him back inside. He flew straight back to his nest box, where he began to dance and sing for his hen.

# Acknowledgements

I have had the help of many people writing this book. I thank all the members of the East London North Road Pigeon Racing Club, in particular Alby Stockwell, Bob Brock, Brian 'Woodo' Woodehouse, Chris Schofield, George Chalkley, Johnny Boyle, Johnny Stockwell, John Purton, Steve Chalkley and Steve Tate, for sharing their stories, welcoming me at Leyton House, and teaching me how to race. I also thank those who did not wish to be named.

I thank Ian Evans of the Royal Pigeon Racing Association for his time and mentorship.

I thank Nicholas Blake for sharing my childhood fascination with pigeons, and all the members of the Pigeon Updates WhatsApp group for sustaining it. For help with training the birds I thank Damian Le Bas, Daniel Wilson, Elisabeth Day, Romee Tilanus, Steve Dragicevic and Thomas Hart-George. For help with their care I thank Marcus Sharpe and Yara Evans.

My explanation of theories of pigeon homing was developed during conversations with Oliver Padget and Rupert Sheldrake. I am immensely thankful for their time, knowledge and encouragement. All errors are my own.

'Tony Coles' is a composite: I thank the pest exterminators who formed him.

I thank all my friends for ideas and discussions, especially Althea Wasow, Brian Hurwitz, Dawn Gaietto, Gaby Wood, Lisa Appignanesi, Jacob Gracie-Burrow, Marianna Simnett, Neil Vickers, Robert Macfarlane, Ruth Padel and Patrick Wright.

I thank in particular my early readers: Agostino Inguscio, Alice Spawls, Charlotte Higgins, Damian Le Bas, Edmund Gordon, Olivia Laing, Romee Tilanus and Thomas Marks.

I thank my parents, Romee Tilanus and Peter Day, for love, stories, and translations. My sister Anna helped deliver both my children, my sister Elisabeth helped to train my birds and my brother Ben built them a home. I thank them all.

I thank my editors – Joe Zigmond and Mark Richards – who tolerated my volte-face over the subject of this book, Caroline Westmore and everyone else at John Murray for seeing it through. My agent Peter Straus and his assistant Matthew Turner were equally patient, for which I thank them.

Most of all I thank Natalya, Dora and Ivo, who have shown me what a home can be.

## Illustration Credits

Author's photos: pages 6 and 141. Charles Darwin, *The Variation of Animals and Plants under Domestication*, vol. 1, 1875: page 33. Getty Images: pages 95 and 137. Stiftung Deutsches Technikmuseum, Historisches Archiv. Photo by Julius Neubronner: page 138. Rachel Whiteread, *House*, 1993. An Artangel commission. Photo by Edward Woodman: page 163.

# Bibliography

Colin Osman's *Racing Pigeons* is the best guide to the sport of pigeon racing I have found, and I refer to it throughout. If you are interested in becoming a pigeon racer this is the book to get.

For the account of Darwin's life I am indebted to Janet Browne's magisterial two-volume biography: *Charles Darwin: Voyaging* and *Charles Darwin: The Power of Place*. On the subject of Darwin's pigeons I also made use of the excellent website www.darwinspigeons.com, maintained by John Ross.

On the history of the home, Judith Flanders's *The Making of Home* and Witold Rybczynski's *Home: A Short History of an Idea* were invaluable. Helmut Illbruck's *Nostalgia* and Susan J. Matt's *Homesickness: An American History*, are both fascinating accounts of the origins and afterlives of pathologised homesickness.

On the science of animal homing and pigeon navigation, I am indebted, in particular, to Bernd Heinrich's *The Homing Instinct*, and to G. V. T. Matthews' *Bird Navigation*, as well as Anna Gagliardo's fascinating paper 'Forty Years of Olfactory Navigation in Birds' (2013). The work of the Oxford Animal Navigation Group, which is making great advances in this field, can be found online at https://www.zoo.ox.ac.uk/oxford-navigation. Tim Guilford's enlightening lecture on 'Mysteries of Bird Navigation' can be watched here: https://vimeo.com/116943321

Barbara Allen's *Pigeon* was invaluable on the cultural and natural history of the bird, as were Andrew D. Blechman's *Pigeons* and Colin Jerolmack's *The Global Pigeon*.

In describing Winkie's flight, and the use of pigeons in war more generally, I made use of Gordon Corera's excellent *Secret Pigeon Service*. The story of Leaping Lena is derived from Elena Passarello's *Animals Strike Curious Poses* and Patrick Wright's *Iron Curtain*.

References to works cited in the text, and to others I consulted in the writing of it, can be found below.

## Chapter 1: Homing In

Allen, Barbara, *Pigeon* (Reaktion, 2009)

Brooks, Geraldine, *The Idea of Home* (ABC books, 2011)

Freud, Sigmund, 'The Uncanny' in *The Standard Edition*, vol xvii, trans. and ed. James Strachey and Anna Freud (Hogarth Press, 1948)

Guilford, T., and Biro, D., 'Route Following and the Pigeon's Familiar Area Map', *Journal of Experimental Biology* (71:169–79, 2014)

Hansell, Jean, *The Pigeon and the Wider World* (Millstream Books, 2011)

Haraway, Donna, *Staying with the Trouble* (Duke University Press, 2016)

Heinrich, Bernd, *The Homing Instinct* (William Collins, 2014)

Hustvedt, Siri, *A Plea for Eros* (Hodder & Stoughton, 2006)

Kennedy, Roger, *The Psychic Home* (Routledge, 2014)

Loy, Mina, 'Property of Pigeons' in Mina Loy, *Lost Lunar Baedeker* (Carcanet, 1997)

Miller, Thayer, *Racing Pigeons: A Manual* (Xlibris, 2015)

Moore, Marianne, 'Pigeons' in Marianne Moore, *Complete Poems* (Faber & Faber, 1968)

Pepys, Samuel, *The Diary of Samuel Pepys*, vol. VII – 1666: 1666, ed. Robert Latham and William Matthews (Bell & Hyman, 1983)

Ransome, Arthur, *Pigeon Post* (Jonathan Cape, 1936)

Solnit, Rebecca, *The Encyclopaedia of Trouble and Spaciousness* (Trinity University Press, 2014)

'Squills', *Squills: The International Pigeon Racing Year Book* (Racing Pigeon Publishing Co., 2017)

Stephens, Wilson, *Pigeon Racing* (Ward Lock, 1983)

Uchino E., and Watanabe, S., 'Self-Recognition in Pigeons Revisited' in *Journal of Experimental Animal Behaviour* (Nov 2014)

White, T. H., *The Goshawk* (Cape, 1951)

## Chapter 2: The Birds

Barthes, Roland, *Mythologies*, trans. Richard Howard (Hill and Wang, 2012)

Blechman, Andrew D., *Pigeons: The Fascinating Saga of the World's Most Revered and Reviled Bird* (Grove Press, 2006)

Browne, Janet, *Charles Darwin: vol. 1 Voyaging* (Jonathan Cape, 1995)

——, *Charles Darwin: vol. 2 The Power of Place* (Pimlico, 2002)

Darwin, Charles, *Autobiographies*, ed. Michel Neve (Penguin Classics, 2002)

Dickens, Charles, 'Spitalfields', in *Household Words* (5 April 1851)

Graham, James E., et al, *Acrobats of the Air* (Hambly Bros., 1944)

Mynott, Jeremy, *Birds in the Ancient World* (Oxford University Press, 2018)

Naether, Carl, *The Book of the Racing Pigeon* (Read Books, 2013)

Rijs, Aad, *Fancy Pigeons* (Rebo Publishers, 2006)

Rogers, James, *The Pigeon Fancier's Guide* (1844)

Ross, John, http://darwinspigeons.com/

Zim, Herbert, *Homing Pigeons* (William Morrow & Co., 1970)

## Chapter 3: Homemaking

Chamberlain, Edgar, *The Homing Pigeon* (Homing Pigeon Publishing, 1907)

Cieraad, Irene (ed.), *At Home: An Anthropology of Domestic Space* (Syracuse University Press, 1999)

Corera, Gordon, *Secret Pigeon Service: Resistance and the Struggle to Liberate Europe* (William Collins, 2018)

Flanders, Judith, *The Making of Home* (Atlantic Books, 2014)

George, Rosemary Marangoly, *The Politics of Home* (University of California Press, 1996)

Leclerc, George-Louis, *A Natural History, General and Particular; Containing the History and Theory of the Earth, a General History of Man, the Brute Creation, Vegetables, Minerals, &c, &c.*, trans. William Smellie (Richard Evans and John Bourne, 1817)

Lukacs, John, 'The Bourgeois Interior', in *The American Scholar* (Vol. 39, No. 4, Autumn 1970)

——, *The Passing of the Modern Age* (Harper Torch, 1977)

Osman, Colin, *Racing Pigeons: A Practical Guide to the Sport* (Faber & Faber, 1996)

Rybczynski, Witold, *Home: A Short History of an Idea* (Penguin, 1987)

Said, Edward, *Reflections on Exile* (Granta, 2001)

Thoreau, Henry David, *Walden* (Penguin, 2016)

Vidler, Anthony, *The Architectural Uncanny* (MIT Press, 1992)

——, *Warped Space*, (MIT Press, 2001)

## Chapter 4: Ranging

Bachelard, Gaston, *The Poetics of Space*, trans. Maria Jolas, trans. (Orion, 1964)

Berger, John, *The Shape of a Pocket* (Bloomsbury, 2002)

——, *And Our Faces, My Heart, Brief as Photos* (Bloomsbury, 2005)

——, and Mohr, Jean, *A Seventh Man* (Verso, 2010)

Darwin, Charles, 'Origin of Certain Instincts' in *Nature* (7, 179, 24 April 1873)

Eliade, Mircea, *The Sacred and the Profane*, trans. Willard R. Tras (Harcourt, 1957)

Green, Henry, *Living* (Hogarth Press, 1929)

Kavanagh, Patrick, 'The Parish and the Universe', in Patrick Kavanagh, *Collected Prose* (MacGibbon & Kee, 1967)

——, 'Innocence', in *Patrick Kavanagh: The Complete Poems* (Goldsmith Press, 1972)

——, *By Night Unstarred: An Autobiographical Novel*, ed. Peter Kavanagh, ed. (Goldsmith Press, 1977)

Oliver, Mary, *Upstream: Selected Essays* (Penguin Random House, 2016)

Tegetmeier, W. B., *Pigeons: Their Structure, Varieties, Habits and Management* (London, 1868)

——, *The Homing or Carrier Pigeon (le Pigeon Voyageur): Its History, General Management, and Method of Training* (George Routledge, 1871)

# Chapter 5: Homegoing

Baker, Alf, *Winning Naturally* (Racing Pigeon Publishing Co., 1991)

Chadwick, Bruce, *Law & Disorder: The Chaotic Birth of the NYPD* (Thomas Dunne Books, 2017)

Crasset, Matali, *The Pigeon Loft* (Pyramyd, 2004)

Fisher, John, *Airlift 1870: The Balloon and Pigeon Post in the Siege of Paris* (Max Parish and Co., 1965)

Freud, Sigmund, 'A Difficulty in the Path of Psycho-Analysis', in *The Standard Edition*, vol. XVII, trans. and ed. James Strachey and Anna Freud (Hogarth Press, 1948)

Haraway, Donna, 'A Cyborg Manifesto' (1985)

——, *When Species Meet* (University of Minnesota Press, 2008)

——, *Staying with the Trouble* (Duke University Press, 2016)

Hayhurst, J. D., *The Pigeon Post Into Paris* (Self-published, 1970)

Osman, W. H., *Pigeons in World War II* (Racing Pigeon Publishing, 1950)

Skinner, B. F., 'Pigeons in a Pelican', *American Psychologist* (15(1), 28–37, 1960)


# Chapter 6: Homelands

Hughes, Ted, 'Swifts', in Ted Hughes, *Collected Poems* (Faber & Faber, 2005)

Passarello, Ellen, *Animals Strike Curious Poses* (Jonathan Cape, 2017)

Rees, Richard, *Simone Weil: A Sketch and a Portrait* (Oxford University Press, 1966)

Sebald, W. G., *Austerlitz*, trans. Anthea Bell (Hamish Hamilton 2001)

——, *The Emigrants*, trans. Michael Hulse (Vintage, 2002)

——, *The Rings of Saturn*, trans. Michael Hulse (Vintage, 2002)

——, *After Nature*, trans. Michael Hamburger (Penguin, 2003)

——, *On the Natural History of Destruction*, trans. Anthea Bell (Penguin, 2003)

——, 'Feuer und Rauch: Über eine Abwesenheit in der deutschen Literatur', in *Saturn's Moons: W. G. Sebald: A Handbook*, ed. Jo Catling (Routledge, 2011)

——, *A Place in the Country*, trans. Jo Catling (Hamish Hamilton, 2013)

Weil, Simone, *The Need for Roots* (Routledge Classics, 2002)

Wright, Patrick, *Iron Curtain* (Oxford University Press, 2007)

## Chapter 7: Liberation

Able, Kenneth P., 'The Debate Over Olfactory Navigation by Homing Pigeons', *Journal of Experimental Biology* (199, 121–4, 1996)

——, *Gatherings of Angels* (Comstock Books, 1999)

Baldaccini, N. E., Benvenuti, S., Fiaschi, V., and Papi, F., 'Pigeon Navigation: Effects of Wind Deflection at Home Cage on Homing Behaviour', *Journal of Comparative Physiology* (99, 177–86, 1975)

Benjamin, Walter, *Berlin Childhood Around 1900: Hope in the Past* (Harvard University Press, 2006)

Birkhead, Tim, *Bird Sense* (Bloomsbury, 2012)

Dorrian, Mark, and Pousin, Frederic (eds), *Seeing From Above* (I. B. Tauris, 2013)

Fontcuberta, Joan, 'Dronifying Birds, Birdifying Drones', trans. Graham Thomson, in *The Pigeon Photographer, by Julius Neubronner & His Pigeons* (Rorhof, 2017)

Freud, *Beyond the Pleasure Principle*, trans. John Reddick (Penguin, 2003)

Gagliardo, Anna, 'Forty Years of Olfactory Navigation in Birds', *Journal of Experimental Biology* (216: 2165-2171, 2013)

Guilford, Tim, and Graham K. Taylor, *Animal Behaviour* (Nov. 97: 135–43, 2014)

Holmes, Richard, *Falling Upwards* (William Collins, 2014)

Kramer, Gustav, 'Experiments on Bird Orientation and Their Interpretation', *Ibis* (99: 196–227, 1952)

Ludovici, L. J., *The Challenging Sky: The Life of Sir Alliott Verdon-Roe* (Herbert Jenkins, 1956)

Matthews, G. V. T., *Bird Navigation* (Cambridge University Press, 1968)

Moholy-Nagy, László, 'The New Vision', in *The New Vision and Abstract of an Artist* (Wittenborn, Schultz, 1947)

Papi, F., 'The Olfactory Navigation System of Homing Pigeons', *Verhandlungen der deutschen Zoologischen Gesellschaft* (69, 184–205, 1976)

——, and Fiore, L., Fiaschi, V., and Benvenuti, S., 'Olfaction and Homing in Pigeons', *Monitore Zoologico Italiano* (6, 85–95, 1972)

Solnit, Rebecca, *A Field Guide to Getting Lost* (Canongate, 2006)

Walcott, Charles, 'Pigeon Homing: Observations, Experiments, and Confusions', *The Journal of Experimental Biology* (199, 21–7, 1996)

Wallraff, H. G., *Avian Navigation: Pigeon Homing as a Paradigm* (Springer, 2005)

——, 'Ratios Among Atmospheric Trace Gases Together with Winds Imply Exploitable Information for Bird Navigation: A Model Elucidating Experimental results', *Biogeosciences* (10, 6929–43, 2013)

Wiltschko, R., and Wiltschko, W., 'Avian Navigation: From Historical to Modern Concepts', *Animal Behaviour* (65, 257–72, 2003)

## Chapter 8: Homebound

Berger, John, *Why Look at Animals?* (Penguin, 2009)

Sheldrake, Rupert, *A New Science of Life* (Blond and Briggs, 1981)

——, *Seven Experiments that Could Change the World* (Park Street Press, Vermont, 2006)

——, *The Sense of Being Stared At* (Arrow, 2010)

——, *Dogs That Know When Their Owners Are Coming Home* (Arrow, 2011)

——, *The Presence of the Past* (Icon, 2011)

——, *The Science Delusion* (Coronet, 2012)

Skinner, B. F., '"Superstition" in the Pigeon', *Journal of Experimental Psychology* (38, 168–72, 1947)

Uexküll, Jacob von, *A Foray Into the Worlds of Animals and Humans: With a Theory of Meaning*, trans. Joseph O'Neill (University of Minnesota Press, 2010)

## Chapter 9: Homeless

Heidegger, Martin, 'Building Dwelling Thinking', in *Basic Writings* (Routledge, Kegan & Paul, 1978)

——, *Pathmarks*, ed. William McNeill (Cambridge University Press, 2010)

Humphries, Courtney, *Superdove* (HarperCollins, 2008)

Jerolmack, Colin, *The Global Pigeon* (University of Chicago Press, 2013)

Nagy, Melsi, and Johnson Phillip David II (eds), *Trash Animals* (University of Minnesota Press, 2013)

Racz, Imogen, *Art and the Home* (I. B. Tauris, 2015)

Sinclair, Iain, *Lights Out for the Territory: 9 Excursions in the Secret History of London* (Granta, 1997)

Waggoner, Matt, *Unhoused: Adorno and the Problem of Dwelling* (Columbia University Press, 2018)

Ward-Aldam, Digby, 'Ghost House', *Apollo* (https://www.apollo-magazine.com/house/, 2013)

## Chapter 10: Waiting

Gilman, Charlotte Perkins, *The Home, its Work and Influence* (Charlton, 1910)

——, *The Living of Charlotte Perkins Gilman* (University of Wisconsin Press, 1990)

——, 'The Yellow Wallpaper', in *The Yellow Wallpaper and Other Stories*, ed. Robert Shulman (Oxford World Classics, 2009)

Rowbotham, Sheila, *Dreamers of a New Day: Women Who Invented the Twentieth Century* (Verso, 2010)

Spawls, Alice, ' "Never to Touch Pen, Brush, or Pencil again" – The Madness of Charlotte Perkins Gilman', (https://www.versobooks.com/blogs/2272-never-to-touch-pen-brush-or-pencil-again-the-madness-of-charlotte-perkins-gilman, 2015)

## Chapter 11: Homesick

Burton, Robert, *The Anatomy of Melancholy* (NYRB Classics, 2001)

Chamberlain, Edgar, *The Homing Pigeon* (Homing Pigeon Publishing, 1907)

Fiennes, William, *The Snow Geese* (Picador, 2002)

Illbruck, Helmut, *Nostalgia: Origins and Ends of an Unenlightened Disease* (Northwestern University Press, 2012)

Kant, Immanuel, *Anthropology from a Pragmatic Point of View*, trans. Victor Dowdell (Southern Illinois University Press, 1978)

Keyssler, Johann, *Travels through Germany, Bohemia, Hungary, Switzerland, Italy and Lorrain: Giving a True and Just Description of the Present State of Those Countries* (London, 1756)

Matt, Susan J., *Homesickness: An American History* (Oxford University Press, 2011)

Millett Thompson, S., *Thirteenth Regiment of New Hampshire Volunteer Infantry in the War of the Rebellion, 1861–1865. A diary, etc.* (Houghton, Mifflin & Co., 1888)

## Chapter 12: Homecoming

Anon, *Ancrene Wisse*, trans. Hugh White (Penguin, 1993)

Benjamin, Marina, *Insomnia* (Scribe, 2018)

Cassin, Barbara, *When Are We Ever at Home?*, trans. Pascale-Anne Brault (Fordham University Press, 2016)

Douglas, Mary, *Thinking in Circles: An Essay on Ring Composition* (Yale University Press, 2010)

Maistre, Xaviere de, *Voyage Around my Room*, trans. Stephen Sartarelli (New Directions, 1994)

Montaigne, Michel de, 'Of Idleness', in Michel de Montaigne, *The Complete Essays*, trans. M. A. Screech (Penguin, 1993)

Perec, Georges, *Species of Spaces and Other Pieces*, trans. John Sturrock (Penguin, 1999)

——, *An Attempt at Exhausting a Place in Paris*, trans. Marc Lowenthal (Wakefield Press, 2010)

Wilson, Emily (trans.), *The Odyssey* (W. W. Norton & Company, 2018)

# Index

# Index

Note: Page numbers in *italic* refer to illustrations. The abbreviations JD stand for the author, Jon Day.